Communications in Computer and Information Science   1479

More information about this series at http://www.springer.com/series/7899

Gabriele Kotsis · A Min Tjoa ·
Ismail Khalil · Bernhard Moser ·
Atif Mashkoor · Johannes Sametinger ·
Anna Fensel · Jorge Martinez-Gil ·
Lukas Fischer · Gerald Czech ·
Florian Sobieczky · Sohail Khan (Eds.)

Database and Expert Systems Applications - DEXA 2021 Workshops

BIOKDD, IWCFS, MLKgraphs, AI-CARES, ProTime, AISys 2021
Virtual Event, September 27–30, 2021
Proceedings

 Springer

Editors
Gabriele Kotsis
Johannes Kepler University of Linz
Linz, Austria

A Min Tjoa ⓘ
Vienna University of Technology
Vienna, Austria

Ismail Khalil
Johannes Kepler University of Linz
Linz, Austria

Bernhard Moser
Software Competence Center Hagenberg
Hagenberg, Austria

Atif Mashkoor
Johannes Kepler University of Linz
Linz, Austria

Johannes Sametinger
Johannes Kepler University of Linz
Linz, Austria

Anna Fensel
University of Innsbruck
Innsbruck, Austria

Jorge Martinez-Gil
Software Competence Center Hagenberg
Hagenberg, Austria

Lukas Fischer
Software Competence Center Hagenberg
Hagenberg, Austria

Gerald Czech
Software Competence Center Hagenberg
Hagenberg, Austria

Florian Sobieczky
Software Competence Center Hagenberg
Hagenberg, Australia

Sohail Khan
Sino-Pak Center for Artificial Intelligence
Haripur, Pakistan

ISSN 1865-0929   ISSN 1865-0937 (electronic)
Communications in Computer and Information Science
ISBN 978-3-030-87100-0   ISBN 978-3-030-87101-7 (eBook)
https://doi.org/10.1007/978-3-030-87101-7

This Springer imprint is published by the registered company Springer Nature Switzerland AG
The registered company address is: Gewerbestrasse 11, 6330 Cham, Switzerland

Preface

The Database and Expert Systems Applications (DEXA) workshops are a platform for the exchange of ideas, experiences, and opinions among scientists and practitioners – those who are defining the requirements for future systems in the areas of database and artificial technologies.

This year DEXA featured six international workshops:

- The 12th International Workshop on Biological Knowledge Discovery from Data (BIOKDD 2021)
- The 5th International Workshop on Cyber-Security and Functional Safety in Cyber-Physical Systems (IWCFS 2021)
- The Third International Workshop on Machine Learning and Knowledge Graphs (MLKgraphs 2021)
- The First International Workshop on Artificial Intelligence for Clean, Affordable and Reliable Energy Supply (AI-CARES 2021)
- The First International Workshop on Time Ordered Data (ProTime 2021)
- The First International Workshop on AI System Engineering: Math, Modelling and Software (AISys 2021)

DEXA workshops included papers that focus mainly on very specialized topics on applications of database and expert systems technology.

We would like to thank all workshop chairs and Program Committee members for their excellent work, namely Lukas Fischer and Bernhard Moser, the co-chairs of the BIOKDD workshop; Atif Mashkoor and Johannes Sametinger, the co-chairs of the IWCFS workshop; Anna Fensel, Bernhard Moser, and Jorge Martinez-Gil, the co-chairs of the MLKgraphs workshop; Sohail Khan and Thomas Strasser, the co-chairs of the AI-CARES workshop; Paolo Meloni, Maqbool Khan, Gerald Czech, Thomas Hoch, and Bernhard Moser, the co-chairs of the AISys workshop; Siegfried Hörmann and Florian Sobieczky, the co-chairs of the ProTime workshop.

DEXA 2021 was the 32nd in the series of annual scientific conferences on Database and Expert Systems Applications after Vienna, Berlin, Valencia, Prague, Athens, London, Zurich, Toulouse, Vienna, Florence, Greenwich, Munich, Aix en Provence, Prague, Zaragoza, Copenhagen, Krakow, Regensburg, Turin, Linz, Bilbao, Toulouse, Vienna, Prague, Munich, Valencia, Porto, Lyon, Regensburg, and Linz.

Due to the pandemic and for the safety of all participants as well as other restrictions preventing travel and gatherings, this year's DEXA was held as a virtual conference in the Central Europe time zone.

We would like to express our thanks to all institutions actively supporting this event, namely, once again:

- Johannes Kepler University Linz (JKU)
- Software Competence Center Hagenberg (SCCH)

- The International Organization for Information Integration and Web based applications and Services (@WAS)

Finally, we hope that all the participants of the DEXA 2021 workshops enjoyed the program that we put together.

September 2021

Gabriele Kotsis
A Min Tjoa
Ismail Khalil

Organization

Steering Committee

Gabriele Kotsis	Johannes Kepler University Linz, Austria
A Min Tjoa	Technical University of Vienna, Austria
Robert Wille	Software Competence Center Hagenberg, Austria
Bernhard Moser	Software Competence Center Hagenberg, Austria
Ismail Khalil	Johannes Kepler University Linz, Austria

AI-CARES 2021 Chairs

Sohail Khan	Sino-Pak Center for Artificial Intelligence, Pak-AustriaFachhochschule: Institute of Applied Sciences and Technology, Pakistan
Thomas Strasser	AIT Austrian Institute of Technology, Austria
Ismail Khalil	Johannes Kepler University Linz, Austria

AI-CARES 2021 Program Committee

Josep M. Guerrero	Aalborg University, Denmark
Reza Arghandeh	Western Norway University of Applied Sciences, Norway
Peter Palensky	TU Delft, The Netherlands
Stefan Übermasser	AIT Austrian Institute of Technology, Austria
Zaffar Haider	Sino-Pak Center for Artificial Intelligence, Pak-AustriaFachhochschule: Institute of Applied Sciences and Technology, Pakistan
Saima Jabeen	Pak-Austria Fachhochschule: Institute of Applied Sciences and Technology, Pakistan

AISys 2021 Chairs

Paolo Meloni	University of Cagliari, Italy
Maqbool Khan	Pak-Austria Fachhochschule: Institute of Applied Sciences and Technology, Pakistan
Gerald Czech	Software Competence Center Hagenberg, Austria
Thomas Hoch	Software Competence Center Hagenberg, Austria
Bernhard Moser	Software Competence Center Hagenberg, Austria

AISys2021 Program Committee

Jan Bosch	Chalmers University of Technology, Sweden
Gabriele Gianini	University of Milan, Italy
Mihhail Matskin	KTH Royal Institute of Technology, Sweden
Helena Holmström Olsson	Malmö University, Sweden
Pierre-Edouard Portier	INSA Lyon, France
Dou Wanchun	Nanjing University, China

BIOKDD 2021 Chairs

Lukas Fischer	Software Competence Center Hagenberg, Austria
Bernhard Moser	Software Competence Center Hagenberg, Austria

BIOKDD 2021 Program Committee

Jamal Al Qundus	FU Berlin, Germany
Matteo Comin	University of Padova, Italy
Manuela Geiss	Software Competence Center Hagenberg, Austria
Michael Giretzlehner	RISC Software GmbH, Austria
Adrien Goeffon	LERIA, Université d'Angers, France
Robert Harrison	Georgia State University, USA
Daisuke Kihara	Purdue University, USA
Mohit Kumar	Software Competence Center Hagenberg, Austria
Martin Leucker	University of Lübeck, Germany
Maad Shatnawi	United Arab Emirates University, UAE
Peter F. Stadler	Leipzig University, Germany
Emanuel Weitschek	Italian Competition Authority, Italy
Dominique Lavenier	CNRS, IRISA, France
Maad Shatnawi	United Arab Emirates University, UAE
Stefan Thumfart	RISC Software GmbH, Austria
Emanuel Weitschek	Uninettuno International University, Italy
Malik Yousef	Zefat Academic College, Israel

IWCFS 2021 Chairs

Atif Mashkoor	LIT Secure and Correct Systems Lab, Austria
Johannes Sametinger	Johannes Kepler University Linz, Austria

IWCFS 2021 Program Committee

Yamine Ait Ameur	IRIT, INPT-ENSEEIHT, France
Paolo Arcaini	National Institute of Informatics, Japan
Miklos Biro	Software Competence Center Hagenberg, Austria
Jorge Cuellar	Siemens AG, Germany
Angelo Gargantini	University of Bergamo, Italy

Osman Hasan	National University of Sciences and Technology, Canada
Jean-Pierre Jacquot	LORIA, Henri Poincaré University, France
Irum Inayat	National University of Computers and Emerging Sciences, Pakistan
Xabier Larrucea	Tecnalia, Spain
Rene Mayrhofer	Johannes Kepler University Linz, Austria
Martín Ochoa	AppGate Inc., Colombia
Rudolf Ramler	Software Competence Center Hagenberg, Austria
Neeraj Singh	University of Toulouse, France
Edgar Weippl	University of Vienna, Austria

MLKgraphs 2021 Chairs

Anna Fensel	University of Innsbruck, Austria
Jorge Martinez-Gil	Software Competence Center Hagenberg, Austria
Bernhard Moser	Software Competence Center Hagenberg, Austria

MLKgraphs 2021 Program Committee

Anastasia Dimou	Ghent University, Belgium
Lisa Ehrlinger	Johannes Kepler University Linz and Software Competence Center, Hagenberg, Austria
Agata Filipowska	Poznan University of Economics, Poland
Isaac Lera	University of the Balearic Islands, Spain
Vit Novacek	National University of Ireland, Galway, Ireland
Femke Ongenae	Ghent University, Belgium
Mario Pichler	Software Competence Center Hagenberg, Austria
Artem Revenko	Semantic Web Company GmbH, Austria
Marta Sabou	Vienna University of Technology, Austria
Harald Sack	Leibniz Institute for Information Infrastructure and KIT Karlsruhe, Germany
Iztok Savnik	University of Primorska, Slovenia
Sanju Mishra Tiwari	Universidad Autonoma de Tamaulipas, Mexico
Marina Tropmann-Frick	Hamburg University of Applied Sciences, Germany

ProTime 2021 Chairs

| Siegfried Hörmann | TU Graz, Austria |
| Florian Sobieczky | Software Competence Center Hagenberg, Austria |

ProTime 2021 Program Committee

| David Gabauer | Software Competence Center Hagenberg, Austri |
| Manuela Geiß | Software Competence Center Hagenberg, Austria |

Anna-Christina Glock   Software Competence Center Hagenberg, Austria
Hans Manner   University of Graz, Austria
Sebastian Müller   TU Graz, Austria

Organizers

Contents

AI System Engineering: Math, Modelling and Software

Time Ordered Data

Biological Knowledge Discovery from Big Data

Artificial Intelligence for Clean, Affordable and Reliable Energy Supply

Cyber-Security and Functional Safety in Cyber-Physical Systems

Mode Switching for Secure Web Applications – A Juice Shop Case Scenario

Michael Riegler$^{(\boxtimes)}$ ⓘ and Johannes Sametinger$^{(\boxtimes)}$ ⓘ

LIT Secure and Correct Systems Lab, Department of Business Informatics,
Johannes Kepler University Linz, Linz, Austria
{michael.riegler,johannes.sametinger}@jku.at
https://www.jku.at/en/lit-secure-and-correct-systems-lab
https://www.se.jku.at

Abstract. Switching modes is a general mechanism that is used in many domains. We have suggested to use it for security purposes to make systems more resilient when vulnerabilities are known or when attacks are performed. OWASP provides several vulnerable web applications for testing and training security skills. We have the idea of applying mode switching to one of these applications in order to demonstrate its usefulness in increasing security. We have chosen *Juice Shop* as our sample application. In this paper (i) we suggest a multi-modal architecture for web applications; (ii) we present *Juice Shop* as our web application scenario; and (iii) we show first reflections on how mode switching can reduce attack surfaces and, thus, increase resilience.

Keywords: Mode switching · Web application · Web shop · Security · Resilience

1 Introduction

Multiple modes are common in many domains like automotive, aviation and energy. We pursue the idea of using modes to increase the resilience of software. We have presented first findings of a systematic literature review [10] and a web server case study using a multi-purpose mode switching solution [11]. The case study has shown that mode switching can reduce the window of exposure from 536 to 8 days and provides 98.9% of the time with zero (known) risk.

In this paper, we will go one step further. We present opinions and first reflections on how to use mode switching to make web applications more secure and resilient. For that purpose, we have analyzed vulnerabilities and common weaknesses of a popular security testing web shop. We plan to simulate attacks, to investigate how to detect them, and to identify methods of how to react and mitigate them. Our focus is on a multi-modal architecture to resiliently defend against attacks and to overcome the time until a vulnerability is fixed. Eventually, we strive for answers to the following questions: (i) What does it

© Springer Nature Switzerland AG 2021
G. Kotsis et al. (Eds.): DEXA 2021 Workshops, CCIS 1479, pp. 3–8, 2021.
https://doi.org/10.1007/978-3-030-87101-7_1

take to include mode switching behavior into an existing web application? (ii) Which are the modes that are useful for a web application? (iii) How much more resilient does mode switching make a web application?

In Sect. 2, we present the idea of mode switching and its use in several domains. In Sect. 3, we describe the used example web application *Juice Shop* and discuss approaches to harden it in Sect. 4. First considerations about the use of mode switching in *Juice Shop* will be presented in Sect. 5. We discuss our results in Sect. 6 and draw conclusions in Sect. 7.

2   Mode Switching

Modes are used to divide and manage complexity. They consist of a configuration and specific behavior. Some web applications use modes already, e.g., a regular mode, a maintenance mode where only registered users with special rights can see the front end, and a development or debug mode where errors and further information are provided. Depending on the screen resolution, the display mode *desktop* or *mobile* is chosen. Users can switch between *light* and *dark* mode of the graphical user interface. Registered users can switch from *view* mode to *edit* mode in order to modify articles. Progressive web apps support functionalities like a native app, e.g., an *online* and *offline* mode, where contents and inputs are cached and synchronized if there is a connection. Web Application Firewalls (WAFs) provide a *detection* and *prevention* mode [7]. In *detection* mode, the WAF is just monitoring and logging, while in *prevention* mode it actively blocks intrusions and attacks.

Multiple modes are also used in other domains like automotive, aviation and energy. First findings of a systematic literature review on mode switching are provided by [10]. Self-driving cars may have modes for manual driving, adaptive cruise control, lane keeping assistant, parking and emergency [1]. Airplanes switch among the modes of parking, taxiing, take-off, manual and automatic flying and as well landing. Power plants provide multiple modes for power operation, startup, hot standby, hot shutdown, cold shutdown and refueling [13]. Special accident and emergency systems and a degraded mode of operation [3] provide resilience if there is any kind of malfunction.

Moving target defense (MTD) makes it more difficult for attackers to find out the underlying systems and to attack them in a targeted manner. For example, Thompson et al. rotate web servers to increase uncertainty and resilience [12]. In our case study [11], we have used MTD as an adaptive security strategy and combined traditional web application hardening and mode switching to mitigate software vulnerabilities.

3   Juice Shop

The *Open Web Application Security Project* (OWASP) provides a directory of vulnerable web applications for testing security skills and tools for attack and defense. One of the flagship projects is *Juice Shop* [8]. Like a common e-commerce application, it provides typical actions of a web shop. We can search and browse products, register as a user and login, choose products and proceed to the checkout. But *Juice Shop* is a consciously insecure web application including vulnerabilities of the OWASP Top Ten security risks [9]. It has been used in Hackathons [6] and Capture-The-Flag training events. The front end of *Juice Shop* consists of a single page application with Angular and Material Design [5]. An Express application on a Node.js server builds the back end. Sequelize and finale-rest are used for the connection to an SQLite database.

Web developers can study the application for vulnerabilities, perform attacks, and sharpen security awareness. In [5] the 94 vulnerabilities of the *Juice Shop* are presented as challenges with difficulty levels between 1 and 6. Hints and step-by-step instructions are provided to execute attacks. Hacking tools like browser development tools, *PostMan* and *ZAP* are recommended to detect vulnerabilities and to exploit them [5]. Other common tools are *nmap* for scanning open ports and *sqlmap* to find and take advantage of SQL injections.

4   Securing Juice Shop

According to *Security by Design* principles, web applications should be built secure right from the start. OWASP provides a list of the top 10 web application security risks, how to test applications and how to prevent and mitigate them [9]. NIST provides general security and privacy controls for information systems [4]. Common approaches are least privilege and defense-in-depth. Web servers and other software should run within non-privileged accounts, restrict file and directory access, enable protection mechanisms, disable default behavior like directory browser listing, and remove the server version banner.

Static and dynamic vulnerability detection tools can be used for analysis. *Static Application Security Testing* (SAST) uses white-box testing to find vulnerabilities in the source code. For example, the *NodeJsScan* vulnerability scanner finds 40 issues in the source code of *Juice Shop*.

Dynamic application security testing (DAST) has a focus on black-box testing. Tools like *OWASP Zap* help to perform and simulate attacks and to scan for vulnerabilities.

5   Mode Switches in Juice Shop

The *Juice Shop* has many security vulnerabilities. Even if we try to build software with security in mind, vulnerabilities will show up sooner or later. With mode switching, we try to make systems more resilient to security problems. The idea is to check how *Juice Shop* with several modes and with the same vulnerabilities will behave differently. In this paper, we present the general idea, first considerations as well as first results.

As a first step, we will use log-file analysis and file integrity checks to detect anomalies, attacks and manipulations on the server side. Attacks can occur at different levels and in different system components like front end, back end and database. For example, the log-file analysis tool *Fail2ban* has default filters for *sshd, apache, qmail, proftpd* and others [2]. We can define further filters with regular expressions to detect attacks, failures, etc. We imagine detecting attacks, like a brute-force attack on authentication or SQL injection, and to lockout single attackers. These tools allow to ban IP addresses after a specific number of failed attempts within a certain time for a predetermined time. For distributed attacks like a *Denial-of-Service* (DoS), such block list will not be effective. In this case, we imagine a mode switch, for example after a specified number of blocked IP addresses, to restrict the number of connections and to mitigate further attacks. After the detection of anomalies, we want to switch to a mode with extended log level for further investigation, to disable not absolutely necessary legacy encryption protocols and to deny 3rd party access in certain circumstances. In case of a detected injection, e.g., reading confidential data from a database, we want to switch to a protected mode immediately to prevent further data loss, to prevent fines according to the *General Data Protection Regulation* (GDPR), and to prevent loss of reputation.

Modes can be implemented at different architecture levels like operating system, web server, database, web application, and others. At the network and firewall level, this can be blocking IP addresses and at the front end/back end to deny registration, restrict login or specific cash options. From an economic perspective, we can limit access to countries with the most sales or block countries where the most frequent attacks originate from. If we have only a small number of known customers, we may use an *allow list* mode where only specific users are granted access and all others are locked out, or a mode with an additional access code for the web shop. In an extended authentication mode, we can enforce two-factor authentication (2FA).

In some situations, it might be an option to switch specific software components to older versions with less functionalities but without newly introduced bugs and vulnerabilities. Based on the MTD strategy, see above, we can switch some components to another implementation. Manipulated components like *Docker* containers can be exchanged with a fresh installation from a repository.

6   Discussion

Mode switching is not a silver bullet to solve security problems. SAST and DAST should be implemented during the whole development life-cycle to find typical problems. Fuzzing and other black-box testing tools can reveal previously unknown vulnerabilities. Vulnerabilities need to be fixed at their core. This needs time, money and attention. There should not be more bugs and vulnerabilities after an update than before the update. Quality assurance with comprehensive testing is important. Mode switching may provide an important security advantage that helps even when updates are not available or administrators do not install available updates for whatever reason.

In order to answer research question (RQ) 1 (What does it take to include mode switching behavior into *Juice Shop*?), we have adapted *Juice Shop* to support modes. For that purpose, we needed to define triggers for mode switches, the current mode information and actions to start and stop modes. We installed *Fail2ban* and implemented log file filters using regular expressions to detect attacks and trigger mode switches. As reaction, shell scripts are executed to start/stop modes, which change configuration files, services and permissions, and save the current mode information in a special file. In addition we used the process manager *PM2* to provide auto-restart functionality if something happens. Another mode switching trigger we want to investigate are file integrity checks to detect manipulations.

For answering *RQ2* (Which are the modes that are useful for *Juice Shop?*), we have identified several useful modes at different levels. For example, at the database level, we detect SQL injection attacks by checking log files, block attacker's IP address, inform the administrator and after a certain number of such attacks we change the database mode from normal to read-only automatically to restrict further attacks. Another example are static and dynamic web application modes, which we have implemented with two *Docker* containers. In case of detected high risk vulnerabilities or a manual intervention, we can switch from the dynamic mode to the static mode that provides at least contact information or some kind of static content for users to bridge the risky time. Brute force attacks can be restricted by blocking single IP addresses after some false attempts. Another way or extension is to add *captchas* and to automatically enforce the authentication mode with 2FA, e.g. when the user wants to login from an unknown IP address.

For answering *RQ3* (How much more resilient does mode switching make *Juice Shop?*), we simulated attacks like SQL injection to trigger mode switches. The first results have shown that mode switching makes *Juice Shop* more resilient as it prevents further attacks, because immediately after a detected attack, modes are switched, functionality decreased and security increased. But development and evaluation are still in progress.

7   Conclusion

Early work on our use case has provided a first impression on how to make web applications with mode switching more secure and resilient. We have taken the vulnerable OWASP web shop *Juice Shop* as an example. We want to simulate attacks, detect them with off-the-shelf software and resiliently respond to them with a switch to a less risky mode. We are only at the beginning of our work and have presented our ideas for discussion. In the future, we want to generalize the findings to make recommendations of mode switching for specific OWASP Top 10 Web Application Security Risks, because similar vulnerabilities exist in real world applications.

Acknowledgement. This work has partially been supported by the LIT Secure and Correct Systems Lab funded by the State of Upper Austria.

References

1. Chen, T., Phan, L.T.: SafeMC: a system for the design and evaluation of mode-change protocols. In: 2018 IEEE RTAS, pp. 105–116 (2018). https://doi.org/10.1109/RTAS.2018.00021
2. Fail2ban: Manual Fail2ban 0.8. https://www.fail2ban.org/wiki/index.php/MANUAL_0_8
3. Firesmith, D.: System Resilience: What Exactly is it? https://insights.sei.cmu.edu/blog/system-resilience-what-exactly-is-it/
4. Joint Task Force Interagency Working Group: Security and Privacy Controls for Information Systems and Organizations. US NIST, revision 5 edn. (2020). https://doi.org/10.6028/NIST.SP.800-53r5
5. Kimminich, B.: Pwning OWASP Juice Shop. OWASP Foundation, Inc. (2021). https://pwning.owasp-juice.shop/
6. Liu, Y., Cannell, J.C., Coffman, J.H.: Gannon university hackathon: a combination of virtual and onsite education event to recruit high-school students within cybersecurity major. In: 2020 IEEE FIE, pp. 1–4 (2020)
7. Microsoft: What is Azure Web Application Firewall on Azure Application Gateway? - Azure Web Application Firewall (2020). https://docs.microsoft.com/en-us/azure/web-application-firewall/ag/ag-overview
8. OWASP: OWASP Juice Shop. https://owasp.org/www-project-juice-shop/
9. OWASP: OWASP Top Ten. https://owasp.org/www-project-top-ten/
10. Riegler, M., Sametinger, J.: Mode switching from a security perspective: first findings of a systematic literature review. In: Kotsis, G., et al. (eds.) DEXA 2020. CCIS, vol. 1285, pp. 63–73. Springer, Cham (2020). https://doi.org/10.1007/978-3-030-59028-4_6
11. Riegler, M., Sametinger, J., Vierhauser, M., Wimmer, M.: Automatic mode switching based on security vulnerability scores. In: Submitted for Publication (2021)
12. Thompson, M., Mendolla, M., Muggler, M., Ike, M.: Dynamic application rotation environment for moving target defense. In: 2016 Resilience Week (RWS), pp. 17–26, August 2016. https://doi.org/10.1109/RWEEK.2016.7573301
13. US Nuclear Regulatory Commission (NRC): Standard Technical Specifications - Operating and New Reactors - Current Versions (2019). https://www.nrc.gov/reactors/operating/licensing/techspecs/current-approved-sts.html

A Conceptual Model for Mitigation of Root Causes of Uncertainty in Cyber-Physical Systems

Mah Noor Asmat[1]([✉]) , Saif Ur Rehman Khan[1], and Atif Mashkoor[2]

[1] Department of Computer Science, COMSATS University Islamabad (CUI),
Park Road, Tarlai Kalan, Islamabad 45550, Pakistan
saif_rehman@comsats.edu.pk
[2] LIT Secure and Correct Systems Lab, Institute for Software Systems Engineering,
Johannes Kepler University, Altenbergerstraße 69, 4040 Linz, Austria
atif.mashkoor@jku.at

Abstract. Cyber-Physical Systems (CPS) are widely used in different domains. The major application domains of CPS are healthcare, transportation, manufacturing, industrial control systems, automatic pilot avionics, robotics systems, and so on. Uncertainty is one of the major issues that challenge the reliability of a CPS. In the literature, various approaches have been proposed to deal with uncertainty. However, fewer studies have focused on handling the root cause analysis of uncertainty and also suggesting the corresponding mitigation strategies. Inspired by this, we propose a conceptual model effective in mitigating the root causes of uncertainty in CPS. Moreover, some potential future research dimensions are outlined.

Keywords: Cyber Physical Systems · Uncertainty · Root causes · Challenges

1 Introduction

Nowadays, Cyber-Physical Systems (CPS) are widely used in every field of life. Basically, CPS is a set of heterogeneous physical units that collect physical data from the real world, communicate through the Internet, and execute complex tasks to accomplish certain goals [1,2]. Due to the multi-disciplinary interaction, the complexity of CPS significantly increases with the heterogeneity of components, which brings several challenges including security, privacy, trust, robustness, uncertainty, and architectural issues [3–6]. Security and uncertainty are the main challenges faced by CPS [7,11]. Notice that security and privacy related issues occurred at run time, while uncertainty issues happened at the

The research reported in this paper has been partly supported by the Austrian Science Fund (FWF) within the IVOIRE project (grant # I 4744-N), and the LIT Secure and Correct System Lab funded by the province of Upper Austria.

© Springer Nature Switzerland AG 2021
G. Kotsis et al. (Eds.): DEXA 2021 Workshops, CCIS 1479, pp. 9–17, 2021.
https://doi.org/10.1007/978-3-030-87101-7_2

design level. Generally speaking, uncertainty is described as a lack of information about a particular state of the system, about changes in the environment, or about the form of data or the outcome [1].

In the literature, the causes of uncertainty are handled through diverse approaches. Generally, the known uncertainties are minimized and mitigated through modeling and simulation, while unknown uncertainties can only be detected and addressed at run time [1]. Furthermore, to predict unknown uncertainty in CPS, it is essential to first classify the root causes of the uncertainty. The current state-of-the-art reported few studies that focused on uncertainty in CPS [8–10]. Moreover, some studies mentioned the root causes of uncertainty in CPS [9,11–15]. As previously discussed, uncertainty is handled in prior work through modeling. However, to the best of our knowledge, the reported studies lack in mentioning the root causes of uncertainty in CPS. Moreover, it is also observed that the majority of the conducted studies lack in explicitly focusing on mitigating the root causes of uncertainty in the context of CPS. Motivated by this, we propose a conceptual model for handling the root causes of uncertainty in CPS. The main contributions of this work are as follows:

- Reports state-of-the-art tools and techniques for mitigating the uncertainty in CPS.
- Describes the root causes of uncertainty in CPS.
- Propose a conceptual model for handling the uncertainty in CPS.

The remaining part of this paper is organized as follows: Sect. 2 discusses the conducted literature review in the targeted research context. In contrast, Sect. 3 elaborates the root causes of uncertainty in CPS. Furthermore, the proposed conceptual model is presented in Sect. 4. Finally, Sect. 5 concludes this work and also outlines potential future research directions.

2   Literature Review

This section provides a critical analysis of the state-of-the-art in order to highlight the research gap in the context of uncertainty in CPS. Moreover, existing techniques, tools, and evaluation parameters are discussed along with the root causes. Table 1 mentioned the studies covering the targeted research perspectives.

Zhang et al. [11] focused on handling uncertainty at run time through test modeling. Notice that test-ready models are explicitly captured in the "Uncertainty-wise Test-Modeling (UncerTum)" framework that supports Model-Based Testing (MBT) in CPS for solving uncertainty. The authors used IBM RSA simulation tool[1] to model the framework. Furthermore, they collected uncertainty requirements in order to validate the simulation results for the correctness of the framework. In contrast, another study [9] handled the uncertainty through uncertainty-aware model-based testing. The authors applied on-the-fly

---

[1] https://www.ibm.com/products/rational-software-architect-designer.

MBT and Bayesian inference as inverse uncertainty approach in order to improve the quantification of uncertain software systems. They modeled uncertainty and also performed run time verification using a machine learning-based algorithm proposed by An et al. [12]. Moreover, to explain the interactions of agents in Intelligent Transport Systems (ITSs), the parameterized modeling language sto-hChart(p) (parameterized stochastic hybrid statecharts) is characterized. Additionally, the authors handled the uncertainty at run time in CPS. This is due to the fact that run time verification provides assistance to autonomous vehicles in making "smarter" decisions during run time.

Using SysML/MARTE, Du et al. [13] investigated a standard-based solution. The authors used various heterogeneous UML diagrams, CCSL, and logical clocks in order to mark synchronization points. They handled uncertain environment by regulating the heating system of a building and real-world information from the user preferences and behavior. In contrast, another study [14] discussed the orthogonal uncertainty modeling approach effective for early documentation of uncertainties. However, the authors lack in empirically validating the proposed model. Xiong et al. [15] focused on mitigating the uncertainty caused by the network congestion. The authors proposed an architecture to prioritize the event-based messages and reduce network congestion. However, they handled the uncertainty at run time.

In comparison to the previously reported work, Hu et al. [16] conducted a survey on systematicness, stability, and security based on the concepts, models, and implementation. Notice that systematicness is the interaction of sensors and actuators. While, stability is the stable sensing and actuation of CPS through attacks or noisy input data. The authors reported that lack of information, changes in the environment, and lack of real-time computation are the main causes of uncertainty identified in CPS. Thus, to handle the uncertainty, they implemented the AcmeStudio framework. Also, they applied Eclipse plugin based on the Eclipse modeling framework to handle uncertainty in CPS during engineering [17].

From the analysis of the current state-of-the-art, it can be concluded that existing work mainly focused on handling the uncertainty in CPS during the operation/testing phase. However, it is of vital importance to handle the uncertainty in early phases of the development life cycle (design phase). Surely, it would help in optimally dealing with the uncertainty in the CPS context. Furthermore, existing work lack in focusing on the root causes of uncertainty in CPS. Moreover, it is observed that uncertainty is considered subjectively. However, it is suggested to consider the uncertainty as objectively together with subjectively. Motivated by this, we propose a conceptual model to mitigate the root causes of uncertainty in CPS. Moreover, we focus on finding the root causes of uncertainty from the state-of-the-art in uncertainty in the CPS context. Also, the possible solution effective to mitigate the root causes of uncertainty in CPS are outlined.

Table 1. Current state-of-the-art about mitigation of uncertainty in CPS.

Author(s)	Methodology/ Tool(s)	Technique(s) used	Evaluation measure(s)	Root cause(s)	Limitation(s)
Camilli et al. [9]	Eclipse IDE	Inverse uncertainty quantification approach	Error and precision are used for the measurement of accuracy	Functional dependency	Lack of mitigation of causes of uncertainty. Uncertainty is taken on subjectively basis
Zhang et al. [11]	UML Testing Profile, CertifyIt, IBM RSA	UncerTum	Probability or percentage	Change in Environment	Handling uncertainty during CPS operation. Uncertainty is taken subjectively
An et al. [12]	UPPAAL-SMC and MATLAB	Machine learning algorithm and stohChart(p)	Probability distribution	Changes in environment	Handling uncertainty during CPS operation. Lack of mitigation of causes of uncertainty
Du et al. [13]	CCSL, Logical clocks, and Statistical Model Checking (SMC)	SysML/MARTE, a standard-based technique is recommended	Probability distribution	Imprecise understanding of environment, Changes in environment	Handling uncertainty during CPS operation
Bandyszak et al. [14]	Orthogonal uncertainty modeling	Orthogonal modeling language	—	Lack of information, Changes in the environment	Lack of empirical evaluation to validate the results
Xiong et al. [15]	The formal expression of event-based CPS	Information theory, Markov chain matrix, and Kalman filter algorithm	Level of information entropy of sensor data in uncertain times	Communication failure	Handling uncertainty during CPS operation
Hu et al. [16]	A Gaussian Markov Random Field (GMRF) is used for the evaluation of random variable and their dependency	AcmeStudio framework	Coherency and accuracy	Lack of information, changes in the environment, lack of real-time computation	In the human-tier, there is not any multi-interface data service to correct any action that is caused by uncertainty
Angelo et al. [17]	Eclipse plugin based on Eclipse modeling framework, Physical modeling tool	MAPE-K	The physical system metrics and the network level metrics	Functional dependency	The proposed framework can only be applied during the engineering of CPS

3   Root Causes of Uncertainty in CPS

In this section, the main root causes of uncertainty in CPS are discussed according to a taxonomy [18], and their origin in CPS components [1]. Generally, uncertainty may occur in CPS due to three main reasons: (i) human behavior, (ii) technological process, and (iii) natural process. It is worth to mention that the main uncertainty's reason includes various root causes. Figure 1 shows a thematic taxonomy of the root causes of uncertainty in CPS.

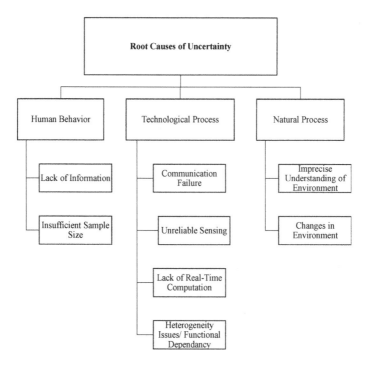

Fig. 1. Thematic taxonomy of root causes of uncertainty in CPS.

3.1   Human Behavior

Human behavior greatly impacts the reliability of CPS. We found two main root causes of human behavior including lack of information and sufficient sample size. Lack of information about technological and environmental processes leads to the unreliability of CPS. In contrast, incorrect user input and insufficient sample size collected for computation also lead to unreliable results.

Lack of Information. It is mostly reported root cause of uncertainty in CPS [9,12–14]. The lack of information could be about software, hardware, or any CPS component. Also, the lack of information could be due to the lack of human expertise. Thus, it is crucial to avoid human errors/mistakes.

Insufficient Sample Size. Data collection and usage play a significant role in CPS. Insufficient sample size effects on the accuracy of the results. Although, one may argue that insufficient sample size is a minor issue. However, it leads to incorrect output; thereby, affecting the targeted goal of CPS.

3.2   Technological Process

Heterogeneous hardware and software units are the core components of a CPS. This reason covers the root causes from a technological viewpoint.

Communication Failure. Network failure or network congestion are the main reasons for communication failure. The sensors and actuators may not be able to work reliably due to communication failure.

Unreliable Sensing. The sensor's unreliability can lead to poor data collection. The sensors are regarded as a crucial part of a CPS. Thus, it is important to mitigate this type of uncertainty in CPS. Obviously, uncontrollable data is generated from sensors [19] that causes uncertainty and consumes storage.

Lack of Real-Time Computation. Real-time computation is one of the major traits of CPS. Consider the scenario which may have lack of real-time computation and also contains a delay in data processes or computation. Surely, it would lead to severe damage in CPS. For example, An et al. [12] reported real-time performance as a core challenge in driving an autonomous vehicle.

Heterogeneity Issues/Functional Dependency. Limited system resources, including power usage, may cause ineffective sensing that could lead to unreliable sensing such as poor data collection. As a result, CPS may be negatively impacted by the decision-making challenges [20]. This mainly because of the multi-domain interaction of the cyber and physical world.

3.3   Natural Process

Natural processes affect the reliability of CPS. It could be a sudden change in the environment or a lack of understanding about the environment.

Imprecise Understanding of Environment. It is also crucial to collect complete information about the environmental occurrences.

Change in Environment. The majority of CPS becomes unreliable due to a sudden change in the environment. For example, uncertain environment data is gathered to predict the uncertain driving behavior of vehicles in ITS for an autonomous vehicle [12].

Based on the discussed causes of uncertainty in CPS, it is essential to mitigate the uncertainty causes in order to ensure the quality and reliability of CPS. For this reason, a conceptual model is proposed to mitigate the causes of uncertainty during the design phase of CPS development.

4   Conceptual Model

This section presents the proposed conceptual model as illustrated by Fig. 2. Notice that a button-shaped rectangular box represents the action steps, while the bullets represent the suggested steps necessary to perform the corresponding action steps. Similarly, the upward arrow after the validation step indicates the next step of the development phase of CPS (Fig. 2). Moreover, due to the unavailability of resources, underdevelopment CPS may not be used. However, we have focused on an interactive scenario from a case study or real-time CPS example instead of under-development CPS.

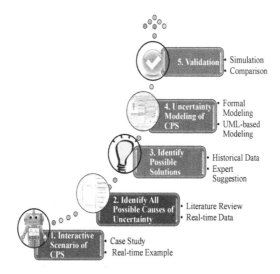

Fig. 2. High-level view of proposed conceptual model.

The proposed model contains five main steps during the design phase:

1. Interactive Scenario of CPS: The first step is to collect an interactive scenario. Notice that interactive scenarios and causes of uncertainty are identified from the literature or real-time example.
2. Identify the Possible Causes of Uncertainty: The second step is to identify all of the possible causes of uncertainty in a particular scenario, either case study from literature review or real-time data from real-time example.
3. Identify the Possible Solutions: The third step is to identify the possible solutions for the mitigation of the identified causes of the uncertainty in CPS. The possible solutions could be determined from the literature or stakeholders of a CPS of a particular scenario. Thus, historical data or expert judgment can be used in this step.
4. Uncertainty Modeling of CPS: Fourth step is to model the uncertainty causes along with the best possible solution for CPS. Modeling can be performed based on suggestions including formal modeling or UML-based modeling.

5. Validation: Lastly, the fifth step focuses on the validation of the performed modeling. To achieve this, data validation can be performed based on current state-of-the-art simulation tools.

5   Conclusion and Future Work

In this study, the root causes of uncertainty are discussed in the context of CPS. It is essential to mitigate the root causes of uncertainty in order to achieve a reliable and robust CPS. To accomplish this, a conceptual model is proposed for the design phase in order to mitigate the root causes of uncertainty in CPS.

The future work focuses on modeling and validating the proposed conceptual model using various cases scenarios. Similarly, another research direction could be on providing a detailed set of guidelines for mitigation of root causes of uncertainty using different CPS scenarios.

References

1. Ali, S., Yue, T.: U-test: evolving, modelling and testing realistic uncertain behaviours of cyber-physical systems. In: 2015 IEEE 8th International Conference on Software Testing, Verification and Validation, ICST 2015-Proceedings, pp. 2–3. IEEE (2015). https://doi.org/10.1109/ICST.2015.7102637
2. Biro, M., Mashkoor, A., Sametinger, J., Seker, R.: Software safety and security risk mitigation in cyber-physical systems. IEEE Softw. **35**(1), 24–29 (2018)
3. Mashkoor, A., Biro, M., Messnarz, R., Palacios, R.C.: Selected functional safety and cybersecurity concerns in system, software, and service process improvement and innovation. J. Softw. Evol. Process. **30**(5), e1955 (2018)
4. Törngren, M., Sellgren, U.: Complexity challenges in development of cyber-physical systems. In: Lohstroh, M., Derler, P., Sirjani, M. (eds.) Principles of Modeling. LNCS, vol. 10760, pp. 478–503. Springer, Cham (2018). https://doi.org/10.1007/978-3-319-95246-8_27
5. Lukas, E., Radu, G.: Cyber-physical systems: challenge of the 21st century. J. Chem. Inf. Model. **53**(9), 1689–1699 (2016). https://doi.org/10.1017/CBO9781107415324.004
6. Ong, L.M.T., Tran, N.C., Nguyen, N.T., Huynh, H.X., Luong, H.H.: Cyber physical system: achievements and challenges. In: ACM International Conference Proceeding Series, pp. 129–133. ACM (2020). https://doi.org/10.1145/3380688.3380695
7. Mashkoor, A., Sametinger, J., Biro, M., Egyed, A.: Security- and safety-critical cyber-physical systems. J. Softw. Evol. Process. **32**(2), e2239 (2020)
8. Zhang, M., Selic, B., Ali, S., Yue, T., Okariz, O., Norgren, R.: Understanding uncertainty in cyber-physical systems: a conceptual model. In: Wasowski, A., Lönn, H. (eds.) ECMFA 2016. LNCS, vol. 9764, pp. 247–264. Springer, Cham (2016). https://doi.org/10.1007/978-3-319-42061-5_16
9. Camilli, M., Gargantini, A., Scandurra, P.: Model-based hypothesis testing of uncertain software systems. Softw. Test. Verification Reliab. **30**(2), 1–27 (2020). https://doi.org/10.1002/stvr.1730

10. Bandyszak, T., Daun, M., Tenbergen, B., Weyer, T.: Model-based documentation of context uncertainty for cyber-physical systems: an approach and application to an industry automation case example. In: 2018 IEEE 14th International Conference on Automation Science and Engineering (CASE), Munich. IEEE (2018)

11. Zhang, M., Ali, S., Yue, T., Norgren, R., Okariz, O.: Uncertainty-wise cyber-physical system test modeling. Softw. Syst. Model. **18**(2), 1379–1418 (2019). https://doi.org/10.1007/s10270-017-0609-6

12. An, D., Liu, J., Zhang, M., Chen, X., Chen, M., Sun, H.: Uncertainty modeling and runtime verification for autonomous vehicles driving control: a machine learning-based approach. J. Syst. Softw. **167**, 1–12 (2020). https://doi.org/10.1016/j.jss.2020.110617

13. Du, D., Huang, P., Jiang, K., Mallet, F.: pCSSL: a stochastic extension to MARTE/CCSL for modeling uncertainty in cyber physical systems. Sci. Comput. Program. **166**, 71–88 (2018). https://doi.org/10.1016/j.scico.2018.05.005

14. Bandyszak, T., Daun, M., Tenbergen, B., Kuhs, P., Wolf, S., Weyer, T.: Orthogonal uncertainty modeling in the engineering of cyber-physical systems. IEEE Trans. Autom. Sci. Eng. **17**(3), 1250–1265 (2020). https://doi.org/10.1109/TASE.2020.2980726

15. Xiong, J., Wu, J.: Construction of approximate reasoning model for dynamic CPS network and system parameter identification. Comput. Commun. **154**(February), 180–187 (2020). https://doi.org/10.1016/j.comcom.2020.02.073

16. Hu, F., Lu, Y., Vasilakos, A.V., Hao, Q., Ma, R., Patil, Y.: Robust cyber-physical systems: concept, models, and implementation. Future Gener. Comput. Syst. **56**, 449–475 (2016). https://doi.org/10.1016/j.future.2015.06.006

17. D'Angelo, M., Napolitano, A., Caporuscio, M.: CyPhEF: a model-driven engineering framework for self-adaptive cyber-physical systems. In: Proceedings of the 40th International Conference on Software Engineering: Companion Proceedings, pp. 101–104 (2018)

18. Ramirez, A.J., Jensen, A.C., Cheng, B.H.: A taxonomy of uncertainty for dynamically adaptive systems. In: ICSE Workshop on Software Engineering for Adaptive and Self-Managing Systems, pp. 99–108. IEEE (2012). https://doi.org/10.1109/SEAMS.2012.6224396

19. Truong, H.L., Berardinelli, L.: Testing uncertainty of cyber-physical systems in IoT cloud infrastructures: combining model-driven engineering and elastic execution. In: TECPS 2017 - Proceedings of the 1st ACM SIGSOFT International Workshop on Testing Embedded and Cyber-Physical Systems, co-located with ISSTA 2017, pp. 5–8. ACM (2017). https://doi.org/10.1145/3107091.3107093

20. Cao, R., Hao, L., Gao, Q., Deng, J., Chen, J.: Modeling and decision-making methods for a class of cyber-physical systems based on modified hybrid stochastic timed petri net. IEEE Syst. J. **6**, 1–10 (2020)

Security-Based Safety Hazard Analysis Using FMEA: A DAM Case Study

Irum Inayat[1]([⊠]), Muhammad Farooq[1], Zubaria Inayat[2,3], and Muhammad Abbas[4]

[1] Department of Software Engineering, National University of Computer Emerging Sciences, Islamabad, Pakistan
{irum.inayat,i191235}@nu.edu.pk
[2] Department of Computer Science, Bahira University, Islamabad, Pakistan
zubaria.buic@bahria.edu.pk
[3] Univeristy of Twente, Enchede, The Netherlands
[4] Research Institutes of Sweden, Västerås, Sweden
muhammad.abbas@ri.se

Abstract. Safety and security emerge to be the most significant features of a Cyber-Physical System (CPS). Safety and security of a system are interlaced concepts and have mutual impact on each other. In the last decade, there are many cases where security breach resulted in safety hazards. There have been very few studies in the literature that address the integrated safety security risk assessment. Since, the need of the time is to consider both safety and security concurrently not even consequently. To close this gap, we aim to: (i) perform hazard analysis using Failure Mode Effect Analysis (FMEA) of a cyber physical system case i.e., Dam case study, and (ii) perform risk identification, risk analysis and mitigation for the said case. As a result, we extracted the potential failure modes, failure causes, failure effects, and the risk priority number. In addition, we also identified the safety requirements for the modes of the subject.

Keywords: Safety-security hazard analysis · Risk assessment · Safety requirements · FMEA · Cyber-physical systems

1 Introduction

Cyber-physical systems (CPS) have changed the way humans and machines (computational resources) connect with each other. CPS have many open issues such as data query, latency, storage, real-time data processing, and security among many [1]. Security being the prime factor to let the consumer trust on technology, surfaces the most. Intricate systems like smart homes, industrial automation systems, and automotive rely on secure communication to prevent the risk of life and property. A total of 490 cyberattacks were reported on CPS in the last one decade (2010–2020) published by an American think tank (Center for Strategic & International Studies) [2, 3]. Some of the famous cyberattacks of the decade are Stuxnet [4], Shamoon [5] etc. It is worth mentioning here, that the connection between security and safety is inevitable for CPS [6]. Safety is a

© Springer Nature Switzerland AG 2021
G. Kotsis et al. (Eds.): DEXA 2021 Workshops, CCIS 1479, pp. 18–30, 2021.
https://doi.org/10.1007/978-3-030-87101-7_3

non-functional requirement/trait of the system and is defined as specific, mandatory and minimum amount of safety for system to remain in safe state. Safety has a specific metric assigned to it referred as functional safety of the system [7]. ISA 99/IEC62443 (a safety standard) states that risk management for Industrial Control Security (ICS) (which is a CPS) should cover three parts, functional safety (according to ISA 84/IEC61511 & IEC61508 functional safety focuses on protecting and monitoring the devices or equipment from accidental failures or maintaining a safe state during the operating process), physical safety (Physical safety issues cause hazards such as fire breakout, explosion, flood, chemical spills, biochemical spill and crash of a vehicle [8, 9]), and cybersecurity (ISA 99) [8].

Studies and reports framed many safety incidents and security attacks that happened in industries. Recently, more cases have surfaced where the attackers compromised the safety of CPS by intruding the security of a certain CPS [4]. Some of the recent examples are explained here. For instance, Maroochy Shire Sewage Spill (MSSS) [10] where a SCADA based plant controls more than 142 sewage pumping stations, where each pumping station has their own computer system that receives the command from master station and sends it back to the center. It is one of the largely quoted case of cyber-crime disrupting SCADA. Stuxnet virus attack on the SCADA control system of Iranian Nuclear enrichment plant [11]. The worm was particularly devised to target equipment of SCADA utilized by the targeted country in their nuclear power improvement processes. The attack maimed hardware and burnt centrifuges in the Natanz facility of Iran. The cyber-attack on the German Still mill [4] making its furnace go out of control causing physical damage. The ransomware attack on US natural gas pipeline made the supply halt for two days causing chaos and business loss [12]. The Aramco, which pumps 10% of global oil supply, experienced its largest cyber-attack to date in August 2012, when a Shamon virus attack damaged around 30,000 computers and was aimed at stopping oil and gas production at the biggest OPEC exporter [13].

The examples showed the cases where security vulnerabilities facilitated attackers to compromise the safety of the system [4]. Therefore, the interlaced concepts of security and safety of CPS have become highly relevant in the recent past. CPS utilizes both cyber and physical layers for the communication. It is also noteworthy that in recent years, most of the cyber-attacks commenced with security vulnerability that helped the intruder to inject the malfunction or virus into the system. Therefore, it ends up with compromising the functional safety of the system, that could be fatal to a user life that works in the surrounding. These issues highlight the importance of restructuring the process for development of CPS. If the failure and the vulnerabilities were addressed at design stage there will be less chances of system, failure. That is why, the study includes FMEA that is safety hazard analysis which help to mitigate the risk at design stage. Therefore, in this study we aim to: (i) to identify the hazards from FMEA hazards analysis method, (ii) derive the safety requirements by aligning the identified hazards with IEC-61508 standard and, (iii) identify, analyze and mitigate the risk from DAM case study.

The remaining part of the study is aligned as follows. Section 2 describes the background of different hazard analysis methods and other aspects of the paper. Section 3 provides the designing process of case study. Section 4 contains the results of the process. Section 5 holds the discussion on the results and Sect. 5 concludes/summarizes the paper and discusses the future work.

2 Background

Risks are the uncertain events that lead to hazard. The risk management process can help in eliminating or reducing the probability of occurrence of such events. However, the need of the hour is to consider safety and security risks together and not in succession [10]. Here we summarize the key features that lack in the existing risk management techniques for security-safety risks. Boolean logic driven Markov Process (BDMP) is a graphical modeling approach designed for four kinds of events (i.e., basic, security, safety, and instantaneous events) for CPS [12]. The technique facilitates to draw the security features like Confidentiality, Integrity and Availability (CIA) and addresses the security-safety interlink. However, risk assessment and analysis are not addressed in BDMP. STPA-SafeSec claims that security has an impact on safety and demonstrates its evaluation through a causal model [13]. Bayesian Relief Networks (BRN) is a process used in the industrial control and security over the last two decades that deals with decision making for the uncertain situations [14]. It estimates the likelihood of occurrence of a failure in achieving safety and security requirements. Six-Step Model (SSM) and Information Flow Diagram (IFD) integration approaches help in identifying safety-security requirements by providing significant communication channel vulnerabilities. The risk assessment method combines the attack tree and simulation of CPS resources [15]. The Failure Mode Effect Analysis (FMEA) is type of risk assessment method. The method was applied on autonomous braking system [14] and helps to find risk and assess them in quantitative manner.

Keeping the mentioned gaps in view, this study aims to identify, analyze, plan, control, and track the safety security risks for CPS demonstrated with a case study example of a hydroelectric plant.

3 Case Study Design

The Taum Sauk project [15] is located in the Mountain region of St. Francois in southwest of Missouri which is a region of United States. The plant was developed between 1960–1962. It consists of turbines, power station, tunnels and reservoirs. Basically, Taum Sauk has two dams referred as Upper and lower dam. The main purpose of its design (as shown in Fig. 1) was to fulfill the electric demand in peak hours. It started its operation from 1963 and the water was flowing from the upper reservoir to lower reservoir. Because of the absence of natural flow, the law of thermodynamics enforces to consume more power to pump the water into the upper reservoir for electricity generation. Although, it was still running on economic cost because the upper reservoir got filled at night. It was referred as the biggest battery because of its vast capability of storing energy. It is generally controlled with microwave signal system from Osage Plant. The minimum water level in lower reservoir of the dam is 736 feet and maximum water level 749.5 feet. The instrumentation of the dam is divided into two parts (as shown in Fig. 2):

Pressure sensors and conductivity sensors. Different kinds of PLC were installed to operate under dispatch controller and operation. The complete system depends upon the two kinds of PLC (Programmable logic controllers) known as Common PLC and Upper Reservoir PLC (UR PLC). In December 2005, the upper reservoir of the dam witnessed a catastrophic failure and stop its operation until it was redeveloped and commenced its operation in 2010. In 2005, the Northwest side of UR got overtopped during it refilling process. As a result, 38000000 m^3 amount of water released in just around 12 min, which is equal to 1 billion US gallons. All the crew members survived the flood. According to the investigation and press notes, gauges that were used to monitor the water level in the upper reservoir were crashed/malfunction [15].

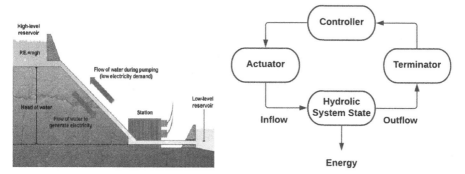

Fig. 1. Taum Sauk Dam   **Fig. 2.** Control diagram

4 Results

4.1 Security-Based Safety Hazard Analysis of DAM Case Study Using FMEA

Failure mode effect analysis (FMEA) is a bottom-up risk analysis approach. It is used at the design stage to prevent the potential failures. It can be applied in the design phase of the system by following the five basic steps: (i) System partitioning, (ii) Assign function to every component, (iii) Determine failure modes for the system, (iv) Risk evaluation with RPN (Risk's priority number), (v) Risk mitigation mechanism.

After performing the FMEA on Taum Sauk project, we managed to identify 58 hazards for the five basic components of the system i.e., Operator, dispatcher, PLC, Sensors, gates. Once identified the hazards, RPN was calculated to analyze the severity level of the risks. The analysis led to the fact that by compromising the system authentication and launching the DDoS attack the data may be altered to make the system components perform in an anomalous way. This abnormal behavior can result into sudden release of water causing disaster (flooding). Another major cause of accident is the failure of the physical components i.e., turbines, PLC, spillways, or sensors etc. All the components must be fully functional in order to generate electricity. The power station is controlled by the microwave signal, so the jamming attack can disturb the whole system. This will end up in shutting down the hydroelectric power station. Most of the data sent from the HMI (Human Machine Interface) controller and the operator sends that information

Table 1. FMEA

System	Component	Application function	Potential failure mode	Potential cause of failure	Potential failure effect	Risk assessment			
S	C	AF	FM	CF	FE	B	A	E	RPN
Conductivity sensors	Sensor	HI sensor	Pump stop at HI_HI sensor level	Structural instability	Faulty HI Sensor	3	2	2	12
					Delay in Stop signals to pump	3	3	3	27
Conductivity sensors	Sensor	HI_HI Sensor	The pump does not stop at HI_HI sensor	UR toppled	Faulty HI_HI Sensor	4	2	2	16
				Upper reservoir toppled	Delay in stop signals	4	2	3	24
Upper-reservoir PLC	PLC	UR PLC	The pump does not stop till S_HI_HI level	Upper reservoir toppled	Incorrect data to the operator control center	4	3	2	24
Common PLC	PLC	Common PLC	The pump does not stop till S_HI level	Structural instability due to over water capacity	Fault in PLC	3	2	3	18
				Structural instability due to over water capacity	S_HI faulty data	3	3	2	18
Logical gates	Conditions	AND I OR	Data interruption	Gate failure	Delay	2	3	1	6

(continued)

Table 1. (*continued*)

System	Component	Application function	Potential failure mode	Potential cause of failure	Potential failure effect	Risk assessment				RPN
S	C	AF	FM	CF	FE	B	A	E		RPN
Operator	Operator controller	Operator control center	Feedback not reported	Provide wrong signal	Display irrelevant message	3	3	2		18
Taum sock unit	Operator controller	Operator control center	Operator Controller failure	Primary sensor sending wrong information	Unable to access remotely	3	2	2		12
Firewall	Operator controller	Authentication	Intrusion into System	IDS not working	Loss of data	2	4	1		8
Pump turbine	PLC	Pump	(Pump turbine)	System spilled	Pump not started	3	5	3		45
Dispatch control center	Dispatch Control software	Send Megawatt generation instruction	Attacker modifies the sent Megawatt instruction	No encryption	False or no Megawatt generation	5	2	1		10
			Megawatt generation instruction sent too late or lost	Jamming attack	No electricity generation	2	2	1		4

(*continued*)

Table 1. (*continued*)

System	Component	Application function	Potential failure mode	Potential cause of failure	Potential failure effect	Risk assessment			
S	C	AF	FM	CF	FE	B	A	E	RPN
				Network issue	electricity generation in low demand hours	2	2	1	4
		Reception of generation data from operator	Generation feedback not received/lost feedback/feedback Received late	Jamming attack	No feedback regarding dam operation	1	2	1	2
Operator control center	Common PLC	Water Level	Erroneous calculation	SW Defect	Overtopping	2	4	3	24
			Obsolete data	Network congestion	Pumps are not stopped	2	4	3	24
		Activation of generators	Activate generator command sent lost	Jamming attack or network issue	No electricity generation	5	2	2	20
			Activate generator command altered by the attacker	No encryption	No electricity generation during the required hours	5	3	3	60

(continued)

Table 1. (*continued*)

System	Component	Application function	Potential failure mode	Potential cause of failure	Potential failure effect	Risk assessment			
S	C	AF	FM	CF	FE	B	A	E	RPN
			Activate generator command not sent	HW-failure	No electricity generation	5	1	3	15
		Deactivation of generators	Deactivate generator command lost	Jamming attack or Network issue	UR empty	1	2	5	10
			Deactivate generator command altered by the attacker	No encryption		1	2	3	6
			Deactivate generator command not sent	HW-failure		1	2	3	6
			Deactivate generator command sent late	Erroneous implementation of event	Water level reaches below minimum level	1	2	3	6
		Deactivation of pump	Stop pump command delay to the plc pump	Erroneous implementation of events and queues	Potential overtopping of upper reservoir	5	2	4	40

to other integrated components, if such data is compromised with MITM (Man in the Middle) attack. The end situation will create safety hazards that can demolish the whole structure. The detailed FMEA analysis done on the Dam case is explained in the Table 1, below. For the dispatch control software which is a part of dispatch control system has the application function "send megawatt instruction" which could fail due to security breach causing "no electricity generation" as the effect. This shows the interconnection of safety and security risks in a CPS. Likewise, for the Operator control center which is responsible for activation/deactivation of generators and water pump has a risk of jamming attach due to weak or no message encryption. As a result, there will be no electricity generation during the scheduled hours. The deactivation of generators could cause the UR empty causing the water level reaching minimum.

4.2 Safety Requirements

Table 2 presents the complete description safety requirements and constraints derived from the FMEA hazard analysis.

Table 2. Safety requirements

Modes	Safety requirement
Pressure sensor failure	The pressure sensor shall trigger the shutting down of pump if level of water in reservoir reaches above its desired level
Conductivity sensor failure	The conductivity sensors shall activate if the water level rises above the safe level
Incorrect monitoring	The sensors LO and LO-LO shall be activated as soon as the water level becomes too low
Malfunctioning	HI sensor shall activate the automatic shutdown of the pumps if pressure sensors start operating incorrectly
	The HI and the HI-HI sensors shall be used for emergency shutdown when extremely high-water levels occur
	HI-HI sensor shall activate a hard emergency stop of the pumps if pumping mode is not terminated
	The reversible pumps shall be deactivated when the water level in the upper reservoir becomes high
	The system shall be able to notify the operator when an operation is about to occur between the safe and unsafe states of the pressure sensors (p1, p2, and p3)

(*continued*)

Table 2. (*continued*)

Modes	Safety requirement
	The system shall be able to notify the operator when an operation is about to occur between the safe and unsafe states of the conductivity sensors that are placed in pairs above and below the water levels
	Problem-free circuity shall design for the elements that have failure results probabilities greater than 0.00001 for any explosion or damaged
	The system shall be able to notify the operator when an operation is about to occur between the safe and unsafe states of the conductivity sensors that are placed in pairs above and below the water levels
Incorrect reading of k-n-gates measure normally it is (2/3) voter	The system shall be able to be written in the specified probability of the fault detections, probability of the fault isolations that has been taken as input from the pressure sensors The system components shall return the hardware to an assigned safe state when unsafe hardware states are identified
Software components associated with the high level and low-level water has failures	All elements shall provide a permissible error rate to ensure that the HMI components software is operating properly System shall be able to alarmed when HMI software components cannot work properly
HCI producing apparently correct but infect wrong result	System shall display a message in HMI in case of the software elements are failures The system shall identify leading severity failures in an outer safety-critical appliance, I/O device devices, operator control center, modules, and interfaces The system shall revert to a safe state upon all the high severity occurrence
After water level touches the high, H1 sensors does not alarmed and did not sent signals to common PLC which sends instruction to PLC pump to shut down the pump	The H1 sensors conditions shall be detected by Common PLC System shall be able to be alarmed when the water touches the highest water level System shall send instructions to pump to shut down the operation aft

(*continued*)

Table 2. (*continued*)

Modes	Safety requirement
Feedback from common-PLC and UR-PLC that are not reported in the operator-control-center	System shall be able to report the feedback from common-PLC and UR-PLC Feedback circuit shall reserve 10 s after operator control center switch is actuated System shall display a message in HMI for users about the feedback every 1 h
Operator-soft gets incorrect feedback showing the highest water level value; it would send an instruction to common-PLC to shut down the pumping-unit	System hardware devices shall be able to send feedback from hardware components to UR-water level The common operation shall not create system injury while compiling a particular function at a specific period under certain conditions System shall get the hardware components UpToDate and valid System shall be able to measure the water highest level and send feedback to common-PLC
PUMP PLC	Water Pump shall not be stopped when water in upper reservoir is bellow low level water level reported by low sensor shall be validated using water level value of pressure sensors
	SCADA shall ON alarm on failure of high-level sensor Operator control center shall shutdown water pump when high level sensor fails
	SCADA shall ON alarm on HI-HI sensor failure Notification of high sensor failure shall be sent to operator control center Water Pump shall shutdown after HI-HI sensor failure notification received at operator control center
	System shall calculate water level using pressure sensor after failure of LO-LO sensor and start water pump
Water shortage in upper reservoir	Water Pump shall not be stopped when water in upper reservoir is below low level
Pressure Sensor	The pressure sensor shall trigger the shutting down of pump if level of water in reservoir reaches above its desired level
Conductivity Sensors	The conductivity sensors shall activate if the water level rises above the safe level

(*continued*)

Table 2. (*continued*)

Modes	Safety requirement
HI_HI Sensor	The HI and the HI-HI sensors shall be used for emergency shutdown when extremely high-water levels occur
L0-L0 Sensor	The sensors LO and LO-LO shall be activated as soon as the water level becomes too low
HI Sensor	HI sensor shall activate the automatic shutdown of the pumps if pressure sensors start operating incorrectly

5   Conclusion and Future Work

Secure CPS are the safe ones. Vulnerabilities in CPS can be exploited to cause destruction and damage to property and life. With increasing connectedness, the vulnerabilities and backdoors are also escalating. However, for CPS security breach can be detrimental to physical assets along with data and can have serious consequences. It is predicted to have a ransomware attacks on businesses every 11 s in 2021 as compared to 40 s in 2016 causing loss of billions of dollars. Therefore, it is the need of the time to consider security and safety as one. In this work, we have performed risk analysis of a CPS i.e., Dam case study using FMEA to identify the potential safety and security risks, modes, effects and the risk priority numbers. The failure modes and their underlying effects helped us to identify the relevant safety requirements. We have identified safety requirements for all the identified modes of the case under discussion. This shows that safety requirements may be identified while identifying security breaches of a system. Our results show that the dispatch control system and operator control center have security risks that can cause damages like "no electricity generation" and "emptying the UR to let the water touch minimum level".

Close at hand, we plan to align our safety requirements with the safety standards and comparing our results by evaluating the case using other hazard analysis methods. We also aim to replicate the analysis on another CPS to discuss on the differences system dynamics might have on risk identification.

References

1. Kayan, H., Nunes, M., Rana, O., Burnap, P., Perera, C.: Cybersecurity of industrial cyber-physical systems: a review. Cryptogr. Secur. 32 (2021)
2. Lewis, J.A.: Significant Cyber Incidents since 2006, Center for Strategic and International Studies, p. 57 (2021)
3. Al-Mhiqani, M.N., et al.: Cyber-security incidents: a review cases in cyber-physical systems. Int. J. Adv. Comput. Sci. Appl. 9(1), 499–508 (2018)
4. Lee, R.M., Assante, M.J., Conway, T.: German Steel Mill Cyber Attack, ICS Def. Use Case, p. 15 (2014)

5. Dehlawi, Z., Abokhodair, N.: Saudi Arabia's response to cyber conflict: a case study of the Shamoon malware incident. In: IEEE ISI 2013 - 2013 IEEE International Conference on Intelligence and Security Informatics Big Data, Emergent Threats, and Decision-Making in Security Informatics, pp. 73–75 (2013)

6. Alladi, T., Chamola, V., Zeadally, S.: Industrial control systems: cyberattack trends and countermeasures. Comput. Commun. **155**(March), 1–8 (2020)

7. Fu, R., Bao, X., Zhao, T.: Generic safety requirements description templates for the embedded software. In: 2017 9th IEEE International Conference on Communication Software and Networks, ICCSN 2017, p. 5 (2017)

8. De Azevedo, M.T., Martins, A.B., Kofuji, S.T.: ISA99 - Security Standards in water treatment plants. In: Water/Wastewater Automatic Controls Symposium, pp. 1–15 (2013)

9. Gall, H.: Functional Safety IEC 61508 / IEC 61511 the impact to certification and the user. In: AICCSA 08 - 6th IEEE/ACS International Conference on Computer Systems and Applications, pp. 1027–1031 (2008)

10. Sayfayn, N., Madnick, S.: Cybersafety analysis of the maroochy shire sewage spill cybersafety analysis of the maroochy shire sewage spill. Cybersecurity Interdiscip. Syst. Lab. 1–29 (2017)

11. Lu, T., Zhao, J., Zhao, L., Li, Y., Zhang, X.: Towards a framework for assuring cyber physical system security. Int. J. Secur. its Appl. **9**(3), 25–40 (2015)

12. Scaife, N., Traynor, P., Butler, K.: Making sense of the ransomware mess (and planning a sensible path forward). IEEE Potentials **36**(6), 28–31 (2017)

13. Alelyani, S., Harish Kumar, G.R.: Overview of cyberattack on Saudi organizations. J. Inf. Secur. Cybercrimes Res. (2018)

14. Sulaman, S.M., Beer, A., Felderer, M., Host, M.: Comparison of the FMEA and STPA safety analysis methods-a case study. In: Lecture Notes in Informatics (LNI), Proceedings - Ser. Gesellschaft fur Inform., vol. P-292, pp. 175–176 (2019)

15. Kriaa, S., Bouissou, M., Laarouchi, Y.: SCADA safety and security joint modeling (S-cube): case study of a dam (2016)

Privacy Preserving Machine Learning for Malicious URL Detection

Imtiyazuddin Shaik[1]([✉]), Nitesh Emmadi[1], Harshal Tupsamudre[4],
Harika Narumanchi[2], and Rajan Mindigal Alasingara Bhattachar[3]

[1] Cyber Security and Privacy Research Group, TCS Research and Innovation,
Tata Consultancy Services, Hyderabad, India
{imtiyazuddin.shaik,nitesh.emmadi1}@tcs.com
[2] Cyber Security and Privacy Research Group, TCS Research and Innovation,
Tata Consultancy Services, Chennai, India
h.narumanchi@tcs.com
[3] Cyber Security and Privacy Research Group, TCS Research and Innovation,
Tata Consultancy Services, Bangalore, India
rajan.ma@tcs.com
[4] Tata Consultancy Services, Pune, India
harshal.tupsamudre@tcs.com

Abstract. Phishing remains the most prominent attack causing loss of billions of dollars for organizations and users every year. Attackers use phishing to obtain sensitive information from users, install malware and obtain control over their systems. Currently, web browsers counter this attack using blacklisting method, however it fails to detect newly generated malicious websites, hence ineffective. In the recent times, machine learning based URL classification techniques where trained models are deployed on server side, emerged as an effective solution to detect new malicious URLs and provide it as a service to the user. While malicious URL detection continues to be a problem, another potential concern is the user's query privacy (when offered as malicious URL detection as a service, where server can learn about the URL). Hence to address the query privacy, we propose privacy enabled malicious URL detection.

In this work, we focus on privacy enabled malicious URL detection based on FHE using 3 methods (i) Deep Neural Network (DNN) (ii) Logistic regression (iii) Hybrid. In the hybrid approach, the feature extraction is done using DNN and classification is done using logistic regression model, gives practical performance. We designed the models based on split architecture (client/server). We present our experiments with the models trained using a dataset of 100,000 URLs (50,000 valid and 50,000 phished URLs). Our experiments show that malicious URL detection in encrypted domain is practical in terms of accuracy and efficiency.

1 Introduction

In recent years, phishing has been the most prominent and successful attack vector that enables attackers to maliciously obtain sensitive information such as username, password or financial information from users and also install malware

© Springer Nature Switzerland AG 2021
G. Kotsis et al. (Eds.): DEXA 2021 Workshops, CCIS 1479, pp. 31–41, 2021.
https://doi.org/10.1007/978-3-030-87101-7_4

or trojans on target's system by posing as a trusted entity. Malicious URLs are typically sent to users via e-mails, text or pop up messages and the pages pointed by these URLs can host malicious content in the form of viruses, trojans and attack scripts. An investigation report from Verizon 2019 [1] reveals that 32% of the data breaches in 2018 involved phishing. State of Phish 2019 [2] report shows that 83% of its survey respondents experienced phishing in 2018.

Safe browsing is a method used by web browsers to alert users about malicious websites. Prominent web browsers such as Google Chrome, Apple Safari, Mozilla Firefox, Internet Explorer and others provide safe browsing capability to the end-users. Safe browsing classifies websites into two categories namely malicious and benign [3]. Though the blacklist method is most practical approach, it lacks the ability to protect against zero-hour phishing attacks. 63% of the phishing campaigns end within the first two hours, whereas 47% to 83% of phishing URLs appeared in blacklists only after 12 hours [4]. These approaches detect malicious URLs based on common characteristics found in the previously reported phishing attacks. Hence, machine learning based classification algorithms can be employed to classify the malicious URLs [5–7].

However, there have been concerns on privacy that some organizations during safe browsing activity have been sharing user's data such as log IP address to third party organizations [8] which can be used to determine a user's browsing patterns [9]. To address this, safe browsing methods use *differential privacy* [10] to protect query privacy. However, Google and Yandex safe browsing can still be used as tools to identity classes of individuals based on user's browsing data [3,11]. Gerbet *et al.* [3] observe that one can recover the prefix lists of Google and Yandex and tamper their databases enabling tracking of users.

Hence, in this paper, we focus on end to end query privacy of users using malicious URL detection service based on machine learning with a goal to preserve user's privacy. To preserve privacy of user's data, several privacy preserving computation methodologies have evolved, we use fully homomorphic encryption (FHE) [12] as it is more suitable in the context of end-user privacy. Most of the real world ML applications that use Deep Neural Networks (DNN) have many layers and hence expensive to realize in FHE. The malicious URL detection usecase is one of the few problems that have practical performance with lower number of layers and is more suitable for FHE domain. The challenge is to realize such applications using polynomial approximation for activation functions such as sigmoid, RELU functions with minimal loss in performance and accuracy.

Our Contribution: In this paper, we present a FHE based privacy preserving machine learning model for malicious website detection. We assume a client-server model wherein the client is the user that queries malicious URL detection server through a web browser. Considering the limitations of FHE schemes, we present an optimal solution based on three classifiers: (i) DNN (ii) Logistic Regression (iii) Hybrid. The hybrid approach in encrypted domain gives practical performance with minimal loss in accuracy (<4%) when compared to state-of-the-art approach, URLNet.

Related Work: Several machine learning approaches have been explored that can efficiently detect malicious URLs [13–16]. Most of these existing machine learning approaches have limitations such as inability to effectively capture semantic meaning and sequential patterns in URL strings; requiring substantial manual feature engineering; and inability to capture new features and generalize to test data. To address these challenges, Hung *et al.* [17] present URLNet, an end-to-end deep learning framework to learn a nonlinear URL embedding for Malicious URL Detection directly from the URL. This uses Convolutional Neural Networks for both characters and words of the URL String to learn the URL embedding in a jointly optimized framework enabling model to capture several types of semantic information, which was not possible by the existing models. URLNet [17] also presents advanced word-embeddings to solve the problem of too many rare words observed in this task. Hence, we consider URLNet architecture [17] for privacy preserving malicious URL detection.

In the context of privacy preserving malicious URL detection, Chow et al. [18] recently studied privacy preserving phishing web page classification that relies on visual features of the web page being visited. However, the visual similarity based techniques are complex than the text based techniques and require extensive image matching mechanisms that require computational overhead [19] and are in general vulnerable to adversarial machine learning attacks. Furthermore, visual similarity based technique requires a user to visit the website, however, URL based techniques enable user to determine if the website (URL) is genuine before actually visiting the page. Also, our solution gives better performance than visual based approach presented in Chow et al. [18].

2   FHE and Privacy Preserving Machine Learning

Computations on encrypted data has immense potential to provide end-to-end privacy for the users. Considered as holy grail of cryptography, FHE enables computations on encrypted data without the need for decryption. Given a set of ciphertexts $C_1, \ldots C_n$ for plaintext messages $m_1 \ldots m_n$ respectively encrypted with a key, one can evaluate an arbitrary function, say $f(m_1 \ldots m_n)$ without compromising privacy of plaintext messages.

An FHE scheme in general supports two primitive operations, addition and multiplication. The two primitive operations, addition and multiplication, can be used to realize any arbitrary computation on ciphertexts.

$$\texttt{Enc(a+b)=Enc(a) + Enc(b)} \quad (1) \qquad \texttt{Enc(a*b)=Enc(a) * Enc(b)} \quad (2)$$

Privacy preserving machine learning has been widely studied in literature [20]. The FHE scheme we chose for our experiments is CKKS [21] which is implemented in HEAAN FHE library [22]. CKKS scheme supports floating point arithmetic on encrypted data which makes it ideal for encrypted machine learning usecases. HEAAN library implementation of CKKS scheme is easy to use and supports wide range of operations like add, mul, negate, rescale, bootstrapping etc.

Limitations of FHE: Any operation on ciphertexts in FHE induces noise. Of the two primitive operations of FHE, multiplication and addition, multiplication induces more noise and hence multiplicative depth is considered important metric to measure performance. To make computations more efficient, one can use approximation functions with low multiplicative depth to get the results with a reasonable accuracy.

Another major drawback of existing homomorphic encryption schemes is that they are inherently slow owing to the large size of ciphertexts. Ciphertext batching [23] enables packing of several plaintexts into a single ciphertext. This enables parallel operations on multiple underlying plaintexts in a SIMD (Single Instruction Multiple Data) manner.

Even though machine learning models have lot of potential to bring immense benefits to both customers as well as organizations, there are concerns being raised on privacy of customers data being collected. FHE based machine learning algorithms can be used that provide end to end privacy to the users. For the malicious URL detection usecase, we focus on DNN and logistic regression algorithms for classifying an encrypted input URL as malicious or benign. In this usecase, we consider private inference for preserving query privacy. This network is made up of several layers with each layer consisting number of neurons, neuron being the building block. A neuron, in this setup takes inputs as feature vector $E(x_i)$ encrypted using FHE, weights w_i and bias vector b, which server learned during training phase, and gives the output by applying the transfer function that returns an encrypted output:

$$\sum_{i=1}^{n} w_i * E(x_i) + b_i$$

This encrypted output is sent to the activation function to get activation output. Non-linear activation functions like Sigmoid, Tanh and ReLU induce non-linearity in the output of a neuron enabling the neural networks to learn from non-linearly separable data and perform complex operations. However, it is a challenge to realize functions with higher multiplicative depth in FHE domain. Therefore, approximations for the high depth activation functions are employed to efficiently compute them.

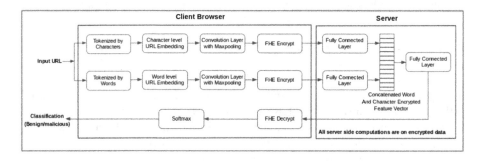

Fig. 1. DNN for privacy preserving malicious URL detection

A simpler form of binary classification can be realized by using a logistic regression based classifier. This does a linear computation of $\sum_{i=1}^{n} w_i * E(x_i) + b$ and the output is given by using an activation function. In other words, a logistic regression can be viewed as DNN with just a single layer and single neuron, which makes it much light in terms of computations. However, it is suitable for only binary type of classification.

3 Our Approach

We realize the privacy preserving malicious URL detection usecase using three approaches namely DNN, logistic regression and hybrid.

- We use DNN based approach for URL classification in specific we chose URL-Net [17] as the malicious URL detection server for our implementation.
- We use logistic regression model as the URL classifier [15]. It uses n-grams based feature extraction method from an input URL.
- We explore a Hybrid approach, where in the features are obtained using the URLNet's feature extraction method and the classification is done using Logistic regression model trained on these feature vectors. This ensures that the features extracted are of high quality and the classification on the encrypted features can be performed in lesser time when compared to DNN.

Feature extraction in these three approaches is performed on client side. Though the feature extraction is being delegated to client-side, it can be updated whenever required. Moreover, the malicious URL detection cannot be delegated completely to client side, as server might not be willing to share the model with the client. Also, server needs to send updated model to the client, whenever model parameters are updated.

We train our model on plaintext data using a dataset of 100,000 URLs divided into 80,000 URLs for training and 20,000 for testing. Training time for 80,000 URLs dataset for model based on (i) DNN is 45 minutes (ii) logistic regression is 2 hours (iii) Hybrid is 3 hours. In DNN based training, we tested for three different epochs as shown in Table 2.

We run our experiments using (i) DNN (ii) Logistic Regression (iii) Hybrid model, coupled with FHE implemented using HEAAN library. Our experiments were run on a system that has Intel Xeon Gold CPU clocked at 2.4 Ghz, 32 GB RAM and run on 32 cores. We perform training using PhishTank and valid URL dataset DMOZ (Refer [15]) for the details of datasets).

Table 1. Time and Memory for private inference using URLNet architecture

FC+concatenated layer	Layer 1	Layer 2	Layer 3	Layer 4	Time(s)	Memory (GB)	Accuracy (%)
2 (1024 × 512)	1024 × 512	512 × 256	256 × 128	128 × 2	**68.3**	**5.5**	**94.8**

3.1 DNN Approach

We model FHE based privacy preserving mechanism on top of URLNet architecture. Our privacy preserving machine learning model for malicious URL detection based on FHE is broadly classified into *encoding component* that changes the input URL u into a matrix format and *inference component* deals with the classification of URL as malicious or benign. Figure 1 depicts the block diagram of our architecture. To get optimal performance using FHE the encoding part is done on client side and inference part is performed on server side.

Encoding Component: Encoding can be performed using

- only character-based CNN
- only word-based CNN
- character and word CNN
- character level word CNN
- character and character level word CNN

Out of these, character and character level word CNN gives optimal performance. In encoding, URL sequence length is taken as 200 characters, above which characters are truncated. In case of lesser length, characters are padded with $<PAD>$ to make it 200.

Inference Component: The outputs of embedding layers are 1024 dimension feature vector. These are encrypted by client to get $\{E(cw_1)\ldots E(cw_n)\}$ which are given as input to server. These encrypted vectors are homomorphically batched to improve the performance of the network. Server passes these encrypted input through a fully connected network to give two 512 dimension feature vectors. These feature vectors are concatenated to form 1024 dimension feature vector. Server then passes this through a fully connected network. Fully connected layer consists of four layers which convert input of 1024 feature vector, into 512, 256, 128 and 2 respectively. The first three layers use ReLU activation function and the output is sent to the client which then decrypts and uses Softmax to get the classification results.

URLNet uses ReLU in the fully connected layers and Softmax for the output layer. ReLU is chosen to add non linearity in the network to perform robust prediction. ReLU function is as follows:

$$ReLU(x) = max(0, x)$$

Let $y_1 \ldots y_n$ be n real numbers. The Softmax function normalizes these into a probability distribution having n probabilities as follows:

$$\frac{e^{y_i}}{\sum_{i=1}^{n} e^{y_i}}$$

These activation functions are computed on encrypted data and usually have more multiplicative depth. Therefore, we use approximation version of activation function ReLU to get optimal performance. ReLU approximation polynomial (more details on ReLU approximation in [24]) is computed using the points

Table 2. Model accuracy based on number of training Epochs

Function	epochs: 5	epochs: 10	epochs: 15
RELU	96.5	97.4	97.95
Approx RELU 1	**93.49**	**94.5**	**94.8**
Approx RELU 2	52.87	49.9	51.1

Table 3. Appoximation polynomials for sigmoid

Approximation	Polynomial	Method	Accuracy
1	$0.5 + 0.25x - 0.0208x^3 + 0.00208x^5$	Taylor series in $[-8, 8]$ [21]	89.26
2	$0.5 + 0.15x - 0.0015x^3$	**Least square approximation** [25]	**91.43**
3	$0.5 + 0.253551x - 0.00148x^2 -$ $0.02587x^3 + 0.00158x^4 + 0.00371x^5$	Lagranges interpolation in $[-7, 7]$	87.57

$X_i, ReLU(X_i)$ where X_i are randomly picked from a standard normal distribution. The ReLU approximation polynomials of degree 4 are as follows:

$$0.1488 + 0.4993X + 0.3007X^2 - 0.0003X^3 - 0.0168X^4 \qquad (3)$$

$$0.1500 + 0.5012X + 0.2981X^2 - 0.0004X^3 - 0.0388X^4 \qquad (4)$$

Experimental Results. Each feature vector is encrypted as a single ciphertext. We used degree 4 approximations of ReLU function. We observed that DNN implemented using Approx RELU 1 (Eq. (3)) outperforms DNN implemented using Approx RELU 2 (Eq. (4)) (see Table 2). While the DNN based classifier gives better accuracy, it is computationally expensive. Client/Server side computation overheads are given in Table 4. We infer that DNN based implementations have higher computational requirements. Table 2 shows model accuracies for varying epochs. Table 1 shows time, memory and accuracies for encrypted inference for the original URLNet DNN architecture. The fully encrypted inference as a service ensures not required end-to-end query privacy for the users. The computation and communication overheads along with corresponding accuracy are tabulated in Table 4.

3.2   Logistic Regression Approach

Although DNN is the best in terms of accuracy, it is computationally expensive in FHE domain due to more number of layers. Therefore, we study a less complex logistic regression based model that gives practical performance and reasonable accuracy. In this section, we leverage logistic regression from [15] to classify URLs as malicious or benign in a privacy preserving manner. [15] uses n-grams based feature extraction technique where a URL is split into tokens based on special characters and converted into bag of n-grams.

Figure 2 shows the architecture for logistic regression based URL classifier using FHE. Here the feature extraction using bag of n-grams is done by the client

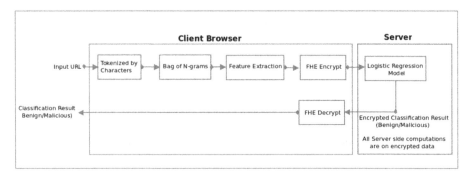

Fig. 2. Logistic regression for privacy preserving malicious URL detection

and the encrypted feature vector is sent to the server, which preserves privacy of user's input. Server does encrypted classification using Logistic regression based on FHE and gives encrypted classification result to the client, who decrypts the result to see whether the URL is malicious or benign. Since feature extraction is done using n-grams based approach, higher n value will give more number of features, which inturn increases computation overhead. Considering computational limitations of FHE, we found tri-grams are more practical and efficient in FHE setting. Each element in the bag of tri-grams represents a feature vector. These feature vectors are given as input to the server for classification. In [15], logistic regression uses sigmoid function to compute the gradient. However, as exponentiation is expensive in FHE domain, we use approximation of Sigmoid function which is a polynomial of some lower degree. The different approximations of Sigmoid are given in Table 3.

Experimental Results. We run our experiments for logistic regression based on FHE on DMOZ dataset (Refer [15]. We observe that approximation sigmoid 2 gives best accuracy in FHE domain (see Table 3). The computation and communication overheads along with corresponding accuracy are given in Table 4.

Table 4. Server and Client side computation overhead

Method	Client				Server		Accuracy
	#features	Ciphertext size (KB)	Encryption times (ms)	Decryption times (ms)	Time (sec)	Memory Usage (Gb)	
DNN	2k	786.4	12.3	7.9	68.3	5.5	94.8
LR	<1k	131.1	5.6	3.2	0.24	0.029	87.5
	5k	524.3	22.1	10.5	1.14	0.101	91.43
Hybrid	**2k**	**131.1**	**5.9**	**3.3**	**0.26**	**0.03**	**93.03**

3.3 Hybrid Approach

We started with state-of-the-art DNN based classification which is able to learn dynamically the features from a dataset and hence act as a better classifier.

However, it is computationally very expensive. Then we explored logistic regression based classification which is simple (and hence be less accurate than DNN based) and requires less computational resources. To overcome both limitations, we study a hybrid approach wherein the feature extraction is done using the embedding matrices and convolution layers from the URLNet architecture and these rich features are then used to train a logistic regression based classifier. This helps us to mitigate the tradeoffs of both the techniques to provide an efficient privacy preserving malicious URL classifier.

Experimental Results. The accuracy of our hybrid approach is given in Table 5. Table 4 shows that hybrid approach is more efficient (i.e. better in terms of memory and computation time than that of DNN and accuracy than that of LR) with less overhead both at client and server side, at the same time maintaining good accuracy. The ciphertext size is less compared to DNN because DNN requires larger parameter set to accommodate more computations (more noise budget). All parameters are set to achieve at least 80 bits of security for ciphertext.

Table 5. Sigmoid Approximations for Hybrid approach based malicious URL detection classifiers

Hybrid	
Activation function	Accuracy
Sigmoid[a]	95.6
Approximate Sigmoid 1	92.8
Approximate Sigmoid 2	92.6
Approximate Sigmoid 3	**93.03**

[a]Though Sigmoid gives good accuracy in plaintext domain, it is expensive to realize in FHE domain. Therefore, we use alternative approximations that perform better in FHE domain.

4   Conclusion and Future Work

In this paper, we presented a privacy preserving malicious URL detection model using Fully Homomorphic Encryption. FHE provides end-to-end query privacy for users. We modelled our solution in a client-server architecture delegating the inference computation to the server in privacy preserving manner. In plain domain, DNN based model gives better accuracy than logistic regression models. However, we note that in encrypted domain, logistic regression model based on approximation of Sigmoid gives better accuracy. We also analysed a hybrid approach which gives us the best of both approaches and highlight tradeoffs between computation requirement and accuracy in encrypted domain. Therefore, we recommend logistic regression based model with DNN based feature extraction for URL classification in encrypted domain.

Acknowledgment. The authors would like to thank Sumedh Gupte from Data and Decision Sciences Group, TCS for his help with the implementation.

References

1. Verizon Business Ready: 2019 data breach investigation report by verizon (2018)
2. Wombat Security: State of phish 2019 (2018)
3. Gerbet, T., Kumar, A., Lauradoux, C.: A privacy analysis of google and yandex safe browsing. In: 2016 46th Annual IEEE/IFIP International Conference on Dependable Systems and Networks (DSN), pp. 347–358. IEEE (2016)
4. Sheng, S., Wardman, B., Warner, G., Cranor, L.F., Hong, J., Zhang, C.: An empirical analysis of phishing blacklists. In: Sixth Conference on Email and Anti-Spam (CEAS), California, USA (2009)
5. Le, A., Markopoulou, A., Faloutsos, M.: Phishdef: URL names say it all. In: 2011 Proceedings IEEE INFOCOM, pp. 191–195. IEEE (2011)
6. Ma, J., Saul, L.K., Savage, S., Voelker, G.M.: Beyond blacklists: learning to detect malicious web sites from suspicious URLs. In: Proceedings of the 15th ACM SIGKDD International Conference on Knowledge Discovery and Data Mining, pp. 1245–1254. ACM (2009)
7. Zhang, Y., Hong, J.I., Cranor, L.F.: Cantina: a content-based approach to detecting phishing web sites. In: Proceedings of the 16th International Conference on World Wide Web, pp. 639–648. ACM (2007)
8. Apple's tencent privacy controversy is more complicated than it looks (2019). https://www.theverge.com/2019/10/14/20913680/apple-tencent-privacy-controversy-safe-browsing-blacklist-explainer
9. Lopatka, M., Bird, S., Segall, S.: Replication: why we still can't browse in peace: on the uniqueness and reidentifiability of web browsing histories. In: USENIX (2020)
10. Dwork, C., McSherry, F., Nissim, K., Smith, A.: Calibrating noise to sensitivity in private data analysis. In: Halevi, S., Rabin, T. (eds.) TCC 2006. LNCS, vol. 3876, pp. 265–284. Springer, Heidelberg (2006). https://doi.org/10.1007/11681878_14
11. How safe is apple's safe browsing? (2019). https://blog.cryptographyengineering.com/2019/10/13/dear-apple-safe-browsing-might-not-be-that-safe/
12. Gentry, C., Boneh, D.: A fully homomorphic encryption scheme, vol. 20. Stanford University Stanford (2009)
13. Saxe, J., Berlin, K.: expose: a character-level convolutional neural network with embeddings for detecting malicious URLs, file paths and registry keys. arXiv preprint arXiv:1702.08568 (2017)
14. Zhang, Y.-L., et al.: Poster: a PU learning based system for potential malicious URL detection. In: Proceedings of the 2017 ACM SIGSAC Conference on Computer and Communications Security, pp. 2599–2601. ACM (2017)
15. Tupsamudre, H., Singh, A.K., Lodha, S.: Everything is in the name – A URL based approach for phishing detection. In: Dolev, S., Hendler, D., Lodha, S., Yung, M. (eds.) CSCML 2019. LNCS, vol. 11527, pp. 231–248. Springer, Cham (2019). https://doi.org/10.1007/978-3-030-20951-3_21

16. Ma, J., Saul, L.K., Savage, S., Voelker, G.M.: Learning to detect malicious URLs. ACM Trans. Intell. Syst. Technol. (TIST) **2**(3), 30 (2011)
17. Le, H., Pham, Q., Sahoo, D., Hoi, S.C.H.: URLNet: learning a URL representation with deep learning for malicious URL detection. arXiv preprint arXiv:1802.03162 (2018)
18. Chou, E.J., Gururajan, A., Laine, K., Goel, N.K., Bertiger, A., Stokes, J.W.: Privacy-preserving phishing web page classification via fully homomorphic encryption. In: ICASSP 2020-2020 IEEE International Conference on Acoustics, Speech and Signal Processing (ICASSP), pp. 2792–2796 (2020)
19. Varshney, G., Misra, M., Atrey, P.K.: A survey and classification of web phishing detection schemes. Secur. Commun. Networks **9**(18), 6266–6284 (2016)
20. Lauter, K.E.: Private AI: machine learning on encrypted data. Cryptology ePrint Archive, Report 2021/324 (2021). https://eprint.iacr.org/2021/324
21. Cheon, J.H., Kim, A., Kim, M., Song, Y.: Homomorphic encryption for arithmetic of approximate numbers. In: Takagi, T., Peyrin, T. (eds.) ASIACRYPT 2017. LNCS, vol. 10624, pp. 409–437. Springer, Cham (2017). https://doi.org/10.1007/978-3-319-70694-8_15
22. HEEAN library (2017). https://github.com/kimandrik/HEAAN
23. Smart, N.P., Vercauteren, F.: Fully homomorphic SIMD operations. Des. Codes Cryptography **71**(1), 57–81 (2014)
24. Chabanne, H., de Wargny, A., Milgram, J., Morel, C., Prouff, E.: Privacy-preserving classification on deep neural network. IACR Cryptol. ePrint Arch. **2017**, 35 (2017)
25. Kim, M., Song, Y., Wang, S., Xia, Y., Jiang, X.: Secure logistic regression based on homomorphic encryption: design and evaluation. JMIR Med. Inform. **6**(2), e19 (2018)

Remote Attestation of Bare-Metal Microprocessor Software: A Formally Verified Security Monitor

Jonathan Certes[(⊠)] and Benoît Morgan

IRIT-ENSEEIHT, University of Toulouse, Toulouse, France
{jonathan.certes,benoit.morgan}@irit.fr

Abstract. Remote attestation is a protocol to verify that a remote algorithm satisfies security properties, allowing to establish dynamic root of trust. Modern architectures for remote attestation combine signature or MAC primitives with hardware monitors to enforce secret confidentiality.

Our works are based on a verified hardware/software co-design for remote attestation, VRASED. Its proof is established using formal methods and its implementation is conducted on a simple embedded device based on a single core microcontroller. A heavy modification of the core, along with a hardware monitor, enforces security properties.

We propose to extend this method to microprocessors where cores cannot be modified. In this paper, we tackle this problem with support from the microprocessor's debug interface and demonstrate that the same security properties also hold.

Keywords: Remote attestation · Security · Formal verification · FPGA

1 Introduction

Remote attestation consists in verifying that a machine called *Prover* satisfies necessary security properties to be trusted by a remote machine called *Verifier* [4]. These security properties are generally verified through a challenge-response protocol as depicted on Fig. 1.

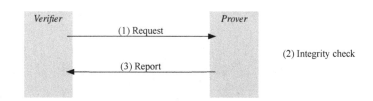

Fig. 1. Remote attestation protocol

© Springer Nature Switzerland AG 2021
G. Kotsis et al. (Eds.): DEXA 2021 Workshops, CCIS 1479, pp. 42–51, 2021.
https://doi.org/10.1007/978-3-030-87101-7_5

At first, the *Verifier* transmits a challenge to the *Prover* to request the attestation (1). The *Prover* computes an authenticated integrity check over its memory and the challenge (2) and reports the result to the *Verifier* (3). From this result, the *Verifier* checks whether the *Prover* memory state is valid (4).

To authenticate the answer, remote attestation requires the execution of a cryptographic challenge in a corrupted environment. Safety for this execution is mandatory to ensure security for the protocol. Authentication for the answer follows one of the following strategies:

1. either the challenge is designed so that a modification of its execution environment from the adversary inevitably alters the computation of the answer (which affects computation time);
2. or an integrity-dependent transformation for the *Prover* is kept secret from the adversary.

We can cite Checkmate [8] and Pioneer [13] as representative of the works from the first category. Works such as SMART [7] and VRASED [12] clearly fit in the second category as they imply maintaining a secret and require hardware support for access control.

Formal methods bring a high level of trust in verified remote attestation security. They allow to establish a proof, based on axioms or demonstrated properties, that the system and its implementation are secure. Formal verification is generally conducted in three steps. First, the system (hardware or software) is modelled, for example as an automaton [14]. Then, properties to be satisfied by the system are formally described, this includes secret confidentiality for remote attestation. In the end, *model-checking* conducts an exhaustive state exploration approach or a proof demonstrates that the system verifies the properties.

Section 2 summarizes the state of the art about remote attestation, usually implemented on simple devices, and its formal verification. An approach to extend verified remote attestation to microprocessors is descried in Sect. 3, the contribution is summarized in Sect. 4 and a verified security monitor is detailed in Sect. 5.

2   State of the Art

Eldefrawy et al. proposed SMART [7], a hardware modification for the *Prover* on microcontroller Texas Instrument MSP430. They dedicated a protected memory region to store the secret. Lugou et al. [10] tried to propose a unified method to verify hardware/software co-designs. They applied this method on SMART and modelled the system with *Proverif*. This method does not scale and comes with imprecisions as explained by Eldefrawy et al. in [6]. In all these works, security properties are enforced by a hardware extension, monitoring the system and capable of restarting it in case of a leak of the secret in its next state. *Model-checking* formally verifies the safety for this monitor.

De Oliveira Nunes et al. proposed VRASED (*Verifiable Remote Attestation for Simple Embedded Devices*) [12], a hardware/software co-design method for remote attestation. Their approach includes the implementation of an attesting software and a hardware monitor. This union guaranties security properties. The implementation is also conducted on microcontroller MSP430.

The attesting software is based on a formally verified cryptographic library (memory safety, functional correctness and secret independence) [15], which computes the *HMAC* of an attested region from a shared secret. The hardware monitor enforces access control to the secret as well as immutability and atomicity for the attesting software. A heavy modification of the core enables the use of the interruption signals, program counter and read/write addresses as inputs for the hardware monitor. The model for the attacker is as follows: the attacker can control the entire software state of the *Prover*, code and data, that is not explicitly protected by the hardware monitor.

The following steps describe how soundness and security proofs are obtained:

1. Soundness and security are expressed using temporal logics. This includes:
   - any direct access to the secret can only be performed by the attesting software (access control);
   - any memory region written by the attesting software (excluding the final results of the computation) cannot be read by the attacker.
2. Properties are described in the same formalism as soundness and security. This includes:
   - The resulting *HMAC* computed by the attesting software is correct (functional correctness).
   - The attesting software cannot be modified by the attacker (immutability).
   - Execution of the attesting software cannot be interrupted, it starts at the first instruction and finishes at the last (atomicity).
3. Proof for soundness and security are obtained through rewritings with *Spot* [5]: when their implication by the conjunction of the properties is a tautology.
4. *Model-checking* with *NuSMV* [3] ensures that the hardware monitor verifies the properties. Conversion tool *Verilog2SMV* [9] translates *Verilog* Hardware Description Language (HDL) into an automaton which is checked against the properties.
5. Some properties are axiomatic as they are converted from the specifications of the formally verified cryptographic library.

This co-design method for remote attestation is adapted to simple embedded devices such as microcontrollers. Our goal is to re-use its proofs for soundness and security as a framework to secure remote attestation on microprocessors.

3   Extension to Microprocessors

Unless working with open-source architectures, it is impossible to conduct modifications on the hardware, thus microprocessor cores. As a consequence, equivalent observations must be achieved from other inputs to deduce the state of the interruption signals, program counter and read/write addresses.

3.1   Environment

Modern Systems on Chip (SoC), such as Xilinx Zynq-7000, integrate ARM microprocessors along with programmable logic in a single device. This combines the flexibility and the parallelism of a Field-Programmable Gate Array (FPGA) with the performances of an Application-Specific Integrated Circuit (ASIC). Spatial partitioning for sensitive memory (such as the secret or the code of the attesting software) and implementation of a hardware extension can take place in the FPGA.

ARM microprocessors come with a debug interface called *CoreSight* which enables real-time instruction flow tracing without slowing down execution. Traces contain information to reconstruct the execution of a program. During the execution of the attesting software, the activation of program flow tracing, combined with the addition of specific instructions, provides data that can be used for monitoring. In particular, *Program Trace Macrocell* (PTM) module outputs a trace when an interruption or an indirect branch occurs and provides the destination address [2].

In order to enforce access control and immutability properties, the hardware extension in the FPGA monitors access signals to the sensitive memory. To enforce atomicity properties, it is coupled with the use of the debug interface. A trace is generated when an interruption occurs during the execution of the attesting software. The first and last instructions are chosen such as a trace is generated and gives the value of the program counter: an indirect branch with the address of the next instruction as a destination.

3.2   Refinement Approach

Extension to microprocessors comes with new constraints and increases the capabilities, thus power of the attacker. To adapt, we follow a stepwise refinement approach, in which we start from a very abstract microprocessor, similar to microcontrollers, down to a model close from reality.

First, we consider single-core microprocessors where we abstract capabilities for the attacker to rely on cache, Memory Management Unit (MMU) and the configuration of *CoreSight*. This system is called model 0: functionalities and targeted applications are identical to those of a microcontroller. The definitions of the soundness and security are identical to the ones described in [12]. They are to be proven.

Then, in a new refined model, a new constraint is added to the definition of security; for example: "the attacker is capable to reconfigure *CoreSight*". The conjunction of a new property, described in temporal logic, is added to the specification. As a consequence, the system must satisfy this new property so that the proof stays valid. Two possible approaches are considered:

– Either the new system is translated in an automaton and the verification of (both old and new) properties are conducted through *model-checking*. This approach is identical to the one introduced by [12], it is adapted to small automata.

– Or a simulation relation is established: if all states of the old model are simulated in the new one, then the new model verifies the same properties [11].
Only the new properties are to be verified through *model-checking*. This approach reduces the effort of verification in case of space-state explosion.

These operations are repeated for each new capability provided by the use of
a microprocessor. At each iteration, proof is established on the new model. The
refinement of the specification can be verified at each step with an implication
of its previous expression.

4   Contribution

To re-use proofs from VRASED and extend them to microprocessors, we re-use
their attesting software and automaton as-is. Due to the immutability of the
core, the inputs of this automaton: interruption signals, program counter and
read/write addresses, have to be deduced from external observations.

In this paper, we propose a solution based on hardware/software co-design
to deduce the value of these useful signals at critical steps of the protocol execution. Axioms describe the behaviour of *CoreSight* in accordance with its documentation and the content of the software. New properties are verified through
model-checking of the hardware. Then, we conduct a proof to show that the
soundness and security properties from [12] also hold on our model 0, even with
no modification of the core.

5   Verified Security Monitor

In this section we describe a method to prove the soundness and security on
model 0. Targeted applications are identical to microcontrollers, i.e. embedded
systems, and no hardware modification for the core is required.

5.1   Attacker Model in Practice

An application is loaded in the DDR, it runs bare-metal on one core of the system and behaves as a code loader. It expects code coming from the Universal
Asynchronous Receiver-Transmitter (UART), to load it in the memory and execute it. Depending on the application, this software might also expect code to
be transferred from the network interface. Any code can be loaded so that the
attacker can control the entire software state of the *Prover*. Memory is limited
so that an entire operating system does not fit.

5.2   Attesting Software and Monitor Architectures

Both the secret and the code of attesting software are stored in dedicated ROM
located in the FPGA. A RAM is also located in the FPGA and is used as
an exclusive stack by the attesting software. *CoreSight* debug interface outputs

program flow traces trough a trace port interface unit to the FPGA. Signals are monitored by the hardware extension to obtain read/write addresses and information about the execution of attesting software.

Figure 2 represents this implementation of a Xilinx Zynq-7000 where partitioned memories are accessible through the Advanced eXtensible Interface (AXI) communication interface [1].

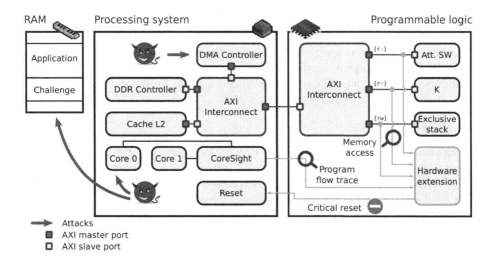

Fig. 2. Implementation on Xilinx Zynq-7000

Attesting software is re-used from [12] and wrapped around with specific instructions to configure *CoreSight* and the MMU. As a consequence, during its execution:

- first instruction is an indirect branch that forces *CoreSight* to output the value of the program counter.
- MMU restricts read/write addresses to the memories located in the FPGA and the challenge location.
- an interruption outputs a trace with exception information.
- last instruction is an indirect branch that forces *CoreSight* to output the value of the program counter.

5.3 Definition of Model 0

To validate our approach, a proof is conducted on model 0, where some of the capabilities of the attacker are abstracted. Here are hypothesis that we assume in the definition of our model:

1. the whole system is synchronous.

2. when a trace containing a destination address is output by *CoreSight*, the program counter takes this address at the next clock cycle; that is, the next system state.
3. the attacker does not reprogram the FPGA.
4. the attacker does not reconfigure *CoreSight* or the MMU.
5. during the execution of the attesting software by one core of the microprocessor, other cores are paused.
6. cache and registers are empty before and after an execution of the attesting software and after a reset.

These hypotheses are expressed using temporal logics and are considered axiomatic. They help proving that security properties hold and will be discarded in the subsequent models. Future refined versions of the hardware extension must verify that they are still enforced.

5.4 Proof Strategy

The hardware extension is described in *Verilog* and converted into an automaton. It contains the hardware monitor from [12]. Since the processor is left unmodified, verified properties from [12] are expressed using deduced values for the monitored signals (not their real values) and cannot be used to prove the remote attestation security anymore. We add axioms and prove that their conjunction implies the initial VRASED security properties. For instance, an axiom can be "if the deduced value of the program counter is in the address range of the attesting software, then its real value is". These axioms form a proof obligation to be discharged by the other modules of the system.

The other modules of the system aim at obtaining *CoreSight* traces and access signals to memories in the FPGA, then process them to deduce values that are accepted by VRASED original automaton. The cornerstone of the deduction process is a transducer that translates the content of *CoreSight* traces into deduced values for the interruption signals, program counter and read/write addresses. The automaton depicted on Fig. 3 represents parts of this transducer. Its outputs are predicates where:

– pc_d represents the deduced value for the program counter
– irq_d represents the deduced value for the interruption signal
– CR (for *Critical Region*) is the address range where the attesting software is located
– CR_{min} is the address of the first instruction of the attesting software
– CR_{max} is the address of the last instruction of the attesting software

Its inputs are events. For each label on the transitions, the event is that *CoreSight* outputs a compressed trace containing branch information. Predicates for these labels are defined as follows:

– @CR_{min}: destination address is equal to CR_{min}
– @CR_{max}: destination address is equal to CR_{max}
– *exception*: trace contains exception information

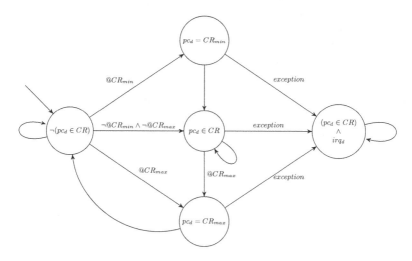

Fig. 3. Transducer *CoreSight* to VRASED : deduction of *pc*

This transducer verifies properties in which deduced values are expressed using the decoded address and exception information. To demonstrate our proof obligation, new axioms must then be added to express this decoded information according to the real values of the program counter and the interruption signals. With the conjunction of these new axioms and the verified properties, we prove the implication of the proof obligation.

These axioms form the next proof obligation for the rest of the system. The hardware is extended to decode addresses and exception information from a decompressed trace delivered by *CoreSight*. This leads to new properties, verified with *model-checking*, that helps to prove the next proof obligation with other axioms.

As a consequence, the design of the hardware extension is an iterative process which can be described as follows:

1. Security properties are defined in [12]. We re-use the same automaton to verify a property P_n expressed from deduced predicates.
2. Axioms A_n are necessary to imply the security property. These axioms form a proof obligation.
3. Axioms A_n are implied by the conjunction of properties P_{n+1} and axioms A_{n+1}. Rewritings with a theorem prover demonstrate that this implication is a tautology.
4. The hardware monitor is extended to verify properties P_{n+1}. This hypothesis is ensured with *model-checking*.
5. Steps 3 and 4 are repeated while incrementing n until the proof is based only on axioms resulting from a translation of *CoreSight* documentation.

At the end of the design process, our hardware extension is a composition of hardware modules: a re-used automaton from [12], a transducer, a trace decoder and a trace decompresser. Figure 4 summarizes our proof strategy.

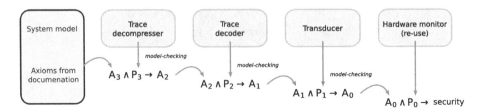

Fig. 4. Proof obligations

The role of the trace decompresser is to identify the type of packet that is transmitted by *CoreSight* and inform the transducer that an event occurred. The trace decoder transmits decoded addresses and exception information to the transducer when an event occurs.

5.5   Results and Future Work

Once we re-used the automaton from [12], our hardware extension allows to deduce all predicates and prove that all security properties from [12] also hold on our model 0. As a consequence, remote attestation security for embedded systems applications has been proven. Soundness has also been formally verified on our model 0 following the same approach as in [12].

To extend formally verified remote attestation to microprocessors, our objective is to refine our model so that each hypothesis defined in Sect. 5.3 is discarded and the attacker capabilities are not restricted. We intend to follow an iterative approach and extend our system to verify new security properties as described in Sect. 3.2.

We also aim at targeting complex applications such as software running on an operating system. The method for remote attestation may be adapted to the application in order to stay sound and secure.

6   Conclusion

VRASED proposed a formally verified hardware/software co-design method, based on *model-checking* and proof, and is implemented on a simple architecture with a heavy modification of the core.

Our approach to extend this method to ARM microprocessors is as follows: *CoreSight* debug interface proceeds to a non-invasive collect of data that traces the execution flow. Combined with a hardware extension and software wrapping, we retrieve appropriate inputs to re-use VRASED hardware monitor. Regarding hypothesis on the attacker capabilities, we have proven that soundness and security for the remote attestation can be ensured for embedded systems applications with no modification of the CPU core.

To extend the use of microprocessors to remote attestation, a refinement approach allows to achieve a formal verification in an iterative manner. When *model-checking* leads to a space-state explosion, we establish a simulation relation between automata and prove that the system meets its specification. Soon, our approach will allow to prove remote attestation soundness and security for embedded systems applications with non-restricted capabilities for the attacker.

References

1. AMBA AXI and ACE Protocol Specification, no. IHI 0022D ID102711 (2003–2011)
2. CoreSight PTM-A9 Technical Reference Manual - Revision: r1p0, no. ARM DDI 0401C ID073011 (2008–2011)
3. Cimatti, A., et al.: NuSMV 2: an OpenSource tool for symbolic model checking. In: Brinksma, E., Larsen, K.G. (eds.) CAV 2002. LNCS, vol. 2404, pp. 359–364. Springer, Heidelberg (2002). https://doi.org/10.1007/3-540-45657-0_29
4. Coker, G., et al.: Principles of remote attestation. Int. J. Inf. Secur. **10**(2), 63–81 (2011). https://doi.org/10.1007/s10207-011-0124-7
5. Duret-Lutz, A., Lewkowicz, A., Fauchille, A., Michaud, T., Renault, É., Xu, L.: Spot 2.0—a framework for LTL and ω-automata manipulation. In: Artho, C., Legay, A., Peled, D. (eds.) ATVA 2016. LNCS, vol. 9938, pp. 122–129. Springer, Cham (2016). https://doi.org/10.1007/978-3-319-46520-3_8
6. Eldefrawy, K., Nunes, I.O., Rattanavipanon, N., Steiner, M., Tsudik, G.: Formally verified hardware/software co-design for remote attestation. arXiv preprint arXiv:1811.00175 (2018)
7. Eldefrawy, K., Tsudik, G., Francillon, A., Perito, D.: SMART: secure and minimal architecture for (establishing dynamic) root of trust. In: NDSS, vol. 12 (2012)
8. Ghosh, A., Sapello, A., Poylisher, A., Chiang, C.J., Kubota, A., Matsunaka, T.: On the feasibility of deploying software attestation in cloud environments. In: 2014 IEEE 7th International Conference on Cloud Computing (2014)
9. Irfan, A., Cimatti, A., Griggio, A., Roveri, M., Sebastiani, R.: Verilog2SMV: a tool for word-level verification. In: 2016 Design, Automation & Test in Europe Conference & Exhibition, DATE 2016, Dresden, Germany, 14–18 March 2016 (2016)
10. Lugou, F., Apvrille, L., Francillon, A.: Toward a methodology for unified verification of hardware/software co-designs. J. Cryptogr. Eng. (2016)
11. Milner, R.: An algebraic definition of simulation between programs. In: Proceedings of the 2nd International Joint Conference on Artificial Intelligence, London, UK, 1–3 September 1971 (1971)
12. Nunes, I.D.O., Eldefrawy, K., Rattanavipanon, N., Steiner, M., Tsudik, G.: VRASED: a verified hardware/software co-design for remote attestation. In: 28th USENIX Security Symposium. USENIX Association, Santa Clara, August 2019
13. Seshadri, A., Luk, M., Perrig, A., van Doorn, L., Khosla, P.K.: Pioneer: verifying code integrity and enforcing untampered code execution on legacy systems. In: Malware Detection (2007)
14. Vardi, M.Y.: An automata-theoretic approach to linear temporal logic. In: Moller, F., Birtwistle, G. (eds.) Logics for Concurrency. LNCS, vol. 1043, pp. 238–266. Springer, Heidelberg (1996). https://doi.org/10.1007/3-540-60915-6_6
15. Zinzindohoué, J.K., Bhargavan, K., Protzenko, J., Beurdouche, B.: HACL*: a verified modern cryptographic library. In: Proceedings of the ACM SIGSAC Conference on Computer and Communications Security, CCS, Dallas, TX, USA (2017)

Provenance and Privacy in ProSA

A Guided Interview on Privacy-Aware Provenance

Tanja Auge[✉], Nic Scharlau, and Andreas Heuer

University of Rostock, Rostock, Germany
{tanja.auge,nic.scharlau,andreas.heuer}@uni-rostock.de

Abstract. Consciously collecting (research) data and respecting privacy aspects are two contradictions, which seem to be mutually exclusive at first moment. However, this does not have to be the case. But before we can address this conflict and its resolution, we want to understand what the terms privacy, provenance, and research data management actually mean. We are not interested in the formal definitions but in the community's understanding of these terms. We have the intention to explore how far the theoretical definitions are known in science and economy. Hence, we interviewed 20 people – scientists and non-scientists – and evaluated their answers for discussing the relevance of combining provenance and privacy in the field of research data management. We discovered that provenance is generally understood as the origin of data or physical objects, and privacy often refers to the protection of personal data. We found that all participants have a very good understanding of their own research data, which in most cases is based on a well-developed research data management. Nevertheless, there is still some uncertainty, especially in the area of provenance and privacy.

Keywords: Provenance · Privacy · Research data management · Guided interview

1 Introduction

A steady and rapid growth of research data can be observed across all disciplines. Depending on the research question and the domain context, re-evaluating existing data sets is a popular way to test or compare newly developed algorithms and concepts. Other research questions, on the other hand, require the acquisition of new data sets. This data we call *research data*. Furthermore, the results of a data analysis are research data as well.

Long-term archiving, provisioning and processing of such data improves the quality and traceability of research results. Furthermore, it opens opportunities for research and innovation. According to the German Research Foundation (DFG[1]), researchers and scientific institutions have to create conditions for the accessibility and reusability of research data. This ensures *Findability, Accessibility, Interoperability*, and *Reusability* (FAIR principles[2]) of digital assets.

---

[1] https://www.dfg.de.

[2] https://www.go-fair.org/fair-principles/.

G. Kotsis et al. (Eds.): DEXA 2021 Workshops, CCIS 1479, pp. 52–62, 2021.
https://doi.org/10.1007/978-3-030-87101-7_6

Collecting, evaluating, analyzing, archiving as well as publishing research data under the conditions above are main tasks of the so-called *research data management*. The aim is to guarantee the FAIR principles. Especially reusability can be supported by *provenance*, which deals in general with the origin of a thing back to its possibly physical source [5]. *Data provenance* describes the tracing of data records back to the original data. For this purpose, a number of additional data is stored together with the query.

In the project *Provenance Management using Schema mappings with Annotations* (ProSA [1,3]), we use provenance to determine which part of a huge amount of data is necessary for reconstructing a query result. The reconstructed data we call *(minimal) sub-database*. Submitting the sub-database and query in addition to the publication itself guarantees reproducibility. This improves the quality and traceablity as mentioned above. In ProSA we answer questions like: (i) **Where** does the data come from, (ii) **why**, and (iii) **how** is a query result calculated, by combining the CHASE – a technique for transforming databases – with data provenance. Next we want to extend our approach by the aspect of privacy. We briefly address potential difficulties and solution approaches in [2]. However, a detailed analysis is still required.

In brief discussions with scientists from various communities, we realized that many were not familiar with the concept of provenance. They appreciate the need for reproducibility and are often willing to publish their data. However, this changes as soon as personal data or partners from industry are involved. Considering privacy, tracing data back to its origins may conflict the need to protect (personal) data, which results in a natural conflict between saving and publishing data. In order to understand the dispute between provenance and privacy, we decided to do this interview study. It gives us the opportunity to obtain the definitions and interpretations of the participants. In addition, it allows an intensive discussion about the concepts of provenance, privacy, and research data management.

We interviewed a total of 20 individuals from different communities – scientists and non-scientists – in the areas of (i) *personal situation*, (ii) *provenance and privacy*, as well as (iii) *research data management*. We try to determine the requirements of research data management for the participants. Thus, the data needed in the long term and which data should be reconstructible in the first place. We expect that publishing their data in full is not always in the best interest of the participants. For example, if there is an exclusive right for using the collected data, even if only for a certain period of time, there is an interest in publishing no more data than necessary. In this context, the concept of privacy does not refer to the privacy of individual persons, but to the protection of (research) data as such. The latter is particularly interesting in the context of scientific funding agencies such as the DFG, which have certain requirements for projects and publications in terms of scientific reproducibility.

The interview series presented in this article is created as part of the ProSA project. We first start with the preparation (Sect. 3) as well as the presentation of the questionnaire (Sect. 4). This article focuses on the main interview results (Sect. 5). The most important terminology is briefly reviewed in Sect. 2.

2   Provenance, Privacy, and Research Data Management

Before we proceed with the interview and its evaluation, let's recap the common definitions of provenance, privacy, and research data management. Additionally, we briefly introduce the Sweeney experiment addressed later in the interview.

Provenance. In a scientific context, *provenance* deals with the origin of a thing back to its possibly physical source. This can be, for example, the result of a database query or the product of a chemical analysis. If the process can be reconstructed without media disruption and purely at the data level, we call it *data provenance*. *Workflow provenance* specializes in the representation of the production process. These are the most common types. In ProSA we focus on data provenance, which has the purpose to answer the questions: (i) ***Where*** does the data come from, (ii) ***why***, and (iii) ***how*** was the result calculated?

Privacy. The concept of *privacy* refers to the protection of personal data against unauthorized collection, storage, and publication. According to Article 4 of the European Data Protection Regulation[3], personal data is defined as "information relating to an identified or identifiable natural person", whereby a person can be recognized "directly or indirectly, in particular by reference to an identifier or to one or more factors [....] of that natural person". In ProSA, we consider not only personal data, but research data of all kinds to be worth protecting. In order to guarantee privacy, there are a number of different measures of anonymity such as *k-anonymity* [6] or *differential privacy* [4].

The Sweeney Experiment. Data protection is by no means trivial, as Sweeney points out with an illustrative example [7]: In 2000, a data set of 135,000 patients was published in the US state of Massachusetts. This contained, among other things, zip codes, dates of birth, gender, and diagnosed diseases. Social security numbers and names were not included, so the data set was classified as anonymous. At the same time, it was possible to acquire a copy of the voter registry, which contained the names, addresses, dates of birth, gender, and more of all eligible citizens. Combining both sets of data permitted the selection of the Massachusetts governor's diagnosis. Thus, removing distinct personal attributes is still not sufficient to ensure the anonymity of a data set.

Research Data Management. *Research data* represent data generated in the process of scientific research. *Research data management* refers to all activities associated with the preparation, storage, archiving, and publication of these research data.

---

[3] https://eur-lex.europa.eu/eli/reg/2016/679/2016-05-04.

3   Preparation

In this section we describe the sampling and evaluation methods. We further discuss the execution and evaluation of the interview.

Method and Sampling. Since for us the personal definitions and interpretations are of primary importance, we chose an interview. A quantitative evaluation is not a priority for us and only serves as a visualization here. In addition, we suspected a significant variation in the answers, which a standardized questionnaire would not be able to cover. It was confirmed in the course of the study.

The sample of participants is by no means representative. They are members of our professional network at the city of Rostock analysing data on a daily basis. Nevertheless, we made sure that the three affiliations university scientists, non-university scientists and non-scientists were equally represented. The same applies to the research areas or departments. The sample consists of sixteen men and five women ranging in age from early 20s to late 50s. We interviewed four undergraduates, five PhD students, two professors, seven non-scientists, and three research assistants for a total of 20 interviews. One interview was conducted with two subjects; all other interviews were single interviews.

Execution and Evaluation. We conducted 20 interviews of 20 to 25 min each. The resulting audio files were transcribed and anonymized. All personal information and too "explicit" formulations were deleted. Direct quotations are marked in italics and with quotation marks. For reasons of data protection, any details of the person quoted are omitted. All participants also signed a data protection statement and proofread the anonymized transcript upon request.

The interview consists of nine questions divided into three parts: (i) *personal situation*, (ii) *provenance and privacy*, and (iii) *research data management*. The first part has been collected and analyzed quantitatively. Parts two and three have been collected qualitatively and are analyzed both qualitatively (indication of quotations) and quantitatively (bar charts and word clouds). The quantitative evaluation is used in particular for visualization.

4   Question Catalog

We are first interested in the nature, dimension, and storage of the accrued data (*personal situation*). In the second part, we ask about the concepts of provenance and privacy (*provenance and privacy*). Finally, we address research data management and the publication of research data (*research data management*).

Personal Situation

(A) *What are you researching or working on? What is your status at the university, or do you have a profession outside the university?* This questions classify the answers into a specific research discipline. Thus, the way data is handled varies depending on environment and experience of the participants.

(B) *What types and amounts of data does your research generate?* Data comes in many different shapes and sizes, which affects how it is handled.

(C) *How long will the data be stored? And who takes care of storing?* Research data is usually stored for years. This applies to both primary and secondary data, i.e. raw and processed data. Managing this data requires some effort, which is therefore often not provided by the researchers themselves.

Provenance and Privacy

(D) *What do you know about provenance? And what about privacy?* First of all, we are interested in our participants' knowledge of the topics. The questions are therefore intentionally kept vague. Neither "data provenance" nor data protection in particular are mentioned.

(E) *Do you think of situations where privacy means non-personal data? If yes, which ones?* Since many people initially think of personal data when they hear the term privacy, this question may serve as a follow-up question. In ProSA, we consider not only personal data but research data in general as data worthy of protection [2]. Thus, they are also covered by privacy aspects.

(F) *Example: Am I allowed to publish this record as it is? If not, what to change?* To explore the understanding of privacy, we present an extraction of a medical sample data set (see Fig. 1a) based on the Sweeney Experiment above. The data set is highly problematic from a data protection point of view. We are interested in how our participants assess this data set and what anonymization approaches they are already familiar with.

Research Data Management

(G) *What are research data and what is meant by research data management?* The concept of research data can be defined very broadly. Definitions vary depending on the research field. However, research data management is independent of the discipline.

(H) *Would you allow another person to see your research data after you have published about it and why? What conditions would you set? How much data would you share?* Research data is often not property of an individual scientist. Thus, the decision whether to publish data does not rest solely with the scientist.

(I) *Does this contradict the idea of Open Science for you? What is your position on this?* The idea behind Open Science is that both scientific publications and the underlying research data are made freely available – that is, free of charge and without restriction.

5   Evaluation

We again distinguish three parts: (i) *personal situation*, (ii) *provenance and privacy*, and (iii) *research data management*. The first part is evaluated quantitatively, the other two parts qualitatively.

Personal Situation. We interviewed 20 people from different status groups and working respectively study areas, including scientists and non-scientists from the fields of science and engineering (5), humanities (2), data management (5) and software development (2), as well as continuing education (2). Among others, we surveyed scientists (10), non-scientists (7), and students (4).

All participants regularly deal with data management. Depending on the area of application, these are their own or third-party research data or publications. It is striking that most of them work with unstructured data. Structured data, such as (relational) databases, are hardly represented.

Often TB of data is stored for several years. This long storage period is partly by the requirements of third-party funders and/or the interest in long-term studies. However, some participants admitted that sometimes it is simply due to the fact that there are no well designed deletion strategies. Thus, data once collected is simply "parked" and never looked at again. We see a correlation between the amount of data and the duration such data is stored (see Fig. 1b). The bigger the data, the longer it is stored. We conclude that small amounts of data are less "valuable" than large amounts and might easily be reproduced.

In most cases, data management remains in-house, i.e., in the library or data center. Only four of the twenty participants are self-hosted or use external providers for data handling.

Provenance and Privacy. In the second part, we address the topics provenance and privacy. About 30% of our participants (scientists and non-scientist) have no association with the concept of provenance. On inquiry it turns out, however, that the topic itself is not unknown. They call it *"intersubjective intelligibility"*, for example. About half of the participants associate provenance with the *"origin of data or physical objects"* such as historical texts, artworks, and artifacts. They also mentioned compensation for *"World War II spoliations"* or food barcodes. With regard to data, this means the traceability of *"data evaluation processes"*, verification of *"published research results"*, and *"error detection"*. *"Legal safeguards in medical interventions"*, and the exclusion of *"fake news"* are also mentioned. More associations are summarized in the word cloud in Fig. 2a.

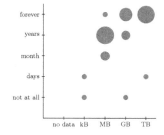

zip code	date of birth	gender	diagnosis
18059	06.03.1998	male	influenza
18055	21.09.1995	female	depression
18106	29.02.1994	male	heart attack
...	...	...	...

(a) Extraction of a medical sample data set   (b) Data size vs. time of storing

Fig. 1. Example data set and correlation of data sive and time storing

Most participants (70%) associate privacy with personal data. In this context, *"any inference about a specific person based on the data or activities must be prohibited."* A few refer to protection of data at all, i.e., personal data, but also (patented) research data and processes. They say *"data is generally worth protecting"*. They made a distinction between *"personal and personally identifiable data"*. So, data does not have to be personally in order to be personal. Others understand privacy as *"process of anonymization and reducing data to a minimum"*. Economists in particular point to the *"creation of and compliance with confidentiality declarations"* and *"data protection aspects"*. Data handling, management of access rights as well as storage duration and management are also addressed, albeit only occasionally. Some participants associate privacy with the *"prevention of re-identification of persons"*, a *"way to prevent that something becomes public knowledge"* or with the *"right to informational self-determination"*.

About a quarter of participants would not consider privacy outside of personal data, and another quarter has no idea what other areas of application there might be. In addition, our participants have the following ideas on where privacy could be used: military and government data, research data, pseudo-anonymized data, as well as data created in collaboration with research partners and companies, or data created using patented processes. The range here is wide.

In order to test the participants' knowledge of data protection in practice, we present them the medical data set shown in Fig. 1a. It consists of a `zip code`, `date of birth`, `gender`, and `diagnosis`. Almost all participants recognize the problems associated with this data set. For example, *"medical data is always worth protecting"* and *"rarely diagnosed diseases allow inferences to be made about individuals, especially if you know someone with matching symptoms."* The question whether the identification rate of 87%, which Sweeney determined in [7], is surprising, half of the participants answered yes, and the other half answered no accordingly. From this we can see no trend. However, our participants' estimates ranged from an identification rate of 5% to 99%.

To avoid re-identification, we will anonymize the medical data set in the next step. As techniques, more than half of the participants mention the omission of entire columns and the generalization of attribute values. In particular, they classify the date of birth as well as the zip code as "dangerous". Thus,

(a) Associations with provenance   (b) Reasons not to publish research data

Fig. 2. Survey results as word clouds

the birthday can be suppressed, generalized to the year, or be abstracted as age. In the case of the zip code, participants recommend aggregating different localities and districts. In this way, rare diseases in particular can no longer be assigned to a direct location. Permuting non-correlating columns, hiding individual tuples or coding attribute values such as A = May 2010 or B = September 2013, are also mentioned. So, we can say: the participants know the most well-known anonymization techniques such as generalization and suppression. However, the anonymization method *"strongly depends on the scientific question asked"*. Finally, there is always a *"loss of information due to anonoymization"*.

Summarized we found out that not all participants were familiar with the concept of provenance. Furthermore, privacy is limited to the protection of personal data. Almost all participants have the same definition of research data and research data management. However, their opinions on open data and open science diverge strongly. But let's take a closer look at this in detail.

Research Data Management. The University of Leeds, for example, defines research data as *"any information that has been collected, observed, generated or created to validate original research findings[4]"*. Similarly, our participants define research data as *"data generated by or needed in the research process"*. This includes primary data (raw data), secondary data (processed (raw) data), and metadata. Aggregated research data is itself research data again, as long as *"the process behind it is clear"*. In general, this includes the *"research method and question, the data generated, hypotheses, positive and negative findings, and the summary and analysis of the data."* Examples of research data types mentioned contain images, animal specimens, experimental data, measurements of all kinds, interviews, patient surveys, social media data, notes, transcripts, code, models and algorithms, network logs, audio and video recordings, simulation results, graphical representations, data files, etc. All in all, any data that is *"collected or aggregated as part of a research project"* can be considered as research data.

All participants describe research data management as the *"handling of research data"*. However, in response to the question of what good research data management looks like, the answers differ quite a bit. Thus, about half of the participants see *"archiving, storing and deleting research data"* as the main task of research data management. This includes not only the storage medium and the *"guarantee of long-term storage"* (compatibility of software and hardware), but also *"structured storage management"*. Because, "otherwise you simply won't find anything and that's just not good with terabytes of data." The protection of personal data and anonymization are mentioned as well by about 40% of the participants. A total of 25% of the participants names the *"guarantee of reproducibility and traceability"* as most important tasks of research data management, while another quarter mention the *"management of access rights"* and the *"protection of data from external influences"*. Further research data management tasks are summarized in Fig. 3.

---

[4] https://library.leeds.ac.uk/info/14062/research_data_management/61/research_dat a_management_explained.

Provenance and data protection are thus self-evident components of research data management for many participants. However, nobody mentioned both aspects. They always focus on one of the two concepts.

Roughly half of the participants is willing to share their data with anyone, *"as long as data protection is guaranteed"*. Some of them are doing so already. They make their data available after completing the associated publication or research project. Twice as many participants make their decision depending on the individual case. For example, data is *"shared within the department at any time"*, but the requests from outside *"is considered individually"*. About 30% of the participants fear the *"risk of competitive scientists"* who might use the data as a basis for publications as well. Accordingly, they are only willing to publish the absolute minimum of the data or merely aggregated data. Publication of data is often justified by the public funding of the individuals/projects. Some participants therefore feel obliged to make their data publicly available. They speak of a conflict between scientific competition and the desire of reproducibility and traceability in the sense of good research. In particular, the *"FAIR principles must be complied"*, i.e. the data must be findable, accessible, interoperable and reproducible. Privacy must be observed as well, as this *"weighs more heavily than traceability in the case of personal data"*.

There are many reasons for not publishing research data. On third of the participants name their *"own reputation"*, *"data protection aspects"*, as well as *"financial and economic interests"* as possible reasons. In some cases (about 20%), it is not the scientist himself who decides whether or not to disclose the data. This is decided by or together with the project partner or funder. In addition, *"economic interests"*, *"patent claims"*, *"political reasons"* as well as the *"financial and time effort during the data collection"* are mentioned. Some participants also mention *"ethical reasons"*, *"concerns about miss or non-citation"*, and the *"freedom of research"*. Others are concerned about the publication of data that contradict their own scientific thesis. A summary of possible reasons can be found in Fig. 2b.

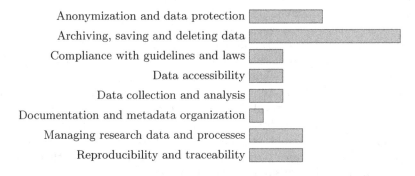

Fig. 3. Tasks of research data management

However, all participants agree that data from third-party funded research should be publicly available after a specified period of time. In this way, the scientist has enough time for first publications before the data become public domain. When asked about the duration of this privilege, the answers vary between one and five years. Furthermore, it is believed that good scientific research, especially in terms of traceability and reproducibility, can only be achieved by *"publishing as much data as possible"*. Additionally, the *"publication of negative research should be given higher priority"*, according to some of our interview partners. Last but not least, one of the participants added that the collection of data itself can be seen as a research effort, too. Therefore, the non-publication of these data would diminish one's own research performance.

Most participants stated that *"publicly funded data should also be publicly available"* iff the data can be considered unobjectionable in terms of privacy and public safety. If not, restricting access is seen as legitimate. Thus, they support the idea of Open Science. Most participants consider the freedom of research to be sacrosanct as well. Thus temporary embargoes, for example for five years, are accepted as a legitimate compromise. We also notice a strong disagreement on the scope of data to be published. Some participants are only willing to publish their results as Open Data or Open Access. While others also want to make their raw data available, too. Often, however, *"not before a corresponding paper has been published or the associated project has ended"*.

6   Conclusion

Consciously collecting (research) data and respecting privacy aspects are two contradictions, which seem to be mutually exclusive at first moment. However, this does not have to be the case. Before we can address this conflict and its resolution, we want to understand what the terms privacy, provenance, and research data management actually mean. For this, we interviewed 21 individuals – scientists and non-scientists – about their understanding of the concepts of provenance and privacy. Additionally, we were interested in the research data management practices of our participants.

We discovered that provenance is generally understood as the origin of data or physical objects, and privacy mostly refers to the protection of personal data. In addition, all participants have a good understanding of their own research data, based in most cases on well-developed research data management. Regarding this, the answers of scientists do not differ much from those of non-scientists as well as students.

Nevertheless, there are still some uncertainties which need to be clarified in the future. Roughly one third of the participants never heard or thought about the concept of provenance. And only two out of twenty participants understand privacy to be more than just the protection of personal data. Even research data management and the reasons for not publishing data differ in various disciplines. Reasons for not publishing research data are diverse, such as personal reputation, external interests, and privacy.

For all these approaches, problems and definitions, literature already exists. However, not all members of the different communities seem to be aware of it yet. Hence, we want to stimulate a discussion about the necessity of provenance, privacy and their combination as well as good research data management for as many community members as possible. After all, there is still a great need for clarification and discussion on this topic.

Acknowledgements. Thanks to all interview partners for their time as well as their exhaustive answers. Thanks also to Tom Ettrich for proofreading our article.

References

1. Auge, T., Heuer, A.: ProSA—using the CHASE for provenance management. In: Welzer, T., Eder, J., Podgorelec, V., Kamišalić Latifić, A. (eds.) ADBIS 2019. LNCS, vol. 11695, pp. 357–372. Springer, Cham (2019). https://doi.org/10.1007/978-3-030-28730-6_22
2. Auge, T., Scharlau, N., Heuer, A.: Privacy aspects of provenance queries. In: Glavic, B., Braganholo, V., Koop, D. (eds.) IPAW 2020-2021. LNCS, vol. 12839, pp. 218–221. Springer, Cham (2021). https://doi.org/10.1007/978-3-030-80960-7_15
3. Auge, T.: Extended provenance management for data science applications. In: PhD@VLDB, CEUR Workshop Proceedings, vol. 2652 (2020). CEUR-WS.org
4. Dwork, C.: Differential privacy. In: Bugliesi, M., Preneel, B., Sassone, V., Wegener, I. (eds.) ICALP 2006. LNCS, vol. 4052, pp. 1–12. Springer, Heidelberg (2006). https://doi.org/10.1007/11787006_1
5. Herschel, M., Diestelkämper, R., Ben Lahmar, H.: A survey on provenance: What for? What form? What from? VLDB J. **26**(6), 881–906 (2017). https://doi.org/10.1007/s00778-017-0486-1
6. Samarati, P.: Protecting respondents' identities in microdata release. IEEE Trans. Knowl. Data Eng. **13**(6), 1010–1027 (2001)
7. Sweeney, L.: Simple Demographics Often Identify People Uniquely. Carnegie Mellon University, School of Computer Science, Data Privacy Lab White Paper Series LIDAP-WP4. Pittsburgh, PA (2000)

Machine Learning and Knowledge Graphs

Placeholder Constraint Evaluation in Simulation Graphs

Stefan Nadschläger[1]([⊠]), Markus Jäger[2]([⊠]), Daniel Hofer[1,3]([⊠]),
and Josef Küng[1]([⊠])

[1] Institute for Application-Oriented Knowledge Processing (FAW),
Faculty of Engineering and Natural Sciences (TNF), Johannes Kepler University
(JKU) Linz, Linz, Austria
{snadschlaeger,dhofer,jkueng}@faw.jku.at
[2] Pro2Future GmbH, Altenberger Strasse 69, 4040 Linz, Austria
markus.jaeger@pro2future.at
[3] LIT Secure and Correct Systems Lab, Linz Institute of Technology (LIT),
Johannes Kepler University (JKU) Linz, Linz, Austria
daniel.hofer@jku.at

Abstract. Simulations can be represented in the form of a graph structure of components. *Placeholders*, where components can be added to the simulation, contain dependency constraint knowledge which is stored in a graph database. In this paper an application for automatic guided simulation creation is presented in the form of a three-step process to evaluate constraints of placeholders and therefore suggest suitable components.

Keywords: Constraint evaluation · Knowledge graph

1 Introduction

Small components can be assembled into an executable simulation, forming graph structures. The components themselves contain knowledge in the form of dependency constraints and a hierarchical set of attributes. In this paper, a three-step process for automatic guided simulation creation is presented. It is based on constraint evaluation of placeholders for simulation components in a graphical user interface. The simulations, the components and the component knowledge is stored in a graph database. Typically such problems are addressed by SAT solvers (see next paragraph), unfortunately these are hardly usable in enterprise application projects (adding (a) lots of complexity concerning data structures and usability for software developers, (b) additional layers in the system significantly reducing the performance of live evaluations). Hence, in this paper, a lightweight alternative to SAT solvers is presented in the form of a three-step process that operates on a knowledge-graph.

An application for solving constraint satisfaction problems are SAT solvers, for example [4,7,9] or its usage in Product Line Engineering [2,3,5]. Algorithms for constraint evaluation can also be found in rule engines, especially in expert

© Springer Nature Switzerland AG 2021
G. Kotsis et al. (Eds.): DEXA 2021 Workshops, CCIS 1479, pp. 65–69, 2021.
https://doi.org/10.1007/978-3-030-87101-7_7

systems (see [1,8]). Particularly the evaluation of the *if* part of *if-then* rules is related to the process described below in Sect. 3. An interesting approach for rule engines, especially in graph databases, is (unfortunately not scientifically published) presented in [6].

In Sect. 2, the functionality of simulation creation is described, as well as the technical aspects, like used frameworks and data structures. In Sect. 3 the three-step process for constraint evaluation is shown. Finally, a summary and outlook is given in Sect. 4.

2 Simulation Creation Process

The user of the system is able to define a simulation by combining components using a graphical user interface. Therefore, the simulation is represented as a tree, showing so-called *placeholders*, where components can be added. These place-holders express a dependency of the component on others, based on specific constraints. Hence, placeholders hold constraints of their parent. Components can be inserted into placeholders by selecting them from a collection of sugges-tions, which result from evaluating the constraints on properties and attributes of components in the database. Adding a component will either result in the addition of further placeholders, or the satisfaction of constraints. If all compo-nents are satisfied (no empty placeholders left), the simulation is in an executable state.

The simulation of a *motor* will be used as a simplified example in Fig. 1.

- The simulation starts with a special component, a so-called *base simulation*. This simulation requires another component to be executable and therefore the graphical user interface shows a placeholder (see (1) in Fig. 1).
- The placeholder requires a *Stator*.
- Again, this component requires another one and therefore a new placeholder is added to the tree, requiring *Material* (see (2) in Fig. 1).

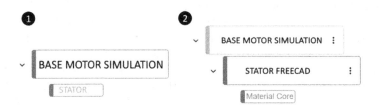

Fig. 1. Example of the Motor simulation. (1) Placeholder *Stator* for base simulation. (2) New placeholder *Material Core* after having added a component.

Every component defines *requirements* and *provisions*. *Requirements* are con-straints that the component needs to be fulfilled in order to become part of an executable simulation. *Provisions* are definitions of simulation specific parts (like data structures, other components, etc.) that are added to the simulation. Other components can require these provisions.

2.1   Technical Aspects

The system is implemented in Java and uses the graph database *Neo4J* for storing the components and representing the assembled simulations.

2.2   Definition of Requirements and Provisions

The basic data structure for *requirements* and *provisions* consists of the following classes:

– *ConstraintSet*: Combines multiple *Constraints* with a logical operator (AND, OR).
– *Constraint*: Combines multiple *ConstraintConditions* with a logical operator (AND, OR).
– *ConstraintCondition*: Represents a condition, for example type = "Stator".

Figure 2 gives an overview of the classes in an UML diagram.

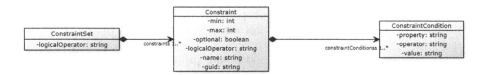

Fig. 2. UML class diagram showing the classes describing a constraint.

Listing 1.1 shows an example for a requirement in JavaScript Object Notation (JSON). The component requires another component with the name "Stator" and its property *path* has to start with "Simulation/Parts/Stator".

Listing 1.1. Example requirement.

```
{
  "logicalOperator": "OR",
  "rules:": [
      "logicalOperator": "OR",
      "ruleConditions": [
          { "property": "type", "operator": "like",
          "value": "Stator" },
          { "property": "path", "operator": "startsWith",
          "value": "Simulation/Parts/Stator" }
      ]
  ]
}
```

This constraint is translated into a *Cypher* query, searching for components that meet these requirements. An example of the result of such a transformation is shown in Listing 1.2. It already contains more logic, including several application specific transformations, e.g., the conversion of the *type* name into an internal *id*.

Listing 1.2. Translated cypher query.

```
MATCH (n: P4230546) −[:REFERENCES
    {name: "95571419−93a0−4a3f−9bcb−973e77047d88"}]−>(c)
MATCH (c)−[:HAS_CONSTRAINT*1..]−>(n2
    {property: "type", value: "2713", operator: "EQ"})
WHERE c.path STARTS WITH "Simulation/Parts/Stator" RETURN n
```

3   Placeholder Constraints Evaluation

The evaluation of the constraints (applies for checking the satisfaction of place-holders, as well as the decision if new placeholders have to be added) in the simulation tree follows a three-step process:

1. Search for components directly assigned to a placeholder. Every placeholder contains a unique ID and therefore direct assignment of a component can easily be identified.
2. Search for components fulfilling multiple constraints.
3. Search for remaining components, not directly assigned to a placeholder.

This process results from two additional properties of constraints and components:

- Constraints can define a *min* and *max* number of placeholders. For example, a constraint having *min* = 2, creates two placeholders requesting the same constraints that have to be satisfied by two different component instances.
- Some components are reusable, others are not. If there are two placeholders requesting the same constraints in the tree, a reusable component can satisfy both of them, a non-reusable component can only satisfy one of them.

The evaluation steps are run one after another, marking already fulfilled placeholders, so that they will not be evaluated a second time. The first evaluation step is trivial. The second step is necessary because several placeholders can have the same constraints, but cannot be fulfilled by the same component because it might not be reusable. Therefore, in this step the number of available components has to match the number of placeholders, excluding the components that are already assigned directly to a placeholder. The third step checks if there are components already assigned to other placeholders and that are reusable, so they could fulfil the remaining placeholders. The information if a component is reusable or not, is defined by inference using its attributes.

4   Summary

In this short paper, a constraint evaluation process is presented for combining single components to a simulation. Therefore, placeholders in a graphical user interface are used to automatically guide a user creating such a simulation.

A three-step process evaluates if constraints are fulfilled, or if new placeholders have to be added. The evaluation of the constraints themselves results in a list of suitable components the user can choose from.

In contrast to complex constraint evaluation solutions, like SAT solvers, a simple (in terms of code complexity and understandability), yet functional, process for applications has been presented. In contrast to SAT solvers and similar systems, this solution avoids proprietary software and only uses applied and trusted libraries/frameworks known from the domain of enterprise applications.

In this paper, work-in-progress of a running project about a simulation creation application is presented. The first project section dealt with the creation of a knowledge-graph for simulation components and constraint evaluation. In the next section the applicability of machine learning is analyzed.

Acknowledgements. This work has been supported by the FFG-COMET-K2 Center of the Linz Center of Mechatronics (LCM) funded by the Austrian federal government and the federal state of Upper Austria.

This work has been supported by the FFG-COMET-K1 Center "Pro^{2}Future" (Products and Production Systems of the Future), Contract No. 881844.

References

1. Akerkar, R., Sajja, P.: Knowledge-Based Systems. Jones & Bartlett Publishers, Burlington (2009)
2. Dhungana, D., Grünbacher, P., Rabiser, R., Neumayer, T.: Structuring the modeling space and supporting evolution in software product line engineering. J. Syst. Softw. **83**(7), 1108–1122 (2010)
3. Dhungana, D., Neumayer, T., Grunbacher, P., Rabiser, R.: Supporting evolution in model-based product line engineering. In: 2008 12th International Software Product Line Conference, pp. 319–328. IEEE (2008)
4. Eén, N., Sörensson, N.: An extensible SAT-solver. In: Giunchiglia, E., Tacchella, A. (eds.) SAT 2003. LNCS, vol. 2919, pp. 502–518. Springer, Heidelberg (2004). https://doi.org/10.1007/978-3-540-24605-3_37
5. Lee, S.U.J.: An effective methodology with automated product configuration for software product line development. Math. Probl. Eng. **2015** (2015)
6. de Marzi, M.: Building a Boolean logic rules engine in Neo4j (2017). https://maxdemarzi.com/2017/08/25/building-a-boolean-logic-rules-engine-in-neo4j/. Accessed 01 Apr 2021
7. Moskewicz, M.W., Madigan, C.F., Zhao, Y., Zhang, L., Malik, S.: Chaff: engineering an efficient SAT solver. In: Proceedings of the 38th Annual Design Automation Conference, pp. 530–535 (2001)
8. Russell, S., Norvig, P.: Artificial Intelligence: A Modern Approach (2002)
9. Tamura, N., Tanjo, T., Banbara, M.: Solving constraint satisfaction problems with SAT technology. In: Blume, M., Kobayashi, N., Vidal, G. (eds.) FLOPS 2010. LNCS, vol. 6009, pp. 19–23. Springer, Heidelberg (2010). https://doi.org/10.1007/978-3-642-12251-4_3

Walk Extraction Strategies for Node Embeddings with RDF2Vec in Knowledge Graphs

Bram Steenwinckel[1($\boxtimes$)], Gilles Vandewiele[1], Pieter Bonte[1], Michael Weyns[1], Heiko Paulheim[2], Petar Ristoski[3], Filip De Turck[1], and Femke Ongenae[1]

[1] IDLab, Ghent University – imec, Ghent, Belgium
{bram.steenwinckel,Gilles.Vandewiele,pieter.bonte,michael.weyns,
filip.turck,femke.ongenae}@ugent.be
[2] Data and Web Science Group, University of Mannheim, Mannheim, Germany
heiko@informatik.uni-mannheim.de
[3] eBay Research, San Jose, USA
pristoski@ebay.com

Abstract. As Knowledge Graphs are symbolic constructs, specialized techniques have to be applied in order to make them compatible with data mining techniques. RDF2Vec is an unsupervised technique that can create task-agnostic numerical representations of the nodes in a KG by extending successful language modeling techniques. The original work proposed the Weisfeiler-Lehman kernel to improve the quality of the representations. However, in this work, we show that the Weisfeiler-Lehman kernel does little to improve walk embeddings in the context of a single Knowledge Graph. As an alternative, we examined five alternative strategies to extract information complementary to basic random walks and compare them on several benchmark datasets to show that research within this field is still relevant for node classification tasks.

Keywords: Knowledge graphs · Embeddings · Representation learning

1 Introduction

As a result of the recent data deluge, the Semantic Web's (SW) Linked Open Data (LOD) initiative is used more and more to interlink various data sources and unite them under a common queryable interface. The product of such a consolidation effort is often called a Knowledge Graph (KG). In addition to unifying information from various sources, KGs are able to enrich classical data formats by explicitly encoding relations between different data points in the form of edges.

Using these KGs to enhance traditional data mining techniques with background knowledge is a relatively recent endeavour [28]. Because KGs are symbolic constructs, they provide the background information in a more graphical representation. Data mining techniques usually require inputs to be presented as numerical feature vectors and are thus unable to process KGs directly. With this

© Springer Nature Switzerland AG 2021
G. Kotsis et al. (Eds.): DEXA 2021 Workshops, CCIS 1479, pp. 70–80, 2021.
https://doi.org/10.1007/978-3-030-87101-7_8

in mind, some of the earliest knowledge-enhanced data mining approaches proceeded by extracting custom features from specific and generic relations inside the graph [16]. These approaches produce human-interpretable variables, but they have to be tailored to the task at hand and therefore require extensive effort. As an alternative, techniques can be applied to learn vector representations, called embeddings, for each of the entities inside a graph based on a limited set of global latent features [6,12]. These techniques are task-agnostic, allowing them to be used for different downstream tasks, such as predicting missing links inside a graph or categorizing different nodes [17].

Natural language and graphs often share similarities. Node2Vec [5] and other related techniques were among the first to leverage these similarities, by extending successful language modeling techniques, such as Word2Vec [11], to deal with graph-based data. Their proposed techniques rely on the extraction of sequences of graph vertices, which are then fed as sentences to language models. Similarly, work on (deep) graph kernels also relies on language modeling to learn the latent representations of graph substructures [8,24,29]. RDF2Vec is a technique that builds on the progress made by these previous two types of techniques by adapting random walks and the Weisfeiler-Lehman (WL) subtree kernel to directed graphs with labeled edges, i.e. KGs [18].

In this work, we show that this WL kernel, while effective for measuring similarities between nodes or when working with regular graphs, offers little improvements in the context of a single KG with respect to walk embeddings. In response to this observation, we broadened our search and examined alternative walk strategies for RDF data. Some were designed for regular graphs but in this paper, we show their applicability on KGs and compare them against the random and WL strategies on different benchmark datasets.

The remainder of this paper is structured as follows. In Sect. 2, background information is provided on KGs and walk embeddings. Next, Sect. 3 discusses five possible alternative walk strategies, including pseudo-code listings for each algorithm. Section 4 then describes the datasets used to evaluate these alternative strategies and lists the corresponding results. These results are subsequently discussed in Sect. 5. Finally, in Sect. 6 we conclude this work with a general reflection.

2   Background

A knowledge graph is a multi-relational directed graph, $\mathbb{G} = (\mathbb{V}, \mathbb{E}, \ell)$, where $\mathbb{V}$ are the vertices or entities in our graph, $\mathbb{E}$ the edges or predicates and ℓ a labeling function that maps each vertex or edge onto its corresponding label. We can simplify any further analysis by applying a transformation to the knowledge graph which removes the multi-relational aspect, as done by de Vries et al. [26].

Machine learning algorithms cannot work directly on this graph-based data, as they require numerical vectors as input. RDF2Vec is an unsupervised, task-agnostic approach that solves this problem by transforming the information of the nodes in the graph into numerical data, which are called latent representations or embeddings [18]. The goal is to capture as much of the semantics as possible in the numerical representation, e.g. entities that are semantically related should be close to each other in the embedded space. RDF2Vec builds on word embedding techniques, which have shown great success in the domain of natural language processing. These word embedding techniques take a corpus of sentences as input, and learn a latent representation for each of the unique words within the corpus. Learning this latent representation can be done, for example, by learning to predict a word based on its context (continuous bag-of-words) or predicting the context based on a target word (skip-gram) [4,11].

In the context of (knowledge) graphs, we can construct an input corpus by extracting walks. A walk is a sequence of vertices that can be found in the graph by traversing the directed links. We can notate a walk of length n and the labeling function to create a sentence as follows:

$$v_0 \rightarrow v_1 \rightarrow \ldots \rightarrow v_{n-1} \tag{1}$$
$$\ell(v_0) \rightarrow \ell(v_1) \rightarrow \ldots \rightarrow \ell(v_{n-1}) \tag{2}$$

The most straightforward strategy to extract walks is by doing a breadth-first traversal of the graph starting from the nodes of interest. Since the total number of walks that can be extracted grows exponentially in function of the depth, sampling can be applied after each iteration of breadth-first traversal. This sampling can either be guided by some metric, resulting in a collection of biased walks [2], or can be performed at random which results in random walks.

2.1 Weisfeiler-Lehman Kernel for Knowledge Graphs

Ristoski et al. proposed to use the WL kernel in order to relabel nodes as an alternative to extracting random walks [18]. The WL kernel was proposed as an extension to the labelling function and is originally an algorithm to test whether two graphs were isomorphic in polynomial time [27]. The intuition behind the algorithm was to assign new labels to each of the nodes, where each of the newly assigned labels captured the information of an entire subgraph up to a certain depth. This algorithm was later adapted to serve as a kernel, or similarity measure, between graphs [22,25], by counting the number of WL labels two graphs had in common. However, we argue that the WL kernel provides no additional information with respect to entity representations when extracting a fixed number of random walks from a knowledge graph. Entities in RDF are represented by Uniform Resource Identifiers (URI), which need to be unique[1]. As such:

$$\ell(x) = \ell(y) \iff x = y \tag{3}$$

Due to this property, WL relabeling, when applied on RDF data, is nothing more than a bijection from the hops in random walks to the hops in the walks obtained through WL relabeling. This relabelling task compresses a subtree into a new string label. There are no situations where a certain fixed label, present in the random walks, is mapped onto different labels in the WL walks or vice versa, multiple labels within the random walks that get mapped onto the same single

---

[1] https://www.w3.org/DesignIssues/Axioms.html.

label in the WL walks. As Word2Vec simply uses a bag-of-words representation internally, it does not make any difference if the original labels or the compressed WL labels were used. This means that WL relabeling does not add any useful additional information in the context of RDF data.

3   Custom Walk Extraction Strategies

Five different strategies were adapted to work with RDF data:

Community hops: As opposed to iteratively extending the walk with neighbors of a vertex, we could, with a certain probability, allow for teleportation to a node that has properties similar to a certain neighbor. The idea of introducing community hops is to capture implicit relations between nodes that are not explicitly modeled in the KG, and to allow for including related pieces of knowledge in the walks which are otherwise out of reach. In order to group nodes with similar properties together, unsupervised community detection can be applied [3]. In this work, we use the Louvain method [1] due to its excellent trade-off between speed and clustering quality. We provide pseudo-code for this strategy in Algorithm 1. We will refer to this strategy as *community*.

Alg. 1: COMMUNITY_WALK($\mathbb{G}$, v, depth, p, hop_prob)

```
# List of comm and vertex->comm dict
com, com_map = COM_DETECTION(G)
walks = { (v) }
for d in RANGE(depth):
    new = set()
    for walk in walks:
        for n in GET_NEIGHBORS(G, v):
            # Sample neighborhood
            if RANDOM() < p:
                new.ADD(walk + (n))

            # Hop to community
            if RANDOM() < hop_prob:
                c_n = com[com_map[n]]
                hop = CHOICE(c_n)
                new.ADD(walk + (hop))
    walks = new
return walks
```

Hierarchical Random Walk (HALK): The frequency of entities in a knowledge graph often follows a long-tailed distribution, similar to natural language. Entities rarely occurring often carry little information, and increase the number of hops between the root and potentially more interesting entities. As such, the removal of rare entities from the random walks can increase the quality of the generated embeddings while decreasing the memory usage [20]. Pseudo-code for this strategy is provided in Algorithm 2. We will refer to this strategy as *HALK*.

N-grams: Another approach that defines a one-to-many mapping is relabeling n-grams in the random walks. The intuition behind this is that the predecessor nodes two different walks have in common can be different. Additionally, we can inject wildcards into the walk before relabeling n-grams [23]. This injection allows subsequences with small differences to be mapped onto the same label. Pseudo-code for this strategy is provided in Algorithm 3. We will refer to this strategy as *n-gram*.

Alg. 2: HALK(walks, thresholds)

```
# Count nr. of walks a hop occurs
counts = { }
for i in RANGE(|walk|):
    for hop in walks[i]:
        if hop not in counts:
            | counts[hop] = [i]
        else:
            | counts[hop].APPEND(i)

# Skip rare hops
halk_walks = [ ]
for thresh in thresholds:
    for walk in walks:
        new = [ walk[0] ]
        for hop in walk[1:]:
            if |counts[hop]|/|walks| ≥ thresh:
                | new.APPEND(hop)
        halk_walks.APPEND(new)
return halk_walks
```

Alg. 3: NGRAM(walks, n, n_wild)

```
# Introduce wildcards in the walks
extended_walks = walks
for walk in walks:
    idx = RANGE(1, |walk|)
    combs = COMBINATIONS(idx, n_wild)
    for comb in combs:
        new = walk
        for i in comb:
            | new[i] = '*'
        extended_walks.APPEND(new)

# Relabel ngrams in the walk
ngram_walks = [ ]
map = { }
for walk in extended_walks:
    new = walk[:n]
    for i in RANGE(n, |walk|):
        ngram = walk[i-n:i]
        if ngram not in map:
            | map[ngram] = |map|
        new.APPEND(map[ngram])
    ngram_walks.APPEND(new)
return ngram_walks
```

Alg. 4: ANONYMIZE(walks)

```
anon_walks = [ ]
for walk in walks:
    new = [ walk[0] ]
    for hop in walk[1:]:
        | new.APPEND(walk.INDEX(hop))
    anon_walks.APPEND(new)
return anon_walks
```

Alg. 5: WALKLETS(walks)

```
walklets = set()
for walk in walks:
    for i in RANGE(1, |walk|):
        | walklets.ADD((walk[0], walk[i]))
return walklets
```

Anonymous Walks: Random walks can be anonymized by transforming the label information into positional information. More formally, a walk $w = v_0 \rightarrow v_1 \rightarrow \ldots \rightarrow v_n$, is transformed into $f(v_0) \rightarrow f(v_1) \rightarrow \ldots \rightarrow f(v_n)$ with $f(v_i) = \min(\{i \mid w[i] = v_i\})$, which corresponds to the first index where v_i can be found in the walk w [7]. Local graph structures often bear enough information for encoding and reconstructing a graph, even when anonymizing the node labels. Ignoring the labels, on the other hand, allows for computationally efficient generation of the walks. We present pseudo-code for this transformation in Algorithm 4. We will refer to this strategy as *anonymous*.

Walklets: Walks can be transformed into walklets, which are walks of length two consisting of the root of the original walk and one of the hops. Provided a walk $w = v_0 \rightarrow v_1 \rightarrow \ldots \rightarrow v_n$, we can construct sets of walklets $\{(v_0, v_i) \mid 1 \leq i \leq n\}$ [14]. While standard RDF2vec does not consider the distance between two nodes in a walk, walklets are explicitly created for different scales. Hence, they allow for such a distinction between a direct neighbor and a node which is further away. Pseudocode for this approach is provided in Algorithm 5. We will refer to this strategy as *walklet*.

4   Results

To evaluate the impact of custom walking strategies, we measure the predictive performance on different datasets and various tasks.

4.1   Datasets

Four datasets, each describing knowledge graphs, serve as benchmarks for node classification and are available from a public repository set up by Ristoski et al. [15]. The names of these benchmark datasets are AIFB, MUTAG, BGS and AM. For each of these data sets, we remove triples with specific predicates that would leak the target from our knowledge graph, as provided by the original authors. Moreover, a predefined split into train and test set, with the corresponding ground truth, is provided by the authors, which we used in our experiments. Three citation networks [21] were converted to knowledge graphs. These citation networks describe scientific papers and the goal is to categorize each of the papers into the correct research domain. Finally, the English version of the 2016-10 DBpedia dataset [10] was used to obtain embeddings for multiple different downstream tasks: 5 different classification tasks (AAUP, Cities, Forbes, Albums and Movies), document similarity and entity relatedness. More details on each of these tasks can be found in the original RDF2Vec paper [18].

4.2   Setup

For each of the entities in all of the datasets, walks of depth 4 are extracted. Only for the entities of DBpedia, the maximum number of walks per entity is limited to 500. These walks are then provided to a Word2Vec model to create 500-dimensional embeddings. Skip-Gram is used with a window size equal to 5 and the maximum number of iterations is set to 10 with negative sampling set to 25. These configurations are identical to the original RDF2Vec study. For node classification tasks, embeddings are fed to a Support Vector Machine (SVM) classifier with Radial Basis Function (RBF) kernel. The regularization strength of the SVM is tuned to be one of $0.001, 0.01, 0.1, 1.0, 10.0, 100.0, 1000.0$. For tasks other than node classification, an evaluation framework is used [13]. For document similarity, we measure the Pearson's linear correlation coefficient, Spearman's rank correlation and their harmonic mean. For entity relatedness, we measure the Kendall's rank correlation coefficient. For the benchmark datasets and citation networks, a pre-defined train/test split is used and experiments are repeated 5 times in order to report a corresponding standard deviation. For the tasks involving DBpedia data, 10-fold cross-validation is used and experiments are only repeated once for timing reasons. Moreover, the community strategy was excluded from the DBpedia experiments, as it cannot be efficiently performed on large knowledge graphs. For each of the walking strategies, we used the following configurations:

- The *random, anonymous* and *walklet* walkers are parameter-free.
- For the *n-gram* walker, we tune $n \in [1-3]$ and the number of introduced wildcards to be either 0 or 1.
- For the *community* walker, we set the resolution of the Louvain algorithm to 1.0 [9] and the probability to teleport to a community node to 10%.
- For the *WL* walker, we use the original algorithm used by Ristoski et al. [18]. We set the number of iterations of the WL kernel to 4 and extract walks of fixed depth for each of the iterations, including zero.
- For the *HALK* strategy, we extract sets of walks using different thresholds: $[0.0, 0.1, 0.05, 0.01, 0.005, 0.001, 0.0005, 0.0001]$.

4.3   Evaluation Results

The results for the various classification tasks are provided in Table 1. The results for the document similarity and entity relatedness task are provided in Table 2.

Table 1. The accuracy scores obtained by various techniques on different datasets.

	Random	WL	Walkets	Anonym.	HALK	N-Gram	Commun.
AIFB	86.11 ± 2.48	$\mathbf{91.67 \pm 0.00}$	63.89 ± 0.00	41.67 ± 0.00	86.11 ± 0.00	88.33 ± 1.11	88.89 ± 1.76
MUTAG	76.76 ± 0.59	75.00 ± 2.46	72.06 ± 0.00	66.18 ± 0.00	75.00 ± 0.00	$\mathbf{77.65 \pm 2.85}$	74.71 ± 3.99
BGS	79.31 ± 0.00	80.69 ± 6.40	65.52 ± 0.00	65.52 ± 0.00	80.00 ± 4.57	83.45 ± 4.02	$\mathbf{84.14 \pm 3.52}$
AM	75.56 ± 2.70	82.53 ± 1.68	47.47 ± 0.00	34.85 ± 0.00	80.10 ± 0.88	$\mathbf{84.44 \pm 2.22}$	73.94 ± 2.70
CORA	$\mathbf{77.20 \pm 0.00}$	74.32 ± 1.56	58.20 ± 0.00	14.30 ± 0.00	76.62 ± 0.36	76.46 ± 0.78	67.92 ± 1.22
CITESEER	64.68 ± 1.58	64.02 ± 1.46	38.40 ± 0.00	16.00 ± 0.00	$\mathbf{66.90 \pm 0.00}$	65.38 ± 1.22	58.66 ± 0.50
PUBMED	75.66 ± 1.36	73.70 ± 2.87	68.30 ± 0.00	24.20 ± 0.00	75.56 ± 0.08	$\mathbf{78.48 \pm 0.35}$	54.64 ± 2.40
DB:AAUP	67.94	**69.88**	69.27	54.73	60.08	66.96	/
DB:Cities	79.07	79.12	79.08	55.34	73.34	**79.79**	/
DB:Forbes	63.73	**64.60**	62.28	55.16	60.98	63.65	/
DB:Albums	75.24	79.31	**79.99**	54.45	66.89	79.38	/
DB:Movies	80.06	**80.48**	78.89	59.40	68.11	78.84	/

Table 2. Document similarity and entity relatedness results

Strategy	Pears. r	Spear. ρ	μ
Random	**0.578**	0.390	0.466
Anonymous	0.321	0.324	0.322
Walklets	0.528	0.372	0.437
HALK	0.455	0.376	0.412
N-grams	0.551	0.353	0.431
WL	0.576	**0.412**	**0.480**

Strategy	Kendall τ
Random	**0.523**
Anonymous	0.243
Walklets	0.520
HALK	0.424
N-grams	0.483
WL	0.516

5   Discussion

Based on the provided results, several observations can be made. The random and WL strategies were already evaluated in the original RDF2Vec study [18]. As such, the results reported in this study can be seen as a reproduction of those results. It is important to note here that the only reason why the results obtained by the WL and random strategy differ in this and the original work, is because originally the walks are extracted after each iteration of the WL relabelling algorithm. This results in k times as many walks, with k the number of iterations in the relabelling algorithm. If walks from only one of the iterations would be used, the results would be identical to those of the random strategy. We hypothesize that this is due to more weight being given, internally in Word2Vec, to the entities where many walks can be extracted from. While the original WL and random strategies result in very strong performances, especially on all downstream tasks of DBpedia, they are in this evaluation often outperformed by custom strategies proposed in this work.

The results indicate that there is currently no one-size-fits-all walking strategy for all tasks and datasets. It seems that the n-gram strategy results in the best predictive performances on average for node classification tasks. The average rank of the n-gram strategy on the four node classification and three citation network datasets, using all seven techniques, is equal to 1.86, followed by 3 of the HALK strategy and 3.07 of both the random and WL strategy. An average rank of 1 would mean that the technique outperforms all others on each dataset. The average rank of the n-gram strategy on all the node classification tasks, excluding the community strategy, is equal to 2.08, followed by 2.375, 2.875 and 3.67 by random, WL and HALK respectively. The performance of the community strategy varies a lot. On some datasets, such as AIFB and BGS, its performance is among the best while it performs a lot worse than random walks on others. This is due to the fact that the quality of the walks is highly dependent on the quality of the community detection. If the groups of nodes, clustered by the community detection, do not align well with the downstream task, the performance worsens.

Some limitations of this study can be identified. Firstly, no comparisons with other techniques are performed. RDF2Vec is an unsupervised and task-agnostic technique. As such, comparisons with supervised techniques, specifically tailored to the task, such as Relational Graph Convolutional Networks [19] can hold unfair results. In the original work of Ristoski et al. [18] it was already shown that RDF2Vec outperforms other unsupervised variants such as TransE, TransH and TransR. Second, a fixed depth and fixed hyper-parameters for the Word2Vec model were used within this study. While tuning these hyper-parameters could possibly result in increased predictive performances, it should be noted that the number of hyper-parameters and the range of a Word2Vec model are very large and that the time required to generate the embedding is significant.

6   Conclusion and Future Work

In this work, five walk strategies that can serve as an alternative to the basic random walk approach are evaluated as a response to the observation that the WL kernel offers little improvement in the context of a single KG. Results indicate that there is no *one-size-fits-all* strategy for all datasets and tasks, and that tuning the strategy to use, as opposed to simple using the random walk approach, can result in increased predictive performances.

There are several future directions that we deem interesting. First, a formal proof is required to show the non-applicability of the Weisfeiler-Lehman kernel on KGs. Second, it would be interesting to study what the impact on the performance is when the strategies are combined with different biased walk strategies. Third, all of the strategies evaluated in this work are unsupervised, but supervised approaches could be evaluated that sacrifice generality to gain predictive performance. At last, as already mentioned, each of the walking strategies are complementary to each other. Combining different strategies together will potentially result in increased predictive performances.

Code availability
We provide a Python implementation of RDF2Vec which can be combined with any of the walking strategies discussed in this work[2]. Moreover, we provide all code required to reproduce the reported results[3].

Acknowledgements. Gilles Vandewiele (1S31417N), Bram Steenwinckel (1SA0 219N) and Michael Weyns (1SD8821N) are funded by a strategic base research grant of the Fund for Scientific Research Flanders (FWO). Pieter Bonte (1266521N) is funded by a postdoctoral fellowship of the FWO.

References

1. Blondel, V.D., et al.: Fast unfolding of communities in large networks. J. Stat. Mech. Theory Experiment **2008**(10), P10008 (2008)
2. Cochez, M., et al.: Biased graph walks for RDF graph embeddings. In: Proceedings of the 7th International Conference on Web Intelligence, Mining and Semantics, pp. 1–12 (2017)
3. Fortunato, S.: Community detection in graphs. Phys. Rep. **486**, 75 (2010)
4. Goldberg, Y., Levy, O.: word2vec explained: deriving Mikolov et al.'s negative-sampling word-embedding method. arXiv preprint arXiv:1402.3722 (2014)
5. Grover, A., Leskovec, J.: node2vec: scalable feature learning for networks. In: Proceedings of the 22nd ACM SIGKDD International Conference on Knowledge Discovery and Data Mining, pp. 855–864 (2016)
6. Hamilton, W.L., et al.: Representation Learning on Graphs: Methods and Applications. Preprint of article to appear in the IEEE Data Engineering Bulletin (2017)
7. Ivanov, S., Burnaev, E.: Anonymous walk embeddings. arXiv preprint arXiv:1805.11921 (2018)

---

[2] github.com/IBCNServices/pyRDF2Vec.
[3] github.com/GillesVandewiele/WalkExperiments.

8. Kriege, N.M., Johansson, F.D., Morris, C.: A survey on graph kernels. Appl. Network Sci. **5**(1), 1–42 (2019). https://doi.org/10.1007/s41109-019-0195-3
9. Lambiotte, R., et al.: Laplacian dynamics and multiscale modular structure in networks. arXiv preprint arXiv:0812.1770 (2008)
10. Lehmann, J., et al.: Dbpedia-a large-scale, multilingual knowledge base extracted from wikipedia. Semantic Web **6**(2), 167–195 (2015)
11. Mikolov, T., et al.: Distributed representations of words and phrases and their compositionality. In: Advances in Neural Information Processing Systems (2013)
12. Nickel, M., et al.: A review of relational machine learning for knowledge graphs. Proc. IEEE **104**(1), 11–33 (2015)
13. Pellegrino, M.A., Altabba, A., Garofalo, M., Ristoski, P., Cochez, M.: GEval: a modular and extensible evaluation framework for graph embedding techniques. In: Harth, A., et al. (eds.) ESWC 2020. LNCS, vol. 12123, pp. 565–582. Springer, Cham (2020). https://doi.org/10.1007/978-3-030-49461-2_33
14. Perozzi, B., et al.: Don't walk, skip! online learning of multi-scale network embeddings. In: Proceedings of the 2017 IEEE/ACM International Conference on Advances in Social Networks Analysis and Mining 2017, pp. 258–265 (2017)
15. Ristoski, P., de Vries, G.K.D., Paulheim, H.: A collection of benchmark datasets for systematic evaluations of machine learning on the semantic web. In: Groth, P., et al. (eds.) ISWC 2016. LNCS, vol. 9982, pp. 186–194. Springer, Cham (2016). https://doi.org/10.1007/978-3-319-46547-0_20
16. Ristoski, P., Paulheim, H.: A comparison of propositionalization strategies for creating features from linked open data. In: Linked Data for Knowledge Discovery (2014)
17. Ristoski, P., Paulheim, H.: Semantic web in data mining and knowledge discovery: a comprehensive survey. J. Web Semantics **36**, 1–22 (2016)
18. Ristoski, P., et al.: RDF2vec: RDF graph embeddings and their applications. Semantic Web **10**(4), 721–752 (2019)
19. Schlichtkrull, M., Kipf, T.N., Bloem, P., van den Berg, R., Titov, I., Welling, M.: Modeling relational data with graph convolutional networks. In: Gangemi, A., et al. (eds.) ESWC 2018. LNCS, vol. 10843, pp. 593–607. Springer, Cham (2018). https://doi.org/10.1007/978-3-319-93417-4_38
20. Schlötterer, J., et al.: Investigating extensions to random walk based graph embedding. In: 2019 IEEE International Conference on Cognitive Computing (ICCC), pp. 81–89. IEEE (2019)
21. Sen, P., et al.: Collective classification in network data. AI Mag. **29**, 93 (2008)
22. Shervashidze, N., et al.: Weisfeiler-Lehman graph kernels. J. Mach. Learn. Res. **12**, 2539–2561 (2011)
23. Vandewiele, G., et al.: Inducing a decision tree with discriminative paths to classify entities in a knowledge graph. In: SEPDA2019, the 4th International Workshop on Semantics-Powered Data Mining and Analytics, pp. 1–6 (2019)
24. Vishwanathan, S.V.N., et al.: Graph kernels. J. Mach. Learn. Res. **11**, 1201–1242 (2010)
25. Vries, G.K.D.: A fast approximation of the Weisfeiler-Lehman graph kernel for RDF data. In: Blockeel, H., Kersting, K., Nijssen, S., Železný, F. (eds.) ECML PKDD 2013. LNCS (LNAI), vol. 8188, pp. 606–621. Springer, Heidelberg (2013). https://doi.org/10.1007/978-3-642-40988-2_39
26. de Vries, G.K.D., de Rooij, S.: Substructure counting graph kernels for machine learning from RDF data. Web Semantics Sci. Serv. Agents World Wide Web **35**, 71–84 (2015)

27. Weisfeiler, B., Lehman, A.A.: A reduction of a graph to a canonical form and an algebra arising during this reduction. Nauchno-Technicheskaya Informatsia **2**(9), 12–16 (1968)
28. Wilcke, X., et al.: The knowledge graph as the default data model for machine learning. Data Sci. **1**, 39–57 (2017). https://doi.org/10.3233/DS-170007
29. Yanardag, P., Vishwanathan, S.: Deep graph kernels. In: Proceedings of the 21th ACM SIGKDD International Conference on Knowledge Discovery and Data Mining, pp. 1365–1374 (2015)

Bridging Semantic Web and Machine Learning: First Results of a Systematic Mapping Study

Laura Waltersdorfer[1]([✉])[ID], Anna Breit[2][ID], Fajar J. Ekaputra[1][ID],
and Marta Sabou[1][ID]

[1] TU Wien, Vienna, Austria
Laura.waltersdorfer@tuwien.ac.at
[2] Semantic Web Company, Vienna, Austria

Abstract. Both symbolic and subsymbolic AI research have seen a recent surge driven by innovative approaches, such as neural networks and knowledge graphs. Further opportunities lie in the combined use of these two paradigms in ways that benefit from their complementary strengths. Accordingly, there is much research at the confluence of these two research areas and a number of efforts were already made to survey and analyze the resulting research area. However, to our knowledge, none of these surveys rely on methodologies that aim to capture an evidence-based characterization of the area while at the same time being reproducible. To fill in this gap, in this paper we report on our ongoing work to apply a systematic mapping study methodology to better characterise systems in this area. Given the breadth of the area, we scope the study to focus on systems that combine semantic web technologies and machine learning, which we call SWeML Systems. While the study is still ongoing, we hereby report on its design and the first results obtained.

Keywords: Machine learning · Semantic web · Systematic mapping study · Knowledge engineering

1 Introduction

Machine learning (ML) and knowledge engineering have both experienced extensive advancements in research over the last years. Increasing usage of machine learning methods has been achieved recently through deep learning approaches, such as neural networks [9], while symbolic AI is influenced mainly by research on knowledge graphs [4].

However, both areas also have their limitations. On the one hand, modern machine learning techniques need a significant amount of training data and resources to effectively learn complex heterogeneous knowledge which is typically relational and sparse and better captured in symbolic knowledge structures such as ontologies or knowledge graphs. On the other hand, traditional

© Springer Nature Switzerland AG 2021
G. Kotsis et al. (Eds.): DEXA 2021 Workshops, CCIS 1479, pp. 81–90, 2021.
https://doi.org/10.1007/978-3-030-87101-7_9

knowledge engineering approaches are time-consuming in the starting phase and require extensive efforts from domain experts for setup, evaluation, enrichment or validation. To mitigate these shortcomings, interest has grown to combine the strengths of statistical machine learning and symbolic domain knowledge. Such systems are expected to provide improved explainability of results, reduced complexity of AI models and integrating various heterogeneous data sources semantically [1]. In this broad area of hybrid AI systems, our focus is on **Semantic Web Machine Learning Systems (SWeMLS)s**, a subfield of symbolic and statistical technologies and approaches such as neural networks and knowledge graphs.

Despite their importance, there are limited evidence-based findings yet concerning a characterisation and taxonomy of hybrid AI systems in general, and SWeMLSs in particular. A short synopsis of **recent surveys** related to the intersection between semantic web and machine learning (Table 1) reveals that (1) most surveys do not adopt a principled and reproducible methodology for collecting the overviewed papers, but rather choose an ad-hoc paper collection approach [2,7,10] or (2) are scoped around very specific application areas of SWeMLS such as explainable AI or knowledge discovery [6–8].

Table 1. Related survey paper synopsis focusing on the intersection of semantic web and machine learning.

Paper	Survey type	Research area	Scoping
[8]	Systematic review	SWeML	Semantic web technologies and machine learning for explainable AI
[7]	Theoretical work	SWeML	Linked data preparation for usage in ML pipelines; enterprise applications
[6]	Qualitative review	SWeML	Application of semantic web technologies across the knowledge discovery process
[2]	Vision paper	SWeML	Machine learning for the semantic web
[10]	Theoretical work	Neuro-symbolic	Compositional design patterns for neuro-symbolic systems

We therefore conclude that there is a need for a survey of SWeMLSs that adopts a systematic and reproducible methodology to complement current insights with more evidence-based findings. To this end, we are currently performing a *Systematic Mapping Study (SMS)* of SWeMLS focusing on two core research questions: *(i) How are semantic web technologies and machine learning techniques combined? and (ii) How can these interactions be classified in a systematic taxonomy?* From these questions we derived more specific research questions:

- **RQ1 Characteristics of the System:** What kind of SWeMLSs are proposed?
- **RQ2 Application Areas:** What are typical application areas for SWeMLSs?
- **RQ3 Characteristics of ML Module:** What are the characteristics of the machine learning model(s) used in the SWeMLSs?

- **RQ4 Characteristics of the SW Module:** What are the characteristics of the semantic web knowledge structure used in the SWeMLSs?
- **RQ5 Patterns of Connections:** What is the processing flow of the systems in terms of inputs/outputs and the order of processing units?
- **RQ6 Auditability:** Is the auditability/transparency of the system considered?

Systematic Mapping Studies (SMS) are an established method in evidence-based research, also relevant to software engineering [5] for the following reasons: (1) they follow a well-defined paper selection process to identify a *representative set* of primary studies *reducing selection bias* in comparison to ad-hoc study selection; (2) they follow a standard documented process allowing for the study to be *reproduced.*

In this paper, we report on ongoing work on using a SMS method for surveying SWeMLSs. We share the main steps of the method (Sect. 2) and provide initial results (Sect. 3). Conclusions and future steps are discussed in Sect. 4.

2   Survey Methodology: Systematic Mapping Study

The SMS process (Fig. 1), consists of three consecutive stages (1) *Study Planning,* (2) *Study Execution,* and (3) *Analysis and Reporting* stage, which we detail in the next sections.

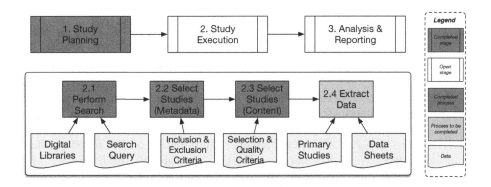

Fig. 1. Overview of the Systematic Mapping Study process.

2.1   Study Planning

In the *Study Planning* stage the goal is to define the scope and methodology of the study and document essential decisions in a *study protocol.* Of key importance in this stage is *study scoping* which involves identifying and analyzing related surveys, related research areas and clearly defining the scope of the survey.

Study Scoping: Definition of Semantic Web Machine Learning Systems. Initially, we defined the topic of interest for our study as Semantic Artificial Intelligence Systems (SAIS). However, after piloting first research questions and keywords, we realized that this definition was too broadly defined: *Firstly*, the retrieved number of papers were unmanageable in size and scope. *Additionally*, it was hard to define a common understanding for the highly heterogeneous approaches. Therefore, we propose the subject of our study to be scoped to SWeMLS, requiring them to fulfill the following three criteria:

1. *They should contain a knowledge structure* module, that represents a domain model, relying on formal logical foundation and encoded in a W3C web-based knowledge representation language such as RDFS, OWL. This might include vocabularies, taxonomies, knowledge graphs, ontologies, and other structures based on linked data.
2. *They should contain a machine learning* module that consists of an inductive model which is able to generalise over a given set of examples. These models include rule learning systems, traditional machine learning models such as support vector machines, random forests, or multi-layer perceptrons, as well as more recent deep learning models.
3. *Task-Based Application.* Application of both aforementioned modules to ensure that the systems have a certain maturity by solving a task or problem in a defined domain.

2.2   Study Execution

During the study execution stage, the study team follows the methodology laid out by the study protocol to (1) retrieve relevant primary studies through search in digital libraries (*Step 2.1*), (2) filter retrieved studies to remove false-positives, i.e., papers that are outside the scope of the survey (*Steps 2.2 and 2.3*) and, finally, (3) read the selected studies and extract relevant data by populating a data extractions sheet defined in the study protocol (*Step 2.4*).

Study Search (Step 2.1). We performed the study search on the following electronic databases: Web of Science[1], ACM Digital Library[2], IEEE Xplore[3] and Scopus[4]. For each digital library, the same search query was used. Our search query is a conjunction of three subqueries ($Q = Q1 \cap Q2 \cap Q3$).

The sub-queries consist of the disjunction (OR) of a number or representative keywords detailed in Table 2 and chosen based on the following rationale:

Query Q1 keywords include (1) name of the overall field of interest (semantic web); (2) most frequent terms referring to semantic structures that have a certain complexity and are established outside of the semantic web community

---

[1] https://www.webofknowledge.com/.
[2] https://dl.acm.org/.
[3] https://ieeexplore.ieee.org/.
[4] https://www.scopus.com/.

Table 2. Sub-queries for the overall search query $Q = Q1 \cap Q2 \cap Q3$. Each sub-query consists of a disjunction (OR) of the relevant search keywords.

Sub-query	Used search keywords
Q1 (SW module)	Knowledge graph, linked data, semantic web, ontolog*, RDF, OWL, SPARQL, SHACL
Q2 (ML module)	Deep learning, neural network, embedding, representation learning, feature learning, language model, language representation model, rule mining, rule learning, rule induction, genetic programming, genetic algorithm, kernel method
Q3 (System)	Natural Language Processing, Computer Vision, Information Retrieval, Data Mining, Information Integration, Knowledge Management, Pattern Recognition, Speech Recognition

(ontolog*, linked data, knowledge graph) as well as (3) a number of W3C recommendations that are likely to be used when implementing semantic web structures.

Query Q2 keywords include terms for machine learning. Since this field is still rapidly evolving, we adopted the following approach for keyword selection. Three external sources were considered as a basis (all visited on Oct 2nd 2020): ACM Computing Classification System (CCS)[5], *Microsoft Academic*[6,7] and specific Wikipedia[8,9] categories. For all three sources child topics or categories to *Artificial intelligence* and *Machine learning* were considered. Keywords appearing in all three sources were selected.

Query Q3 includes task-based keywords to assure that retrieved documents present systems that are aiming to solve specific tasks. We adopted a similar approach to the second research question. Herefore, an intersection of all relevant children of (1) ACM CCS (See Footnote 5) concepts *Artificial Intelligence machine learning, information systems*, (2) *Microsoft Academic* Topics *machine learning* (See Footnote 6) and *artificial intelligence* (See Footnote 7) and (3) Wikipedia categories *artificial intelligence* (See Footnote 8) and *machine learning* (See Footnote 9) was taken into account, where children were considered 'relevant' if they represent an application area.

For these queries 2865 papers were returned from the four digital libraries as depicted in Fig. 2. After merging the result sets of each digital library, 1986 papers remained.

Study Selection (Steps 2.2 and 2.3) identifies those primary studies that will serve as input for the survey. To make the study selection transparent in a distributed team, a set of seven *study selection criteria* was defined. For each

---

[5] https://dl.acm.org/ccs.

[6] https://academic.microsoft.com/topics/41008148,119857082.

[7] https://academic.microsoft.com/topics/41008148,154945302.

[8] https://en.wikipedia.org/wiki/Category:Artificial_intelligence.

[9] https://en.wikipedia.org/wiki/Category:Machine_learning.

criterion, an inclusion as well as a complementary exclusion criterion was formulated. Inclusion criteria (IC) 1–5 focus on metadata such as date, language,
type of publication, accessibility and duplicates. IC6 and IC7 focus on the content and described systems, whether they contain a respective semantic web and
machine learning component and the presence of a solved task by the system,
so whether the system adheres to our definition of SWeMLS.

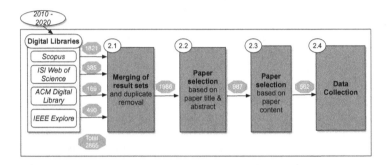

Fig. 2. Initial results of the study selection

The *selection methodology* includes two separate selection steps, first focusing
on meta-data, titles and abstracts. Researchers rule on inclusion or exclusion
considering mainly the two criteria: (1) is there an interconnection of machine
learning and semantic web and (2) is the system solving any task, is there an
evaluation of this task. A second assignee checks unclear cases and 10% of the
decisions of the first researcher. This step reduced the number of papers to 987
papers. In *Step 2.3* all papers are investigated more thoroughly based on the
content of the entire paper, with 562 papers being selected for the study.

3   Initial Results

Based on the ongoing data collection from the remaining 562 papers, we can
report on first initial insights from the study.

Bibliographic Data: From the analysis of the publication count over the years
and publication databases (Fig. 3A), two trends emerge: 1) a progressing absolute
surge in publication numbers over the last three years in all databases and 2)
large portions of the selected papers being available from Scopus. Between 2010
and 2016, the published papers account each year for under 5%, while from 2017
on more than 10% of papers were retrieved, increasing for 2019 and 2020 to over
20%[10].

---

[10] Please note for Fig. 3A, search queries were conducted on November 2nd 2020. Furthermore, papers were counted multiple times for this graphics, in case they were
available in more than one digital library.

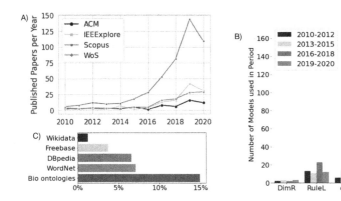

Fig. 3. Published papers about SWeMLSs: (A) Number of papers published in the considered digital libraries over the years; (B) Evolution of the used machine learning algorithms over years; (C) Most frequently used semantic web resources.

RQ2. Targeted Tasks: During the initial phases of study selection, we started with a generic top-down approach of tasks based on related surveys and internal discussions (e.g. data integration, recommender systems,...). During study selection, researchers were able to extend this list based on identified tasks from analysed papers. Thus, we constructed a more comprehensive list based on the input from researchers. Currently, we distinguish between five task types, based on datatype they focus on (i.e., text, graph, image/video), other general tasks and domain-specific tasks. Table 3 lists tasks related to these meta-tasks and exemplary specific tasks.

Table 3. Typical tasks achieved with SWeMLs as collected during study selection.

Task type	Exemplary specific tasks
Text related tasks *(e.g., text annotation or information retrieval)*	Named entity linking, word sense disambiguation, text/document classification, sentiment analysis, hierarchical relation extraction, question answering
(Knowledge) graph related tasks	Knowledge graph creation/extension, ontology creation/extension, association rule learning
Image and video related tasks	Image and video annotation, image and video classification, object detection, emotion recognition
Specific tasks (domain independent)	Recommender system, data integration, data augmentation, data quality assurance, query generation, query expansion, data explanation
Domain-specific tasks *(e.g., from biology, health or finance)*	Gene expression classification, patient outcome prediction, market return prediction

RQ3. Machine Learning Type: We have identified a wide range of different machine learning approaches being used in SWeMLS. The five most prominent categories of ML models, starting with the most frequent ones: (1) *Deep Learning (DL)*, including deep neural network architectures such as transformer-based language models, and Graph Neural Networks, (2) *Artificial Neural Networks (ANN)*, including simple (i.e., non-deep) neural network architectures, such as word2vec, (3) *Classical Machine Learning (cML)*, including e.g., Support Vector Machine, k-nearest neighbor, (4) *Rule Learning (RuleL)*, including e.g., Association Rule Learning, Inductive Logic Programming, and (5) *Dimensionality Reduction (DimR)*, including e.g., PCA, LDA.

The frequency of the presented categories varies a lot, where DL models account for over 45% of all used models in the selected papers, whereas the 5th most prominent category – DimR – covers not even 2% of the used models[11]. Within the DL category, Graph Neural Networks and Graph Embedding models are the most frequent type of model, accounting for half of the DL models, while within ANN models static word embeddings are most common (about 3/5).

Figure 3B depicts the temporal evolution of the use of the five ML categories. While the usage of models (in total numbers) from DimR and RuleL seems approximately stable, the trend for cML models is slightly positive, while the usage of ANN and DL models grew exponentially over the last decade. However, when we correct for the total number of papers published in a given time period, we can clearly see that DimR, RuleL and cML become less popular over time, the application of ANN models is approximately even, while DL models –also with the correction– are on the raise.

RQ4. Semantic Resource: During the study selection stage, we already derived initial insights about the role and characteristics of the semantic resources participating in SWeMLs, as follows. First, these resources can play diverse roles in SWeMLs: they can act as an *input* resource; they can provide additional *background knowledge*; they can be the *outputs* of the process or be used for the purposes of *evaluating* the SWeMLs. Second, the aspect of the semantic resource that is used varies from reusing labels only (altLabels, Synsets), to exploring simple relations (one type and one-hop), hierarchical relations (is_a; also multi-hop) and finally leveraging complex structures in these resources, such as axioms. Third, among the most often used semantic resources (see Fig. 3C) were biological ontologies, WordNet, DBpedia, Freebase and Wikidata.

Finally, we observed that several *types of semantic resources* are used ranging from semantically lightweight structures such as taxonomies and thesauri, to formal ontologies, as well as instantiated semantic structures such as knowledge basis, linked data sets and knowledge graphs. We also observed that, the collected papers, originating from different disciplines, do not share a common understanding of what these terms mean and are often influenced by the trending terminologies (i.e., resources that would be described as a *knowledge base*

---

[11] Please note, that each model is counted separately, so one selected paper could appear as multiple data points in this analysis.

before 2010, might be defined as *Linked datasets* after 2010 and *knowledge graphs* around 2020). In the data extraction step, the concrete type of the used semantic resource will be collected both (i) based on the terminology used by the authors and (ii) through a type assigned by the study team based on an internally defined glossary and definitions of these terms. This will provide an insight into the actual semantic resource types used (by reducing the imprecise use of terminology across various communities and time periods) as well as identify terminology shifts during time.

RQ5. Processing Flow: To answer RQ5, we identify processing flows of systems accordingly to the design patterns already proposed by Van Harmelen and Ten Teije [10], as well as additional patterns not yet proposed. There are two types of components: Inputs and outputs, which are characterised as model-based (also symbolic) or model-free (textual, tabular,...) data. The second type are algorithmic components, which are either deductive (reasoning, querying), and inductive inference (machine learning). During our ongoing data extraction, we encountered process flows that were not captured by these patterns. In Fig. 4 in a) one additional pattern is displayed, with two lines of input, the upper with symbolic and the lower lane with subsymbolic input, i.e. combining word and graph embeddings. For example, this pattern is used in entity extractions of adverse drug events and their respective relations from medical records [3]. In this example shown in Fig. 4b) a graph constructed from FDA Adverse Event Reporting System (FAERS) is used as symbolic input to the LINE algorithm, generating graph embeddings. Additionally, non-contextualised Word2Vec embeddings as well as contextualised ELMO embeddings are pre-trained using discharge summaries from the Medical Information Mart for Intensive Care III (MIMIC-III) database. A bidirectional long short-term memory conditional random field (Bi-LSTM CRF) – exploiting both the knowledge graph embeddings and word embeddings – is then used for recognising and extracting adverse drug events (ADEs) and related information from the clinical notes of patients.

RQ6. Auditability: Complex systems might be subject to audits, investigating their functioning. Since there is no formalised definition of this characteristic yet, we aim to capture information concerning collection of provenance data and relevant parameters of the ML component(s). However, this information is collected during data extraction and not yet available for preliminary analysis.

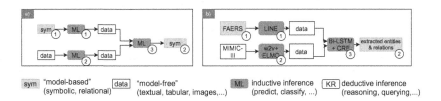

Fig. 4. a) Example of identified processing flow extended from [10] b) instance of flow corresponding to [3]

4   Conclusion and Outlook

In contrast to existing surveys, this work does not focus on a specific domain or application area, but aims to provide a systematic bottom-up definition and representation of research on hybrid AI, specifically SWeMLS. The introduced patterns in [10], proved to be helpful for characterising the data flow of the respective systems. During data extraction we encountered over 40 additional patterns to be described, which we will present synthesised in future work. Furthermore, we will report on specific insights gained, such as a typology of SWeMLSs and respective characteristics of ML and SW components.

Funding and Acknowledgement. This work has been funded by the project OBARIS (http://www.obaris.org), which has received funding from the Austrian Research Promotion Agency (FFG) under grant 877389.

References

1. Bonatti, P.A., Decker, S., Polleres, A., Presutti, V.: Knowledge graphs: new directions for knowledge representation on the semantic web (dagstuhl seminar 18371). In: Dagstuhl Reports, vol. 8. Schloss Dagstuhl-Leibniz-Zentrum fuer Informatik (2019)
2. D'Amato, C.: Machine learning for the semantic web: lessons learnt and next research directions. Semant. Web **11**(1), 195–203 (2020)
3. Dandala, B., Joopudi, V., Tsou, C.-H., Liang, J.J., Suryanarayanan, P.: Extraction of information related to drug safety surveillance from electronic health record notes: joint modeling of entities and relations using knowledge-aware neural attentive models. JMIR Med. Inform. **8**(7), e18417 (2020)
4. Ehrlinger, L., Wöß, W.: Towards a definition of knowledge graphs. In: SEMANTiCS (Posters, Demos, SuCCESS), vol. 48, pp. 1–4 (2016)
5. Kitchenham, B., Charters, S., et al.: Guidelines for performing systematic literature reviews in software engineering version 2.3. Engineering **45**(4ve), 1051 (2007)
6. Ristoski, P., Paulheim, H.: Semantic Web in data mining and knowledge discovery: a comprehensive survey. J. Web Semant. **36**, 1–22 (2016)
7. Sapna, R., Monikarani, H.G., Mishra, S.: Linked data through the lens of machine learning: an enterprise view. In: Proceedings of 2019 3rd IEEE International Conference on Electrical, Computer and Communication Technologies, ICECCT 2019. Institute of Electrical and Electronics Engineers Inc., February 2019
8. Seeliger, A., Pfaff, M., Krcmar, H.: Semantic web technologies for explainable machine learning models: a literature review. In: Proceedings of the 1st Workshop on Semantic Explainability Co-Located with the 18th International Semantic Web Conference (ISWC 2019), vol. 2465, pp. 30–45 (2019)
9. Sutskever, I., Vinyals, O., Le, Q.V.: Sequence to sequence learning with neural networks. In: Advances in Neural Information Processing Systems, pp. 3104–3112 (2014)
10. Van Harmelen, F., Ten Teije, A.: A boxology of design patterns for hybrid learning and reasoning systems. J. Web Eng. **18**(1–3), 97–124 (2019)

On the Quality of Compositional Prediction for Prospective Analytics on Graphs

Gauthier Lyan[1,2(✉)], David Gross Amblard[2], and Jean-Marc Jezequel[2]

[1] Keolis Rennes, Rennes, France
gauthier.lyan@keolis.com
[2] Irisa Lab, Univ Rennes, CNRS, Rennes, France
{david.gross_amblard,jean-marc.jezequel}@irisa.fr

Abstract. Recently, micro-learning has been successfully applied to various scenarios, such as graph optimization (e.g. power grid management). In these approaches, ad-hoc models of local data are built instead of one large model on the overall data set. Micro-learning is typically useful for incremental, what-if/prospective scenarios, where one has to perform step-by-step decisions based on local properties. A common feature of these applications is that the predicted properties (such as speed of a bus line) are compositions of smaller parts (e.g. the speed on each bus inter-stations along the line). But little is known about the quality of such predictions when generalized at a larger scale.

In this paper we propose a generic technique that embeds machine-learning for graph-based compositional prediction, that allows 1) the prediction of the behaviour of composite objects, based on the predictions of their sub-parts and appropriate composition rules, and 2) the production of rich prospective analytics scenarios, where new objects never observed before can be predicted based on their simpler parts. We show that the quality of such predictions compete with macro-learning ones, while enabling prospective scenarios. We assess our work on a real size, operational bus network data set.

Keywords: Compositional · Machine learning · Graph · Prospective · Link weight prediction

1 Introduction

Machine learning techniques have been applied on static, graph-based applications, such as transportation networks or energy grids, to name a few [2,19,20]. These applications have in common an a priori topological model, i.e. a graph, where practical measures are performed on nodes and edges. In a bus transportation network for example, it is possible nowadays to predict the awaiting time in a station or the probable duration of a trip with an acceptable accuracy [22,23].

Recently, micro-learning approaches have been successfully applied to more dynamic, prospective and what-if scenarios (e.g. power grid management [21]).

© Springer Nature Switzerland AG 2021
G. Kotsis et al. (Eds.): DEXA 2021 Workshops, CCIS 1479, pp. 91–105, 2021.
https://doi.org/10.1007/978-3-030-87101-7_10

In these approaches, ad hoc models of local data are built instead of one large model on the overall data set. Micro-learning is typically useful for incremental, prospective scenarios, where one has to perform step-by-step decisions based on local properties. Going back to our bus transportation example, a typical strategical prospective scenario applies when one bus network operator has to plan a new bus line that travels through road sections never used by the bus network until then. A common feature of these graph-based applications is that the predicted properties (such as speed/travel time of a bus line) are compositions of smaller parts (e.g. the speed or travel time on each bus inter-stations along the line). But up to our knowledge, little has been written about the quality of such composite predictions using micro-models, when generalized at a larger scale.

In this paper we propose a generic technique, graph-based compositional prediction, that allows 1) the prediction of the behaviour of composite objects, based on the predictions of their sub-parts and appropriate composition rules, and 2) the production of rich prospective analytics scenarios, where new objects never observed before can be predicted based on their simpler parts. We show that the quality of such predictions compete with macro-learning ones, while enabling prospective scenarios. We assess our work on a real size, operational bus network data set.

The rest of the paper in organized as follows. In Sect. 2 we present our motivational scenario. Our model is outlined in Sect. 3. Section 4 shows our experiments. In Sect. 5 we discuss the related work, and present our conclusion and future work in Sect. 6.

2   Data Model and Motivation Scenario: Rennes City Bus Transportation

In public bus transportation networks, bus speed is considered to be a Key Performance Indicator (KPI) that translates the level of efficacy and attractiveness of a bus network [7–9] Consequently, bus networks operators struggle daily to maintain high bus speed and are in need of reliable, complete and flexible prospective methods to predict the performance (such as speed) of future bus lines.

Running Example. Our running example is the bus network of the French city of Rennes, forming a directed graph $G = (V, E)$, where V is the set of bus stops and $E \subseteq V \times V$ is the set of possibles one-stop trips. Such a graph can be considered as a static graph as long as most of its structure does not evolve in the short term (few months to few years). However, its edges generate a lot of data over time. We consider a non-empty set of features F, associated to each edge, with their corresponding types T_F. A typical set of features associated to each element of E is $F = (time, line, length, road - type, bicycle)$, where *time* is a timestamp, *line* is an integer denoting a bus line number, *length* is the length of the inter-station section, $road - type$ indicates the kind of road the bus runs on (dedicated road or not), and *bicycle* indicates whether bicycles are allowed. Figure 1 gives an overview of a bus network graph in which green vertices are departure terminals, blue vertices are transition/departure bus stops, white vertices are transitional bus stops and red vertices are ending terminals.

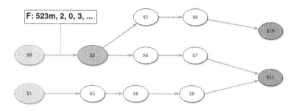

Fig. 1. A bus network with featured edges (F: length of the road, type of line, etc.)

Let us consider a measure $\mathcal{M}$ of the graph, defined on paths p in G. Let $\mathcal{D}$ be a learning data set of examples of $\mathcal{M}$. Let us consider a decision problem in the graph, e.g. Testing different configurations for a future bus line in the network. Given a source and target vertex:

Given a set of paths (i.e. different configurations of the future bus line) S_p, for each path p in S_p from source to target (here $|S_p| = 1$) predict the speed for every sub-section of p. This yields a dataset for every configuration, making it possible for the operator to evaluate which configuration is best suited for the future bus line depending on the speed at either inter-station level, section level, or bus line level.

In the next section we detail the corresponding learning problem associated with the prospective scenario (Fig. 2).

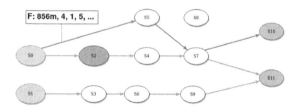

Fig. 2. Prospective scenario: predict $S0-S10$ while edges $S0-S5$, $S5-S7$ and $S7-S10$ do not exist in the data set

3   Micro-learning and Compositional Prediction

As a possible way to envision the prospective scenario, we propose the notion of compositional prediction using micro-learning:

– (Micro-learning) We will first learn a model of $\mathcal{M}$ on each individual edge of G.

– (Compositional prediction) Then we will build the model of $\mathcal{M}$ on a new path by composition.

More precisely, let $p = (e_1, \ldots, e_n)$ be a path in the graph G. Our goal is to predict a given measure $\mathcal{M}(p)$ on any path p on this graph. We possess local measures $m(e)$ of $\mathcal{M}$ on any edge e along this path and, typically, a composition law $\mathcal{C}$ links these measures:

$$\mathcal{M}(p) = \mathcal{C}(m(e_1), \ldots, m(e_n)).$$

Running Example. Consider that $\mathcal{M}$ is the trip duration for a precise bus and date, from the start to the end of the line (the path p). We have observations for $m(e)$, the duration of inter-station trips on p for this bus. Of course in this simple case the value of $\mathcal{M}(p)$ can be obtained by summing durations of trip duration $m(e_i)$ on all edges e_i of p. Similarly, the average speed could be obtained with a slightly different composition law, weighting duration by distances. Besides additive composition laws, multiplicative laws could be foreseen, such as the probability of bus failure (which is a product of one minus the bus failure probability on each edge).

We then define our compositional prediction approach:

Definition 1 (Compositional prediction). *Let $G = (V, E)$ be a directed graph, $\mathcal{M}$ a target measure, a composition law $\mathcal{C}$ and a data set $\mathcal{D}$ of observations $m(e)$ on edges of G. Given a target path $p = (e_1, \ldots, e_n)$, the compositional prediction of $\mathcal{M}(p)$ is given by:*

– *building a model $m^*(e)$ to predict $m(e)$ for each edge $e \in V \times V$, according to edge features $F(e)$;*
– *approximating the prediction of $\mathcal{M}(p)$ by*

$$\mathcal{M}^*(p) = \mathcal{C}(m^*(e_1), \ldots, m^*(e_n)).$$

Running Example. Suppose that we want to estimate the end-to-end duration of trip for a new bus line in a city. Given its path p, we would learn the typical duration of existing bus lines on each inter-stations road fragments (i.e. edges), and simply sum these predictions (the composition law). If a road fragment has never been visited by any other bus in our observation data set, the model approximates it using the most similar road fragment (according to its features such as road type, number of traffic lights, and so on.)

The main advantage of this approach is that predictions are based on the underlying structure of the graph, rather that on macro-observations on it. As shown in the examples, it yields a large flexibility in predictions, without domain specific knowledge (e.g., in the bus network context, multi-agent simulation requires complex modeling hand-made tuning [14]). But this method can also have its drawbacks. When an edge measure is missing, a strategy has to be deployed to fill the missing data, and this is highly related to the amount of describing features on the underlying graph. Also, the cost of building many models for each edge could be tremendous, regarding its macro-level counter-part. Finally, and more importantly, as each model bears its own approxima-tions, errors may sum up along the compositional law $\mathcal{C}$, giving a potentially unusable prediction. We then identify the following research question: **Does micro-learning yield usable predictions with the compositional pre-diction strategy for prospective scenarios, and does it compete with traditional prediction methods (that apply in different contexts)?**

In the following experiments, we evaluate and discuss this question thanks to real data coming from a real bus network (thereby imperfect data, as this is most always the case in the real world [13,18]).

4 Experiments

4.1 Experimental Settings

Reproducibility. All of the experiments are reproducible with code and resources available on a dedicated repository[1].

Experimental Environment. All experiments were run on a 16 cores 32 threads @ 3500 MHz, 64 GB DDR4 3200 MHz 1 TB SSD NVMe, running Ubuntu 20.04 (Budgie flavour). Data were gathered into a normalized data lake built upon Apache Spark 2.4.5/Scala 2.11.12 jobs. All learning tasks were performed using GraalVM 20.2 and Scala SMILE 2.5.3. It took around 70 min for overall model training and 2 min for each of the following predictions.

Experiment with Real Data. We considered the bus transportation system of the French city of Rennes and its metropolitan area (about 500,000 inhabitants) managed by the Keolis Rennes company. Our graph is the graph of 2110 bus stops and 119 bus lines[2], and the features of road portions are automatically extracted from OpenStreetMap (OSM in the sequel).

More specifically, the raw historical data set is composed of readings of bus travels between two contiguous bus stops. Table 1 shows a sample of this data set. The major columns are *line_type* (0 being high frequency, 1 urban, 2 metropoli-tan and 3 express metropolitan lines); *dwell_time*, the time passed at the ori-gin stop (taking and unboarding passengers) and *speed*, the arithmetic speed between *orig* and *dest*. A single trip, which consists of all the measures of a sin-gle bus passing through every single bus stop of a bus line, can be identified by combining the columns *trip_start* which is the instant at which the bus has left the first point of the bus line, *sm* which is the service identifier, *chaining* which is the version of the bus line and *dir* which is the line direction. We considered only real data: no imputation was made in our data set. We considered only full trips for which all data points were present. We also filtered historical data

---

[1] https://gitlab.inria.fr/glyan/compred.
[2] Rennes transportation network: https://data.rennesmetropole.fr.

used to feed the model, dropping invalid speeds/nulls/values and outliers. Using these rules, **we gathered 12 month of data between January 2019 and December 2019, for a total of around 15 millions tuples**[3].

Prediction Task. We targeted the prediction of **the speed of a bus line** depending on time (holidays period, day, time of the day) and line type (urban bus line, metropolitan bus line). We considered predictions for existing lines (classical prediction) and non-existing lines (prospective scenarios, where the lines and some inter-stations data are absent in the training data set).

Candidates. As experimental candidates, we chose 4 groups of bus lines for which we could gather data all along their path. We tested 13 different bus lines in total. The four groups contain different class of bus lines: urbans, inter-district, metropolitans and express.The urban group is composed of urbans bus lines, that cross the city center along their path. The inter-district group are urban bus lines that link different districts, avoiding the city center. The metropolitan group is composed of metropolitan bus lines, that links cities of the metropolitan area to the main city. Those lines contain urban, peri-urban and metropolitan sections. Finally, the express group contain metropolitan lines that allows a faster travel from and to external cities by servicing less bus stops. Note that in the network, each line share some sub-paths with others[4].

Table 1. Sample of the historical data set

Trip start	line	line type	sm	dir	orig	dest	speed	dwell time	order orig	order dest	section	chaining
2018-07-02 00:05:00	02	0		0221	A	2844	2842	25.8	0	1	2	1	21
2018-07-02 00:05:00	02	0		0221	A	2842	2804	21.0	23	2	3	1	21

Road Features with OpenStreetMap. We have built a tool to look for a bus network in OpenStreetMap and to extract its infrastructure information, road per road. We then aggregate the data grouping the roads by inter-stations. We then sum the road lengths, number of traffic signals, stops, giveways, roundabouts, level crossings, crossings, and add the average legal speed of the roads.

Time Discretization. We categorized the time periods into six categories: No holidays, and Autumn/Christmas/Winter/Spring/Summer holidays. For each category we divided each day coded from 0 (monday) to 6 (sunday) in 1 to 3-h period (e.g. 1 am–3 am, or 7 am–8 am). This division is due to obvious pace changes in bus usage, as confirmed by the Keolis company.

---

[3] Data and more material is available at https://gitlab.inria.fr/glyan/compred.

[4] More material about the bus lines is available in the README of the repository.

Micro-learning Data Set. The micro learning data set is made of measures for each inter-station of the network. We simply identified every distinct inter-station and added meta data such as holidays, bus line type, OSM data (that is constant through time), period of time in day and week day[5].

Macro-learning Data Set. The macro learning data set is built using the raw data set, from which we extract **only the overall speed of every complete trip** (i.e. trips for which we have data for each inter-station) of every bus line. We then add the bus line, its type and finally the OSM data aggregated all along the line (i.e. total number of traffic signals, stops, etc.).

Learning Method and Validation Methodology. Our models are built using a classical random forest algorithm parameterized for regression and optimized using grid-search (this choice is motivated by its generality and overall performance, after selecting it amongst others: Lasso, OLS ,SVR, Cart, bayesian ridge and gradient boosting, testing their performance using a small sample of data. It could be naturally adapted to more specific methods, but this is not the scope of our paper). For micro-learning, we build a model of inter-station speed. We then predict the speed of any trip by the natural compositional prediction C_s (summing the road lengths divided by the summed travel times, obtained with the predicted speeds). For macro-learning, we build a model of full bus-line speeds (from start to stop). Learning is performed with OpenStreetMap features, and without OpenStreetMap features on every bus lines in order to assess the impact of these features on the model precision. For validation purposes, we have removed all the data of candidates bus lines from the training data set of each model. To evaluate the classical scenario, we predicted the speed of an entire line with macro and compositional prediction. For the prospective scenario, we measured the compositional prediction quality on non-existing paths in the data set.

In the next sections we are coming back to our initial questions from Sect. 3.

4.2 Results

Accuracy on Real Data. We tested (predicted) ~12'500 trips for the urban bus lines group, ~1'250 trips for the inter-district group, ~5'800 for the metropolitan group and ~800 trips for the express group. All those trips are distributed over the 6 holidays regime, 7 days and 17 periods in day over the 2019 year.

Figure 3 shows the predicted speed of one of the urban bus lines using micro-learning. Each point represents the average predicted speed (purple) and average real speed (dashed) of each inter-station of the line on all the time periods for which data was available. The leftest point of each curve represents the beginning of the bus line, the rightest one being the last stop. Observe that due to the bus line's data deletion from the training dataset, some inter-stations that are specific

---

[5] More information about training data in the repository.

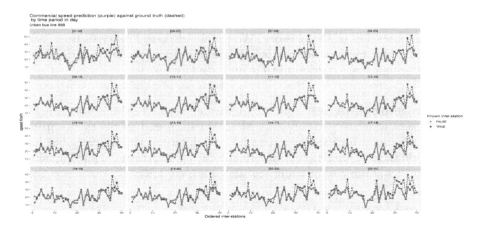

Fig. 3. Speed of urban bus line 858 at inter-stations using micro-learning (purple) vs true speed (dashed). Orange inter-stations where not used by any other bus, i.e. are absent from the training set. (Color figure online)

to this line are totally unknown to the model (orange dots). We also considered metropolitan, express and inter-district bus lines (not displayed)[6]. Visually at first, we can see that micro-learning captures well the daily behaviour of buses, even when the inter-stations are unknown to the model (orange dots).

Table 2 sums up the models's prediction errors for each bus line, group of lines (urban, inter-district, metropolitan and express) and all the lines (global). For each model and bus line (resp. group of lines), the table presents the Root Mean Squared Error (RMSE), the Mean Absolute Error (MAE) and the Mean Absolute Percentage Error (MAPE). RMSE emphasizes large residuals (outliers) while MAE and MAPE are less sensitive to residuals and easier to interpret [17]. RMSE and MAE unit is km/h while MAPE's unit is percentage (difference against truth in percents).

If we take a look at micro predictions in Table 2, we observe that prediction errors for known inter-stations (classical prediction) are better than prediction errors of unknown inter-stations (prospective predictions), except for the express bus lines group. Indeed, RMSE, MAE and MAPE can vary from a 1.2 to 2 factor between micro known and unknown. This shows that the features set used for micro learning might need some enhancement to help the model predicting better. Finally, we observe that global micro predictions precision vary between bus lines groups. However, the urban group gets the best predictions in all aspects when compared to other groups (RMSE:6.7, MAE:4.8, MAPE:26.5%), followed by express (RMSE:6.1, MAE:4.3, MAPE:29.8%), metropolitan (RMSE:7.3, MAE:5.4, MAPE:31.7%) and inter-district (RMSE:9.0, MAE:6.7, MAPE:33.3%) groups.

---

[6] More material is available in the public deposit.

Table 2. Results table

Line	Micro known			Micro unknown			Micro global			Compred			Macro		
	RMSE	MAE	MAPE	RMSE	MAE	MAPE	RMSE	MAE	MAPE	RMSE	MAE	MAPE	RMSE	MAE	MAPE
Urban lines															
858	7.3	5.0	18.2%	6.1	4.5	25.9%	6.9	4.8	22.4%	1.6	1.2	6.2%	2.1	2.0	8.4%
787	5.6	3.9	19.9%	9.1	7.3	44.4%	6.0	4.2	22.2%	1.7	1.3	7.2%	2.2	2.0	9.7%
785	5.9	4.5	22.7%	8.3	6.0	29.2%	7.5	5.4	26.6%	2.6	2.0	9.9%	2.7	2.5	10.4%
889	5.6	4.3	31.1%	8.7	5.9	25.4%	6.3	4.6	30.1%	3.0	2.7	17.4%	2.7	2.6	15.4%
689	6.3	4.6	29.4%	8.2	6.7	53.9%	6.4	4.7	30.7%	3.2	2.8	16.5%	2.4	2.3	12.2%
All urbans	6.3	4.6	25.2%	7.5	5.4	29.4%	6.7	4.8	26.5%	2.6	2.1	12.0%	2.4	2.3	11.5%
Inter-district lines															
696	8.9	6.4	27.1%	9.3	7.4	46.2%	9.0	6.7	33.5%	3.2	2.8	13.7%	4.0	3.8	15.5%
581	6.4	5.1	26.7%	10.3	7.6	31.8%	7.6	5.7	27.9%	3.5	2.8	12.3%	3.9	3.5	13.4%
All inter-Districts	8.8	6.4	27.0%	9.3	7.4	45.9%	9.0	6.7	33.3%	3.2	2.8	13.7%	4.0	3.7	15.5%
Metropolitan lines															
683	5.0	3.8	15.5%	8.4	6.7	26.9%	7.1	5.4	21.8%	3.2	2.5	10.3%	3.1	2.9	9.5%
849	6.3	4.7	37.4%	5.0	4.0	11.9%	6.3	4.7	36.6%	3.2	2.8	12.1%	3.7	3.5	14.3%
532	7.9	5.7	24.2%	12.1	11.9	427%	8.2	6.0	45.4%	4.0	3.3	13.7%	4.8	4.5	15.5%
969	7.2	4.8	25.3%	6.0	4.4	16.1%	7.1	4.8	24.4%	3.6	2.6	9.8%	3.5	3.2	9.9%
All metropolitans	6.7	4.8	25.6%	8.6	6.8	48.3%	7.3	5.4	31.7%	3.5	2.8	11.4%	3.8	3.5	11.9%
Express lines															
711	5.8	4.2	36.6%	4.5	3.6	10.1%	5.6	4.1	32.2%	3.6	2.7	10.3%	7.0	6.9	21.1%
859	6.1	4.2	27.8%	7.9	5.5	21.9%	6.6	4.6	26.1%	7.3	5.6	24.7%	7.0	6.8	20.2%
All express	5.9	4.2	33.4%	6.5	4.6	16.4%	6.1	4.3	29.8%	5.3	3.8	15.6%	7.0	6.8	20.8%
All lines															
All lines	6.6	4.7	25.5%	5.7	7.8	33.7%	7.0	5.0	28.0%	3.0	2.4	12.1%	3.2	2.9	12.2%

Table 3. Models's sensitivity to time features

Group	Compred standard dev.	Macro standard dev.
Urban	1.0	0.5
Inter-district	0.7	0.3
Metropolitan	0.9	0.4
Express	0.9	0.0
Global	0.9	0.4

Urban bus lines are the major lines in the network, hence they produce a significant part of the data used for training. This can explain why the models are more precise when they predict speed for this group.

We noticed a huge prediction error for metropolitan bus line 532 with resp RMSE, MAE and MAPE at 12.1, 11.9 and 427%. We investigated how can the model perform that bad on some cases and found that the average speed of the only unknown inter-station of the bus line 532 is lower than 5 km/h, while its features are alike others inter-stations in the network. The speed calculation business rules used might yield such a low speed, e.g. if the bus has to wait at a bus stop for operational reasons. In other words, inter-stations that have very low average speed with non specific features set is prone to yield important predictions errors (i.e. considered as an outlier).

Globally, micro-learning yields variable quality results, with a higher error rate for unknown inter-stations. The features used for predictions probably need enhancement in terms of noise reduction and/or external data addition such as smart-card data, traffic status, etc.

4.3   Discussion

Micro-learning on graphs at edge level (e.g. bus-inter-stations level) yields variable results on a real data set. Prediction error tends to be more important when no observations on this very edge is available in the learning data set. These results point the importance of having high quality data and choosing the right features set for the model. However, Fig. 3 shows that the micro learning model has a sensitivity to current features, hence this allows for prospective scenarios, when one needs to test different configurations for a future bus line.

Comparing compositional prediction results (Compred) with Macro prediction, raised the following remarks: For urban group, Compred MAPE and RMSE differences are only of 0.5% and 0.2 km/h while Compred's MAE is 0.2 km/h better than macro's. That is to say, macro and Compred are nearly on par when it comes to predict urban bus speed. In other groups, compositional prediction performs slightly better than macro predictions, with MAE, RMSE and MAPE lower for Compred than macro by around 2.5 to +25% depending on the measure we compare. Hence, this suggests that compositional prediction seems to be more capable of catching fine grain variations (i.e. variation on inter-stations) than macro does, as shown in Table 3. This table shows the average predicted speed variation (standard deviation in km/h) of bus lines over time (holidays, days, period). We observed that Compred model seems to be at least twice as sensitive to time features as macro model.

We compared macro-learning (i.e. building models based only on the measures of entire paths) with compositional prediction based on micro-learning (full knowledge of all measures on edges). Macro-learning is disadvantaged by a partial knowledge of the network, while Compred is disadvantaged by a higher volume of data and its obligation to perform an aggregation of small-scale predictions, which is mandatory in prospective scenarios. It appears that the obtained quality is good. Actually our method reaches state of the art performance if we compare with [4]. Finally, the micro-learning mixed with compositional approaches allow the comparison of different configurations at any scale within the bus line.

4.4   Threats to Validity

As internal threats, we acquired the real data set ourselves using our own code, which may be prone to errors. But these data are used in production by the Keolis company, and has been controlled using business rules many times. Also, we used only complete data. No imputation was done. Our code uses a high-level language and state-of-the art libraries for data extraction and machine learning. As construct validity, we choose to use Random forests as ensemble methods model for regression. The choice we made was based on performance amongst a set of models tested on a small sample of data from which random forests performed better (in terms of results and computing time). However, we assumed that the models would behave in an analogous manner with a wider dataset, whereas there is a small risk that this is not the case. Finally, the scope of this paper is to assess the quality of compositional prediction for composite objects in complex environment against traditional macro approaches, we then considered the machine-learning model selection as a secondary issue, hence we probably could have different results with other models. Yet, choosing better models for compositional prediction is another issue that probably needs a dedicated work. As an external threat, our data set, time frame and targets selection might have specificities that could prevent generalization beyond these lines or Rennes Metropolis. On the other side, we gathered 15M tuples over a year from a large city common bus transportation system. The chosen lines are typical and of different kind (urban, inter-district, metropolitan and express).

5   Related Work

5.1   Micro Learning

Hartmann et al. developed Greycat [19, 21], a tool that provides a dynamic temporal graph approach for fast evolving networks. Our concept is different because our goal is to use the history of the network to build a new path in the network using the knowledge we got from the current network.

5.2   Link Weight Prediction

Hou et al. [11] developed Model R a deep neural network model that aims to predict the existence and the weight of new edges (links) within a graph. Our model comes as support for the prediction of weights of both existing and new edges for which features are known, given a timestamp. Also the machine learning model used for the predicting could easily be changed.

Kumar et al. [12] proposed an algorithm to predict edges weight in Weighted Signed Networks (WSN). They predict weight using two vertex based metrics named fairness and goodness, hence their method is vertex centric. A contrario, ours focuses on edges features and aims at predicting variables edges weight given different sets of features.

Zhao et al. [25] proposed a way of predicting the existence of edges and their weight using reliable route approach. They use local similarity measures which consists of examining vertex neighbourhood to determine a reliable route, hence edges and weights. Their work relies on the intrinsic properties of graphs while ours uses graph as a support for real world data representation and exploration. Indeed, while the neighbourhood of nodes is used to predict edges and weight, we only rely on real world features (OSM and historical data) without using any of the graph theory properties.

Fu et al. [10] proposed link weight prediction combining original graph and line graph properties. They also use the graphs intrinsic properties such as degrees to predict link weight over evolving networks. While their work focuses on graph structure to generate features, we gather ours from domain knowledge. Also our method is edge focused and straight forward: We try to keep the network as it is in real life which does not need graph conversion to line graph.

B. Taskar et al. [20] studied the predictability of links within a relational graph. As an example they used neural networks to try to predict relationships between people on social network data. Their work differ from ours to the extent that they try to predict the existence of new edges while we create new edges knowing their properties and use them to predict their weight.

5.3   Bus Travel Time/Bus Speed Prediction

Mendes-Moreira and Barachi [15] imagined a prediction model for networks by predicting sub parts of the networks and re-conciliate the aggregated predictions of the sub-parts with the path they are part of. They do this using a method they called Reconciliation For Regression (R4R) by weighing every sub-predictions using a constraint least square algorithm. Their results show that they reach state of the art performance for bus travel time prediction. However, it is unclear on how far from the reality their model perform without MAPE. One could also raise the following statement: the added complexity of R4R is questionable because it shows that it seems to never offer a better improvement than 3% in prediction precision when compared to other models, including simple ones such as Multivariate Linear Regression (MLR).

Fernandez et al. [9] proposed a statistical model to predict bus commercial speed. Their model needs a lot of calibration made by hand while ours just need data collection.

Petersen et al. [16] predict travel time on known bus lines in order to enhance the quality of service. We try to predict a commercial speed for a not yet existing bus line for strategic purpose, hence giving hints on how a new bus line would likely behave.

A recent work [2] considered prediction in a road network, by decomposing the learning task down to the road segment. They differ with us as their consider a route prediction task (what is the next segment), and do not consider non-existing routes as we do.

Another recent work [24] propose a mathematical model to predict bus time of arrival at bus stop using surrounding traffic and signal control. Their model do it in real time and could be used to enhance travelers information. However their work do not cover the exact same areas as ours.

M. Altinkaya and M. Zontul [1] worked on a review of computational models for bus arrival time predictions. They analyze different methods to predict bus arrival time including statistical and machine learning ones. They suggest that it is needed to focus on data that look alike in order to diminish the prediction error. Which is what we try to do using micro learning and time periods selection.

5.4   Traffic Simulation

Barcelo et al. [3] proposed a software based on AIMSUN NG, a traffic simulation tool, that integrates MACRO, MESO & MICRO simulation in a single framework, sharing a unique database. Doing so allows the solving of the consistency issues when shifting between MACRO, MESO and MICRO scales thanks to data aggregation rules. Their work differ from ours as long as their tools aim is to enhance the capabilities of simulation tools.

Burghout et al. [5] worked on a hybrid mesoscopic-microscopic traffic simulation that lets one apply microscopic simulation on area of interest in mesoscopic areas. They claim that mesoscopic simulation is not as needy as microscopic simulation. We confirm this claim but using a machine learning approach.

Mendes-Moreira and Barachi [15] imagined a prediction model for networks by predicting sub parts of the networks and re-conciliate the aggregated predictions of the sub-parts with the path they are part of. They do this using a method they called Reconciliation For Regression (R4R) by weighing every sub-predictions using a constraint least square algorithm. Their results show that they reach state of the art performance for bus travel time prediction. However, it is unclear on how far from the reality their model perform without MAPE. One could also raise the following statement: the added complexity of R4R is questionable because it shows that it seems to never offer a better improvement than 3% in prediction precision when compared to other models, including simple ones such as Multivariate Linear Regression (MLR).

6   Conclusion and Future Work

In this work, we presented compositional prediction on graphs, an approach to infer path properties from edge properties obtained by micro-learning. Based on a real-size application, we evaluated this approach with respect to classical macro-learning. We showed that it allows to compare different configurations for a future bus line, at variable scale in the bus line, enabling the study of prospective scenarios. This approach exhibits at least comparable and often better quality than the classical approach, while offering state of the art performance with prospective capabilities.

As a future work, we would like to finely understand the quality gap between macro-learning and compositional prediction: while good on small scales, it could be reasonable to switch to macro-prediction on relevant sub-path of the graphs. Also our model must be tested on other scenarios that become crucial for bus network operators such as the fuel consumption along a bus line, or with other composition methods such as product e.g.; computing the risk of accident along a path given its sub-parts individual risks. Eventually given the overestimation of the model one would try to apply arbitrated ensemble methods [6] to re-qualify the model output and enhance its precision. Finally, since the presented model could be embedded within a data exploration model, this paper can be seen as a first step toward declarative languages for prospective scenarios.

References

1. Altinkaya, M., Zontul, M.: Urban bus arrival time prediction: a review of computational models. IJRTE **2**, 164–169 (2013)
2. Amirat, H., Lagraa, N., Fournier-Viger, P., Ouinten, Y.: MyRoute: a graph-dependency based model for real-time route prediction. JCM **12**, 668 (2017)
3. Barceló, J., Casas, J., García, D., Perarnau, J.: Methodological Notes on Combining Macro, Meso and Micro Simulation Models for Transportation Analysis. In: Workshop on Modeling and Simulation. Sedona, AZ (2005)
4. Berger-Wolf, T., Chawla, N. (eds.): Proceedings of the 2019 SIAM International Conference on Data Mining. Society for Industrial and Applied Mathematics, Philadelphia, PA, May 2019. https://doi.org/10.1137/1.9781611975673
5. Burghout, W., Koutsopoulos, H., Andréasson, I.: Hybrid mesoscopic-microscopic traffic simulation. Transp. Res. Rec. J. Transp. Res. Board **1934**, 218–25 (2005)
6. Cerqueira, V., Torgo, L., Pinto, F., Soares, C.: Arbitrated ensemble for time series forecasting. In: Ceci, M., Hollmén, J., Todorovski, L., Vens, C., Džeroski, S. (eds.) ECML PKDD 2017. LNCS (LNAI), vol. 10535, pp. 478–494. Springer, Cham (2017). https://doi.org/10.1007/978-3-319-71246-8_29
7. Cortés, C.E., Gibson, J., Gschwender, A., Munizaga, M., Zúñiga, M.: Commercial bus speed diagnosis based on GPS-monitored data. Transp. Res. Part C Emerg. Technol. **19**(4), 695–707 (2011). https://doi.org/10.1016/j.trc.2010.12.008
8. Courtois, X., Dobruszkes, F.: L'(in)efficacité des trams et bus á Bruxelles, une analyse désagrégée. Brussels Studies. La revue scientifique électronique pour les recherches sur Bruxelles / Het elektronisch wetenschappelijk tijdschrift voor onderzoek over Brussel / The e-journal for academic research on Brussels (2008). https://doi.org/10.4000/brussels.603
9. Fernandez, R., Valenzuela, E.: A model to predict bus commercial speed. Traffic Eng. Control **44**(2) (2003)
10. Fu, C., et al.: Link weight prediction using supervised learning methods and its application to yelp layered network. IEEE Trans. Knowl. Data Eng. **30**(8), 1507–1518 (2018). https://doi.org/10.1109/TKDE.2018.2801854
11. Hou, Y., Holder, L.B.: On graph mining with deep learning: introducing model R for link weight prediction. J. Artif. Intell. Soft Comput. Res. **9**(1), 21–40 (2019). https://doi.org/10.2478/jaiscr-2018-0022
12. Kumar, S., Spezzano, F., Subrahmanian, V.S., Faloutsos, C.: Edge weight prediction in weighted signed networks. In: 2016 IEEE 16th International Conference on Data Mining (ICDM), Barcelona, Spain, pp. 221–230. IEEE, December 2016. https://doi.org/10.1109/ICDM.2016.0033
13. Ma, X., Chen, X.: Public transportation big data mining and analysis. In: Data-Driven Solutions to Transportation Problems. Elsevier (2019)
14. Matsumoto, T., Sakakibara, K., Tamaki, H.: Bus line optimization using multi-agent simulation model of urban traffic behavior of inhabitants applying branch and bound techniques, pp. 234–239. IEEE, July 2015. https://doi.org/10.1109/SICE.2015.7285551
15. Mendes-Moreira, J., Baratchi, M.: Reconciling predictions in the regression setting: an application to bus travel time prediction. In: Berthold, M.R., Feelders, A., Krempl, G. (eds.) IDA 2020. LNCS, vol. 12080, pp. 313–325. Springer, Cham (2020). https://doi.org/10.1007/978-3-030-44584-3_25
16. Petersen, N.C., Rodrigues, F., Pereira, F.C.: Multi-output bus travel time prediction with convolutional LSTM neural network. Expert Syst. Appl. **120**, 426–435 (2019)

17. Pontius, R.G., Thontteh, O., Chen, H.: Components of information for multiple resolution comparison between maps that share a real variable. Environ. Ecol. Stat. **15**(2), 111–142 (2008). https://doi.org/10.1007/s10651-007-0043-y
18. Robinson, S., Narayanan, B., Toh, N., Pereira, F.: Methods for pre-processing smartcard data to improve data quality. Transp. Res. Part C Emerg. Technol. **49**, 43–58 (2014). https://doi.org/10.1016/j.trc.2014.10.006
19. Hartmann, T., Moawad, A., Fouquet, F., Le Traon, Y.: The next evolution of MDE: a seamless integration of machine learning into domain modeling. SoSyM **18**, 1285–1304 (2017)
20. Taskar, B., Wong, M.F., Abbeel, P., Koller, D.: Link prediction in relational data. Adv. Neural Inf. Process. Syst. **16**, 659–666 (2003)
21. Thomas, H., Fouquet, F., Moawad, A., Rouvoy, R., Traon, Y.L.: GreyCat: efficient what-if analytics for data in motion at scale. IS **83**, 101–117 (2019)
22. Treethidtaphat, W., Pattara-Atikom, W., Khaimook, S.: Bus arrival time prediction at any distance of bus route using deep neural network model. In: International Conference On Intelligent Transportation (2017)
23. Zaki, M., Ashour, I., Zorkany, M., Hesham, B.: Online bus arrival time prediction using hybrid neural network and Kalman filter techniques. IJMER **3**, 2035–2041 (2013)
24. Zhang, H., Liang, S., Han, Y., Ma, M., Leng, R.: A prediction model for bus arrival time at bus stop considering signal control and surrounding traffic flow. IEEE Access **8**, 127672–127681 (2020)
25. Zhao, J., et al.: Prediction of links and weights in networks by reliable routes. Sci. Rep. **5**(1), 12261 (2015). https://doi.org/10.1038/srep12261

Semantic Influence Score: Tracing Beautiful Minds Through Knowledge Diffusion and Derivative Works

Pragnya Sridhar[1]([✉])[ID], Deepika Karanji[1][ID], Gambhire Swati Sampatrao[1][ID], Sravan Danda[2][ID], and Snehanshu Saha[2][ID]

[1] Department of CSE, PES University, Bengaluru, India
[2] CSIS and APPCAIR, BITS Pilani K K Birla Goa Campus, Goa, India

Abstract. Articles judged on the basis of raw citations or citation counts (or similar) are biased with "Rich gets Richer" conjecture, and continue to propagate a perceived notion of paper quality and influence among scientific communities. This perception of preferential attachment, overlooking important factors such as context and the age of the paper has been criticized recently. In this paper, we propose 'Semantic Influence Score (SIS)', an unbiased alternative to metrics which rely on raw citation counts. We compute the semantic influence of a paper on its derivative works by developing a multilevel influence network, which takes into account references, domain intersection and influence scores of the articles in the network. SIS provides a robust alternative to the widely used mechanism of raw citation counts i.e., the number of citations it receives.

Keywords: Big scholarly data · Semantic influence · Reference mining · Citation analysis · Machine learning · Research impact networks · AI

1 Introduction

With the tremendous increase in the volume of publications, ranking the articles and authors based on their 'influence' is becoming more relevant and important. The highly cited articles and authors tend to get more citations obeying 'Rich get Richer' conjecture [1]. This renders influence analysis and ranking studies based on citation count inaccurate [3,6]. Additionally, authors are also judged on metrics like h-index which follow the "Rich get Richer" conjecture. Moreover, citations have a temporal aspect. Older papers have greater number of citations than newer papers on similar topics, but aren't necessarily of a better quality. In the list released by Stanford University in 2020 which claims to contain the worlds top 2% of scientists in the field of Artificial Intelligence (AI), the study was primarily based on the number of citations or raw citations. It is possible

Supported by BITS Pilani K K Birla Goa Campus.

for an author to have few, but influential citations. It is also possible for another author to receive many but not as influential citations for articles published in 'questionable forums'. In fact, this is indeed true as we found after a rigorous analysis of some 'influential authors' published in the Stanford list. Hence, the motivation behind this paper is that there exists scant correlation between raw citations and SIS of articles. Centrality Measures are not sufficient to describe influence diffusion [1]. Although metrics such as CiteScore and Article Influence Score are widely used metrics to quantify the quality of a paper, they rely on raw citation counts to compute the scores. It has also been argued that Article Influence Score [2] is not very different compared to raw citation counts. Therefore, the above described inadequacies necessitates the proposal of a new metric - one that does not fall into these quagmires.

In this paper, we present the 'Semantic Influence Score (SIS)' - a scoring mechanism to determine the influence of a paper, impervious to raw citation counts. We also contribute a network of influential papers obtained through vigorous filtering, tag articles to topics with topic modelling, compute Semantic similarity between the papers and their derivative works, computed using their references. Using the above, we built credible corpora of articles to study scholarly influence of base papers on their 'derivative works network'. These networks, which we term as Semantic Influence Networks (SIN), and not the traditional citation networks, are the building blocks for analyzing and quantifying article influence (SIS) via a novel application of the Heat Diffusion Model for the influence score. Our final corpora, carefully filtered, is a sample of 1258 articles with 307696 total citations, an average citation of 244, and median citation of 151.

2 Related Works

There are multiple metrics devised to measure the quality of a journal or article.

The Eigen factor score [2] attempts to give a more accurate representation of the merit of citations rather than raw citation counts. However, it assigns journals to a single category, making it more difficult to compare across disciplines. We utilize a self-developed topic modeling mechanism to tag articles across three categories - Machine Learning (ML), Meta-heuristic Optimization (MO), Deep Learning (DL) and utilize it to comprehensively analyse the score of the article in each topic.

CiteScore [4] uses the average number of citations received in a calendar year by all items published in that journal in the preceding three years as the metric of measuring the citation impact of journals. Source Normalized Impact per Paper (SNIP) [14] also uses only citation counts to compute the metric scores. However, results can be significantly dependent on the dispersion of the number of references as well as their volume. Mingers, John [5] elaborate this issue in greater detail.

The main drawback of raw citation count dependent metrics is that they can be manipulated through coercive citations, self-citations, and even computer generated documents for increasing citation count.

Since our metric is independent of raw citation counts, the Semantic Influence Score has the potential to serve as an impartial and fair alternative popularly used metrics.

3   Data Description

[1]The MAG data set [8,9] obtained from Aminer [15] formed the base of our research. This data-set was over 12 GB in size and could not be loaded in its entirety for analysis. The SIN was created from Connected Papers [12]. In connected Papers, papers are arranged according to their similarity, which is measured by taking into account the number of overlapping citations and bibliographic coupling. This implies that even papers which do not directly cite each other can be strongly connected and positioned close to each other in the graph. For any given base paper, the **derivative works** in this graph is a list of common descendants of the papers in the graph that were influenced by the base paper. The references of a paper are the papers which it cites. In order to obtain this, Semantic Scholar APIs were used. The APIs required an identifier (MAG ID, arxiv ID, semantic scholar corpus ID etc.), The MAG dataset containing only enumerated paper IDs was insufficient for this task. The Semantic Scholar Open Research Corpus (S2ORC) [13] - was used to fetch the corpus IDs of the base papers for this task.

4   Methodology

4.1   Filtering Data-Set

We used the fields of study and developed a validation scheme in determining the class precisely. In order to filter out influential papers from the MAG dataset, we performed a 2-step filter. The first step used the journal or conference name (*venue name* in MAG) of an article as a filter, in the domain of Artificial Intelligence, according to a list of top Journals and Conferences in the field from Google Scholar [7]. This filter reduced the number of papers from 4,894,081 to 92669. The second step involved selecting a citation threshold of 100 for all articles which reduced the number of papers to 5693.

4.2   Tagging Documents into Categories

Tagging of articles according to topics allowed us to compare articles in the same domain rather than compare articles across domains. The articles were tagged separately according to these classes and authors were segregated according to the generated tags. Thus the influence comparison became field and specialization specific. SciBERT [11] is a BERT based language model, pre-trained on the corpus of scientific text for bidirectional representations. Pre-trained

---

[1] We thank Asritha Sai, Shashank J and Rahul JM for their help in data collection.

state-of-the-art model 'en-core-sci-lg' was used to obtain SciBERT embedded vectors of the classes ML, MO and DL and individual fields of study. The similarity metric between each field and each class is computed as: $similarity = cos\theta(fieldVec, classVec)$. The similarity score was multiplied by the weight assigned to the field by topic modelling and then added to that class score. Among 1258 base papers considered, 829 were tagged as ML, 295 as MO and 134 as DL. Some of the papers with the assigned tags are represented in Table 1.

Algorithm 1: Tagging papers with classes

Input: Fields of study with corresponding weights for one paper, classes
Output: Class labels

```
1  // First level classes = ['machine learning','metaheuristic
      optimization']
2  // Second level classes = ['machine learning','deep learning']
3  classesVec = SciBERT.encode(classes);
4  score1=0;
5  score2=0;
6  for field,weight in fieldsOfStudy do
7      queryVec = SciBERT.encode(field);
8      sim = cosSimilarity(queryVec,classesVec[0]);
9      score1 += weights * sim;
10     sim = cosSimilarity(queryVec,classesVec[1]);
11     score2 += weights * sim;
12 end
13 if score1 > score2 then
14     return class[0]
15 if score2 > score1 then
16     return class[1]
```

Table 1. Tagging papers with domain names

Paper title	Label
Transfer learning via dimensionality reduction	ML
Global exponential stability of complex-valued neural networks with both time-varying delays and impulsive effects	MO
The growing hierarchical self-organizing map: exploratory analysis of high-dimensional data	DL

4.3 Creating Semantic Influence Network (SIN) of Influential Papers and Their Derivatives

The papers obtained post filtering, serve as base papers (level 0) for creating SIN. Derivative works of these base papers were obtained by downloading bib files corresponding to each of them from Connected Papers [12]. The name of the base paper was used to manually query the website due to the unavailability of semantic scholar IDs. For the second level of the network, the derivative works of the papers in the level 1 were obtained using web scraping techniques with Selenium[2]. Semantic Scholar ID of the papers in level 1 was used to query the website for the derivative works. To build the adjacency matrices for obtaining influence score and sparse matrices for obtaining similarity score, we had to match the paper name in the filtered dataset to the names in the titles of bib files (in the format "Derivative-works-for-<paperName>.bib") downloaded. In many cases it was observed that there was no direct match between the names in our dataset and the bib file titles. Several paper names contained articles like "The", "An", etc. hyphens which were either diluted in the bib file title owing to the hyphenated formatting. To address the challenge of cleaning the title of the bib file by removing hyphens, and finding the closest match with the actual paper name in our dataset, we used Levenshtein distance.

Levenshtein distance between two words is the minimum number of single-character edits required to change one word into the other. Through eyeballing, we saw that the maximum difference between true matches would be five. Hence *If Lev(cleaned file name, actual paper name) <= 5, declare match.*

4.4 Influence Score

SIN is a network of directed graphs, each of which contains 'base paper' as root node, 'derivative works' and 'derivative of derivative works' as non-root nodes. Edges are directed from source paper to its derivative works, where source paper is a graph node that has outbound edges. The aim is to evaluate and measure the source node's influence in SIN. Our diffusion model is based on the process of Heat Diffusion. Heat flows from a high to low temperature position in a medium. The heat flow in a geometric manifold can be defined using the partial differential equation: $\frac{\partial u}{\partial t} = k\frac{\partial^2 u}{\partial x^2}$. A heat kernel, is a solution to the heat equation that depicts heat flow on a graph as an approximation of the underlying geometric manifold. The temperature distribution does not alter after an equilibration period, and the system reaches a steady state. The heat kernel was modified to reflect the following facts:

1. Each layer of the network comprised nodes that have a direct connection to nodes in the previous layer. The source node's influence diffused on the nodes closer to the source node should be high, intuitively because these nodes represent derivative works of the source article and the impact of a source article on these works is higher compared to farther nodes.

---

[2] GitHub Repository: https://github.com/PragnyaSridhar/Semantic-Influence-Score.

2. The number of incoming and outgoing edges to and from a node depicts the movement of influence from a higher lower-influence region. Intuitively, the more the indegree of a node, the more it gets influenced by the source node since it has been derived from the source node via several direct and indirect paths. The more the outdegree, the more heat it can send to its children nodes.

$$f(t) = e^{H't} f(0). \tag{1}$$

Equation 1 gives the amount of heat present at all the nodes after the diffusion from the source node. Heat obtained and diffused by the node defines the Heat kernel H' in Eq. 1.

$$H'[i,j] = \begin{cases} 1/D[j,i], & \text{if } T[j,i] = 1 \text{ and } D[j,i] \neq 0, \\ -D[j,i]/N, & \text{otherwise.} \end{cases} \tag{2}$$

where D is diffusability of the node and is defined as follows: $D[i] = D[v] - d[i]/N + c[i]/N$. Parameter d is computed by adding the incoming edges to a node and subtracting the outgoing edges. Parameter c indicated the amount of heat node can diffuse to neighbouring nodes, which is computed by taking sum of the distances of all the nodes from the particular node.

4.5   Similarity Score

Definition 1. *Let T_r denote the rooted directed tree with root r. The similarity between two adjacent nodes is defined as the fraction of commonly cited articles. The similarity between r and any other node a in T_r is defined as the product of the similarities between adjacent nodes in the unique path between r and a, denoted by $S(r,a)$.*

The similarity is well-defined as the existence of unique path is guaranteed with the virtue of construction of the graph. Intuitively it makes sense to define the similarity measure this way in the absence of additional information because:

1. If the path between r and b is given by $<r, a, b>$, it is desired that $S(r,b) \leq S(r,a)$, since it is known apriori that nodes farther from root are strictly less similar than those closer.
2. Let $S(r,a) = p_1$ denote the similarity between r and its adjacent node a. Let p_2 denote the similarity between a and its adjacent node b. When $p_1 \approx 1$, $S(r,b)$ is desired to be $\approx p_2$ as virtually r and a behave like the same article and it is already known that $S(a,b) = p_2$. When $p_1 \approx 0$, it is expected that $S(r,b) \approx 0$. This is because of the choice of construction: as b is not adjacent to r, it is known that $0 \leq S(r,b) \leq S(r,a)$ has to be satisfied.

In SIN, edge weights are the reference intersections between a paper and its' derivative, since if a paper and its derivative both cite the same references, it is more likely that paper and its derivative are more similar.

The references were obtained by querying Semantic Scholar API with an identifier. Levenshtein distance was used to match the names in our dataset.

The reference intersection between a paper and its derivative was normalized by dividing the number of common references by the number of references of the parent paper/node. A sparse matrix was made using these weights and similarity scores were computed.

4.6   Semantic Influence Score (SIS)

SIS is a function of the Influence score and the Similarity score. The network structure and the semantic similarity are encoded into SIS. The base contributes the following to SIS $score_0 = SrcHeat(B) * journalprestige(B)$ where B is a Base paper, $SrcHeat$ is the initial heat assigned to the source and $journalprestige$ is a quantitative measure of prestige of the venue B has been published in. The initial heat is the length of the knowledge chain (or the number of derivative works of a base paper). The Journal Prestige is quantified by considering the h5 indices of the paper publication venues. Since conferences tend to have higher values as compared to journals, the scores were normalized separately for conferences and journals.

The contribution of the derivative works or level 1 is computed as:

$$score_1 = w_1 \frac{\sum_{d \in D} (SimScore(B,d) * min(SrcHeat(B), InfScore(d)))}{\sum_{d \in D} bool(SimScore(B,d) \neq 0)} \quad (3)$$

where w_1 is set as 1.0; D is List of derivative works of B; $SimScore$ is the similarity score; $InfScore$ is the influence score and $bool$ is a function that returns 1 if the condition is true and 0 if false. A weighted sum of the influence score was taken by using the similarity score between a paper and its derivative as the weight. The score was normalized by considering the number of non zero similarity scores.

The contributions of level 2 i.e. derivative of derivative works is:

$$score_2 = w_2 \frac{\sum_{d \in D} w_3 \frac{\sum_{dd \in DD} (SimScore(d,dd) * min(SrcHeat(B), InfScore(dd))}{\sum_{dd \in DD} bool(SimScore(d,dd) \neq 0)}}{\sum_{d \in D} bool(\sum_{dd \in DD}(SimScore(d,dd)) \neq 0)} \quad (4)$$

where DD is a List of Lists containing the derivative works of papers in D $w_2 = 0.5$ and $w_3 = 0.25$. Finally, the SIS of base paper B is the sum of the contributions from all the levels of its SIN computed as $SIS_B = score_0 + score_1 + score_2$.

5   Results

Table 2 illustrates some of the SIS scores computed. The table clearly brings out the mismatch between citation count and SIS. 'Scikit-learn', which has the highest citation count in our corpus, scored nearly the same SIS as 'Evolution and development of neural controllers for locomotion, gradient-following, and obstacle-avoidance in artificial insects', which only had 139 citations. On the other hand, a paper with the minimum citation count in our corpus scored a very high SIS of 12.9341. The paper with the highest SIS only had 105 citations, and the paper with the lowest SIS had 133 citations. It was also observed that a feasible regression model between SIS and raw citation count does not exist. This is depicted in Fig. 1. Further, Pearson's correlation coefficient between SIS and raw citation counts was found to be 0.0083. The confidence intervals for the obtained correlation coefficient was computed by using Fisher Z-Transform (Z-score is computed as $z' = 0.5 ln\frac{1+r}{1-r}$ where $[r]$ is the Pearson's correlation coefficient, standard error as $SE = \frac{1}{\sqrt{n-3}}$ and $CI = (tanh(z' - z'_{crit} * SE), tanh(z' + z'_{crit} * SE)$ where CI is the confidence interval) at different confidence levels as shown in Table 3.

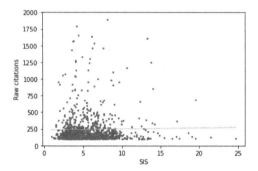

Fig. 1. Regression between raw citation and SIS

Table 2. Semantic influence scores

Paper title	Topic	Raw citation	SIS
Scikit-learn: Machine Learning in Python	ML	12871	5.1665
Evolution and development of neural controllers for locomotion, gradient-following, and obstacle-avoidance in artificial insects	ML	139	5.1667
Some neural network applications in environmental sciences. Part I: forward and inverse problems in geophysical remote measurements	ML	100	12.9341
Neural network controller using autotuning method for nonlinear functions	MO	105	24.7033
Artificial intelligence and molecular biology	ML	133	0.9355
Dlib-ml: A Machine Learning Toolkit	ML	919	1.9742
Constrained K-means Clustering with Background Knowledge	ML	1606	13.3229
Radial basis function network based on time variant multi-objective particle swarm optimization for medical diseases diagnosis	MO	102	13.2623
Toward an architecture for never-ending language learning	DL	1059	2.3356
Advanced ontology management system for personalised e-Learning	DL	120	2.3353
The Unscented Particle Filter	MO	1168	10.6481

Table 3. Confidence intervals for correlation coefficient between SIS and raw citation

Confidence level	Confidence interval
95%	(0.028, 0.1369)
98%	(0.0177, 0.148)
99%	(0.0107, 0.1537)
99.9%	(−0.009, 0.1732)

Table 4. P-values obtained from KS-test

Distribution	p-value
Normal	1.96e−12
Skewed Normal	0.00096
Log Normal	0.22794
Pareto	3.731e−68
Power Law	5.583e−152

From Table 3, we can assert with 99.9% confidence that the maximum value the correlation coefficient can take is 0.1732. This clearly indicates that there exists scant correlation between our metric and raw citation counts, thus proving that SIS is an unprejudiced metric, unaffected by citation counts of papers. Raw citation counts follows Pareto distribution which is an implication of the power law distribution. A minority of the papers contain very high citations. On performing the Kolmogorov-Smirnov (KS) test, we found that our SIS metric does not follow Pareto distribution.

From Table 4, it can be concluded that SIS does not follow Pareto and Power Law distribution as the p-value is less than the significance level (0.01). It can be said with 99% confidence that the SIS metric follows Log-normal distribution instead.

6   Discussion and Conclusion

Let us consider a use case with two Papers, Paper A and Paper B. Consider A having 10000 citations while B has 500 citations. Could the SIS of A be lesser than SIS of B? Let's investigate the network structure of A and B. A has many derivative works which shares a thin percentage of reference intersection with A. This may not the case with the paper B, as we studied the networks thoroughly. A probable example for such small reference intersection is that the citing articles may have just used a core idea/highlight of A (which might be an implementation based article) to complete a task. On closer inspection, we found that the article A is 'Scikit-learn', an implementation toolkit which can be treated as a black-box for several tasks and might have been treated as such by several citing articles/derivative works. This belief is further compounded by a meagre intersection of references, as small as 0.1%, clearly indicating lack of reference evaluation of the cited article by the citing articles. Evolution of knowledge or building a foundation block in the citing article may not have been the priority of the authors. SIS is computed on top of a model based on the assumption of knowledge evolution along the reference/citation chain supported by the rationale that larger intersection of references imply greater influence and dissemination of core foundational knowledge presented in the base paper and the derivative works of the base paper. Therefore, papers with larger citation count but smaller SIS is not an anomaly, but a sensible outcome we expected all along. This establishes the efficacy of the heat diffusion model in the network structure of base papers, knowledge chain and derivative works amply. Thus SIS is a thus robust metric to evaluate the quality and influence of scientific, peer-reviewed publications.

SIS lays the foundation of further investigations in author influence and influence of academic institutions in shaping the future of knowledge creation and dissemination. We plan to define and compute new metrics for evaluating author influence thus providing feasible alternatives to existing metrics such as raw citations, h and i-10 indices.

References

1. Barabási, A.-L., Albert, R.: REPORT emergence of scaling in random networks. Science **286**(5439), 509–512 (1999)
2. Bergstrom, C.T., West, J.D., Wiseman, M.A.: The eigenfactor^{TM} metrics. J. Neurosci. **28**(45), 11433–11434 (2008)
3. Saha, S., Jangid, N., Mathur, A., Narsimhamurthy, A.M.: DSRS: estimation and forecasting of journal influence in the science and technology domain via a lightweight quantitative approach. CollNet J. Scientometrics Inf. Manage. **10**(1), 41–70 (2016)
4. da Silva, J.A.T., Memon, A.R.: CiteScore: a cite for sore eyes, or a VALUABLE, TRANSPARENT METRIC? 21 Jan 2017. https://link.springer.com/article/10.1007/s11192-017-2250-0. Accessed 07 Apr 2021
5. Mingers, J.: Problems with SNIP. J. Informetrics **8**(4), 890–894 (2014). ISSN: 1751-1577
6. Jangid, N., Saha, S., Gupta, S., Rao, J.M.: Ranking of journals in science and technology domain: a novel and computationally lightweight approach. IERI Procedia **10**, 57–62 (2014)
7. Google Scholar Top AI journals and conferences. https://tinyurl.com/yy684539. Accessed 4 Sept 2020
8. Tang, J., Zhang, J., Yao, L., Li, J., Zhang, L., Su, Z.: ArnetMiner: extraction and mining of academic social networks. In: Proceedings of the Fourteenth ACM SIGKDD International Conference on Knowledge Discovery and Data Mining (SIGKDD 2008), pp. 990–998 (2008)
9. Sinha, A., et al.: An overview of microsoft academic service (MAS) and applications. In: Proceedings of the 24th International Conference on World Wide Web (WWW 2015 Companion). ACM, New York, NY, USA, pp. 243–246 (2015)
10. Shen, Z., Ma, H., Wang, K.: A web-scale system for scientific knowledge exploration. In: Proceedings of ACL 2018, System Demonstrations, Melbourne, Australia, pp. 87–92 (2018)
11. Beltagy, I., Lo, K., Cohan, A.: SciBERT: pretrained language model for scientific text. EMNLP arXiv:1904.07248 (2020)
12. Connected Papers Home Page. https://www.connectedpapers.com. Accessed 1 Feb 2021
13. Lo, K., Wang, L.L., Neumann, M., Kinney, R., Weld, D.: S2ORC: The Semantic Scholar Open Research Corpus. Association for Computational Linguistics
14. Moed, H.F.: Measuring contextual citation impact of scientific journals. Computing Research Repository (CoRR)
15. Aminer Homepage. https://www.aminer.cn. Accessed 27 Sept 2020

AI System Engineering: Math, Modelling and Software

Robust and Efficient Bio-Inspired Data-Sampling Prototype for Time-Series Analysis

Michael Lunglmayr[1]([✉]) [ID], Günther Lindorfer[1], and Bernhard Moser[2] [ID]

[1] Institute of Signal Processing, Johannes Kepler University Linz,
Altenbergerstr. 69, 4040 Linz, Austria
`michael.lunglmayr@jku.at`
[2] Software Competence Center Hagenberg, Softwarepark 21,
4232 Hagenberg, Austria
`bernhard.moser@scch.at`

Abstract. Data acquisition is crucial for efficient AI systems. We present a bio-inspired prototype implementation of discrepancy-based adaptive threshold-based sampling on a low-cost microcontroller. We show measurement results demonstrating that an adaptive threshold-based sampling approach can be performed only using onboard components of the microcontroller. To measure the sampling precision, we used sinusoidal signals output by a waveform generator and compared the signals after reconstruction to exact signals with the set parameters. These measurements show that, even with such low-cost components, discrepancy-based adaptive threshold-based sampling can be performed with high precision.

Keywords: Threshold-based sampling · Send-on-Delta · Discrepancy

1 Introduction

The efficiency of learning systems is closely tied to an efficient data acquisition process. Bio-inspired event-based sampling is a promising concept for improving the efficiency of the sampling process in a manifold number of ways. The simple structure of the analog part of data acquisition devices allows for low energy consumption. The event-based data acquisition process results in a low amount of samples representing a signal. This reflects in low data storage requirements and low computational complexity of subsequent processing algorithms for the signals. This is especially important for machine learning algorithms where often the number of required operations scales with the number of samples representing sensor information. Especially when performing learning tasks on edge devices, efficient data acquisition is crucial for a high overall systems efficiency.

Send-on-Delta (SOD) [4] is a prominent member of the class of event-based sampling methods. It represents a signal by a sequence of spikes that are triggered when a signal's amplitude changes by more than a certain threshold value

© Springer Nature Switzerland AG 2021
G. Kotsis et al. (Eds.): DEXA 2021 Workshops, CCIS 1479, pp. 119–126, 2021.
https://doi.org/10.1007/978-3-030-87101-7_12

in the positive or negative direction. If the change was positive, a +1 spike is triggered, if the change was negative a −1 spike is triggered. Typically, a fixed threshold is used for SOD. Recently, a threshold adaption strategy has been proposed [3,5], significantly allowing reducing the number of spikes to represent a signal while maintaining a high reconstruction quality. This adaptive threshold adaption strategy is based on Weyl's discrepancy, which was shown to be the canonical metric for threshold-based sampling [5,6]. This finding is part of a general mathematical framework for threshold-based sampling presented in [5,6]. Within this framework, it was also proved that only quasi-isometry can be achieved between the signal space and the event space but not isometry.

In this work, we present a prototype implementation using a low-cost STM32 microcontroller board (single board costs are around €14). We describe the implementation and present measurement results demonstrating that using the adaptive threshold adaption strategy a high reconstruction precision can be obtained, with, compared to classical SOD, a significantly lower number of spikes. To the best of our knowledge, this is the first prototype implementation of discrepancy-based adaptive threshold-based sampling. This prototype will be used for future research on performing detection and learning tasks in the event space for electrocardiogram (ECG) signals.

1.1   Weyl's Discrepancy

Discrepancy is defined as

$$\|\mathbf{x}\|_D = \sup_{n_1, n_2 \in \mathbb{Z}: n_1 \leq n_2,} |\sum_{i=n_1}^{n_2} x_i|, \tag{1}$$

for a vector $\mathbf{x}$, not necessarily of finite length. This definition is due to its initial introduction for a sequence of numbers from the unit interval by Herman Weyl [9]. For vectors of finite length n, with element indices out of $I_n = \{1, \ldots, n\}$, the discrepancy can be calculated as

$$\|\mathbf{x}\|_D = \max\{0, \max_{k \in I_n} \sum_{i=1}^{k} x_i\} - \min\{0, \min_{k \in I_n} \sum_{i=1}^{k} x_i\}, \tag{2}$$

which allows for an efficient calculation of the discrepancy value. From Eq. (2) an important interpretation of discrepancy can be observed. The discrepancy represents the diameter of a vector and, in the context of threshold-based sampling, also the diameter of the signal that was sampled (because only quasi-isometry can be obtained, discrepancy only approximately represents the diameter of the sampled signal).

1.2   Adaptive Threshold-Based Sampling Approach Based on Quasi-Isometry

The adaptive threshold-based sampling approach used in this work is based on the following principle [3,5]. If a spike is triggered, the discrepancy is calculated for the spike sequence including the currently triggered spike and all past spikes within a pre-defined time window. Figure 1 graphically depicts this concept. This local discrepancy is then used to adapt the currently used threshold value. Here, we used the strategy of halving the threshold if the discrepancy was smaller than a desired lower limit (the discrepancy will go up if the threshold is reduced) and doubling the threshold if the discrepancy was larger than a desired upper limit. The halving or doubling will stop if pre-defined upper or lower limits of the thresholds have been reached. This allows adapting the sampling process to local signal properties. At times where the (local) diameter is large, a large discrepancy value will be calculated in the time window and vice versa. This allows spending samples more efficiently, at times of large changes of the signal (large diameter) one can afford larger sampling errors by using a larger threshold (lower relative error), at times of small signal changes (low diameter) one might want to use a smaller threshold to also maintain a low relative error. Because the spike adaption is done by a deterministic algorithm, using the previously triggered spikes for threshold adaption, the threshold sequence can be unambiguously reconstructed from the spike sequence, e.g. for the reconstruction of the sampled signal.

2 Prototype Development

The threshold-based sampling prototype was fully implemented with the on-board components of an STM32F303VC (STM32F3DISCOVERY board) micro-controller. In the following, the used components are written in parenthesis according to the datasheet [8]. The microcontroller provides two analog comparators (COMP1 and COMP2; allowing to detect threshold crossings) and a digital to analog converter (DAC) with two output channels (DAC OUT 1 and 2) that can be internally connected to each of the comparators, respectively. A 16-bit internal timer (TIM6) is used to measure the time between spikes as described below. The timer used the same clock frequency as the microcontroller core (no prescaler) of 72 MHz. Figure 2a graphically depicts the used components from the microcontroller for the prototype (in addition to its CPU core).

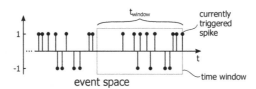

Fig. 1. Local discrepancy calculation in a time window past the currently triggered spike.

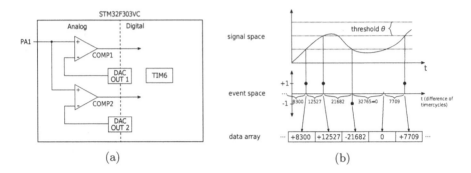

(a)   (b)

Fig. 2. a) Utilized building blocks in the analog and digital domains of the used microcontroller. b) Example sampling scenario with data representation.

2.1 Spike Data Representation and Communication

Spikes not only encode the direction a threshold was crossed but also the time a crossing occurred. For this reason, a representation format was developed allowing for efficient storing, processing, and transmitting of the sampling information in the microcontroller. Figure 2b shows an example representation of a sampled spike sequence. A spike is represented as an array of 16-bit numbers. The number's signs in the array represent the signs of the spikes. Its absolute values represent the timer values when the spikes occurred. After starting the sampling process, the timer runs freely up to an upper limit (32765) and is then reset to zero to cyclically count up again. If a timer reached its upper limit before triggering a spike, a zero is stored to signal such a time duration without triggering a spike. Such time durations will be considered in the subsequent processing by adding its duration to the time information of the following spikes (the value 0 will be interpreted as the maximum timer value). The sampling process is done using two arrays. In one array, the currently sampled spikes are stored while the samples in the other are transmitted via the built-in UART-USB connection (transmission speed 1.024 Mbps) to the computer for further processing. If one buffer is filled, the sampling routine switches to the second buffer and triggers the transmission of the first buffer.

3 Measurement Results

To evaluate the sampling quality, we used the following measurement scenario. We used two STM32F3DISCOVERY boards, one implementing the described threshold-based sampling method and one using its on-board 12-bit successive-approximation analog-to-digital converter (ADC) for reference. The board implementing the threshold-based sampling triggers the start of the conventional (clock-based) sampling process on the second board.

To evaluate the sampling precision we used a RIGOL DG1022A arbitrary waveform generator outputting sine signals of frequencies 100 and 1000 Hz to the described measurement setup, respectively. We set the peak-to-peak output voltage to $V_{pp} = 1$ V using an offset of 1.5 V. To measure the sampling quality, the mean squared error (MSE): MSE $= \frac{1}{N} \sum [y(t_i) - \tilde{y}(t_i)]^2$, $\forall N$ comparison times t_i, was used. As we expect threshold-based sampling to be quite precise at the times a spike is triggered (except thresholding errors of the analog parts) we wanted to evaluate how precise the original function can be reconstructed (the errors of the waveform generator can be considered negligible for this measurement setup). For this reason, we did a spline interpolation between the points acquired by threshold-based sampling and rescaled the interpolation result such that its amplitude fitted within the interval $[-1, 1]$. We then compared the interpolation signal with an exact sine signal of frequency 100 or 1000 Hz, respectively. We sampled the interpolation functions at $1/72$ ms (to match a time grid defined by the clock frequency of 72 MHz of the microcontroller). For performance reference, we compared these results to samples acquired by the second microcontroller board using its onboard ADC using a sampling frequency of 12 kHz. At the sampling times, the sampled value $\tilde{y}(t_i)$ (either from the interpolated signal of threshold-based sampling or using classical sampling) was compared to the values $y(t_i)$ of an exact sine signal with the parameters set in the waveform generator. Table 1 shows the measurement results for the sine signals of 100 and 1000 Hz, respectively. For these test signals, we evaluated different parameter configurations. The first column shows these parameters. Here, $\|\cdot\|_{D,ref}$ refers to the desired discrepancy value, used for the threshold adaption process, in a time window of length t_{window} past the currently triggered spike. For each evaluation, 10 measured periods have been compared to those of an exact sine. The exact sine has been phase-matched to the measured signals for a fair comparison. The random starting phase of the sine leads to slightly different values for the different test cases (e.g. the number of samples/spikes counted in the measurement periods). We compared adaptive

Table 1. Measurement results for test sine signals.

100 Hz	Threshold-based		Conventional ADC	
$\|\cdot\|_{D,ref}/t_{window}$ [ms]	MSE	$\#spikes$	MSE	$\#samples$
2/0.55	$4.8716 \cdot 10^{-4}$	182	$1.1172 \cdot 10^{-4}$	1141
2/0.69	$2.4294 \cdot 10^{-4}$	152	$1.1791 \cdot 10^{-4}$	1081
3/0.55	$1.1727 \cdot 10^{-4}$	349	$2.2025 \cdot 10^{-4}$	1141
No adaption (50 mV)	$4.3318 \cdot 10^{-4}$	324	$1.2923 \cdot 10^{-4}$	1140
1000 Hz	Threshold-based		Conventional ADC	
$\|\cdot\|_{D,ref}/t_{window}$ [ms]	MSE	$\#spikes$	MSE	$\#samples$
2/0.055	$9.0846 \cdot 10^{-5}$	168	0.0022	109
2/0.069	$1.7587 \cdot 10^{-4}$	144	0.0094	109
3/0.055	$4.2768 \cdot 10^{-4}$	319	0.0068	108
No adaption (50 mV)	$1.3820 \cdot 10^{-4}$	342	0.0043	115

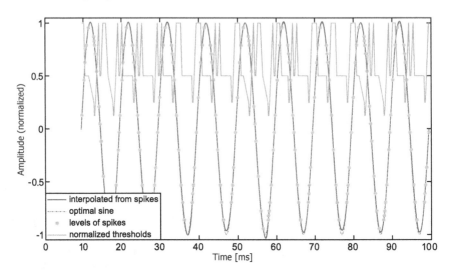

Fig. 3. Measurement data of the first line of Table 1.

threshold-based sampling, allowing the algorithm to select thresholds between 10 mV and 400 mv to SOD with a fixed threshold of 50 mV. For SOD with a fixed threshold, a larger threshold value is necessary as our experiments showed that, especially for the 1000 Hz test cases, choosing a too small threshold leads to aliasing-like effects (the signal changes faster than the SOD sampling unit can adjust its thresholds) resulting in large measurement errors. The adaptive method prevented such effects in the chosen test cases allowing to also use such small thresholds for signal parts requiring a higher sampling precision. This allows for a lower number of spikes and higher precision, as the results of Table 1 demonstrate. Figure 3 shows the threshold-based sampling results of the first line of Table 1. One can see from this figure how the algorithm adjusts the thresholds (here shown normalized) on the signal characteristics.

For this work, the sampling parameters of the prototype have been selected heuristically, it is, however, planned to use machine learning algorithms to optimize these parameters in a data-driven way for the future.

4 ECG Measurements

One of our aims when designing the prototype was to use it as a sampling device for electrocardiogram (ECG) signals. For this use case, it is hard to obtain quantitative results for the sampling precision of ECG signals (one never knows the ground truth). Figure 4 shows an example ECG signal that was sampled by the described prototype. The analog pre-processing and connection to a test person has been done by a "SparkFun Single Lead Heart Rate Monitor" board [7] using an AD8232-chip [1]. For threshold-based sampling, the values $t_{window} = 2.1$ ms and $\|\cdot\|_{D,ref} = 2$ have been used. For this use case, the minimum threshold was

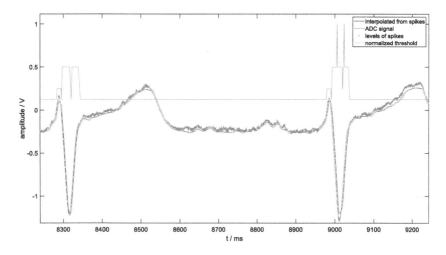

Fig. 4. ECG measurement with the described prototype.

set to 20 mV and the maximum threshold was again set to 400 mV. Setting the minimum threshold higher allows for a better noise reduction, as can be seen in this figure. One can notice that, for this application, the used threshold-based sampling method naturally spends a large number of samples in the regions of most interest of an ECG signal. These are the regions around the sharp peaks (the so-called QRS complexes [2]). In contrast, a low amount of samples is spent for the regions between the QRS complexes. Figure 4 shows part of a recording sequence of approximately 16.8 s. The full signal sampled by the conventional ADC is represented by 202000 samples while the threshold-based sampled signal is represented by a spike train of 40000 spikes. Based on these results, our plan for the future is to obtain quantitative results by performing detection and learning tasks on ECG signals that can then will be compared quantitatively to results obtained via classically sampled signals. We expect the low energy requirements of threshold-based sampling as well as low energy requirements of a subsequent processing algorithm (due to a smaller number of samples) to be especially beneficial for battery-powered wearable computing devices.

5 Conclusion

We presented a prototype implementation of discrepancy-based adaptive threshold-based sampling on a low-cost microcontroller. We showed measurement results for sinusoidal signals demonstrating that adaptive threshold-based can be successfully implemented on such low-cost devices as well as the high reconstruction precision that can be obtained. Compared to classical SOD sampling the number of samples can be significantly reduced while maintaining a high reconstruction precision. A reduction of the number of samples representing a signal of interest has a big impact on the requirements in terms of energy and computational resources which is especially crucial for battery-powered devices.

Acknowledgement. The authors would like to thank the Austrian COMET Program for its support.

References

1. Analog Devices: Single-lead, heart rate monitor front end. https://www.analog.com/media/en/technical-documentation/data-sheets/ad8232.pdf
2. Gacek, A., Pedrycz, W.: ECG Signal Processing, Classification and Interpretation: A Comprehensive Framework of Computational Intelligence. Springer, London (2012). https://doi.org/10.1007/978-0-85729-868-3
3. Lunglmayr, M., Qaisar, S.M., Moser, B.A.: Tradeoff analysis of discrepancy-based adaptive thresholding approach. In: 2019 5th International Conference on Event-Based Control, Communication, and Signal Processing (EBCCSP), pp. 1–4 (2019). https://doi.org/10.1109/EBCCSP.2019.8836905
4. Marek Miskowicz, E.: Event-Based Control and Signal Processing. CRC Press (2017)
5. Moser, B.A., Lunglmayr, M.: On quasi-isometry of threshold-based sampling. IEEE Trans. Signal Process. **67**(14), 3832–3841 (2019). https://doi.org/10.1109/TSP.2019.2919415
6. Moser, B.A.: Similarity recovery from threshold-based sampling under general conditions. IEEE Trans. Signal Process. **65**(17), 4645–4654 (2017)
7. SparkFun Electronics: Sparkfun single lead heart rate monitor - ad8232. https://www.sparkfun.com/products/12650
8. STMicroelectonics: Datasheet for: Stm32f303xb stm32f303xc, October 2018. https://www.st.com/resource/en/datasheet/stm32f303vc.pdf
9. Weyl, H.: Über die Gleichverteilung von Zahlen mod. Eins. Mathematische Annalen **77**, 313–352 (1916)

Membership-Mappings for Data Representation Learning: Measure Theoretic Conceptualization

Mohit Kumar[1,2(✉)], Bernhard Moser[1], Lukas Fischer[1], and Bernhard Freudenthaler[1]

[1] Software Competence Center Hagenberg GmbH, 4232 Hagenberg, Austria
mohit.kumar@scch.at
[2] Institute of Automation, Faculty of Computer Science and Electrical Engineering, University of Rostock, Rostock, Germany

Abstract. A fuzzy theoretic analytical approach was recently introduced that leads to efficient and robust models while addressing automatically the typical issues associated to parametric deep models. However, a formal conceptualization of the fuzzy theoretic analytical deep models is still not available. This paper introduces using measure theoretic basis the notion of *membership-mapping* for representing data points through attribute values (motivated by fuzzy theory). A property of the membership-mapping, that can be exploited for data representation learning, is of providing an interpolation on the given data points in the data space. An analytical approach to the variational learning of a membership-mappings based data representation model is considered.

Keywords: Measure theory · Membership function · Fuzzy theory

1 Introduction

Deep neural networks have been successfully applied in a wide range of problems but their training requires a large amount of data. The issues concerning neural networks based parametric deep models include determining the optimal model structure, requirement of large training dataset, and iterative time-consuming nature of numerical learning algorithms. These issues have motivated the development of a nonparametric deep model [1] that is learned analytically for representing data points. The study in [1] introduces the concept of *fuzzy-mapping* which is about representing mappings through a fuzzy set with a membership function such that the dimension of membership function increases with

Supported by the Austrian Research Promotion Agency (FFG) Sub-Project PETAI (Privacy Secured Explainable and Transferable AI for Healthcare Systems); the Federal Ministry for Climate Action, Environment, Energy, Mobility, Innovation and Technology (BMK); the Federal Ministry for Digital and Economic Affairs (BMDW); and the Province of Upper Austria in the frame of the COMET - Competence Centers for Excellent Technologies Programme managed by Austrian Research Promotion Agency FFG.

© Springer Nature Switzerland AG 2021
G. Kotsis et al. (Eds.): DEXA 2021 Workshops, CCIS 1479, pp. 127–137, 2021.
https://doi.org/10.1007/978-3-030-87101-7_13

an increasing data size. The main result of [1] is that a deep model formed via a composition of finite number of nonparametric fuzzy-mappings can be learned analytically and the analytical approach leads to a robust and computationally fast method of data representation learning. A core issue in machine learning is rigorously accounting for the uncertainties. While probability theory is widely used to study uncertainties in machine learning, the applications of fuzzy theory in machine learning remain relatively unexplored. Both probability and fuzzy theory have been combined to design stochastic fuzzy systems [2–4]. For an analytical design and analysis of machine learning models, a pure fuzzy theoretic approach was introduced [6] where fuzzy membership functions quantifying uncertainties are determined via variational optimization [9]. Although the fuzzy based analytical learning approach to the learning of deep models (as suggested in [1,5,7]) leads to the development of efficient and robust machine learning models, a formal conceptualization of the fuzzy theoretic analytical deep models is still not available. Thus, our aim here is to present a measure theoretic conceptualization of fuzzy based analytical deep models.

The study introduces using measure theoretic basis the concept of *membership-mappings*. The membership-mapping in this study has been referred to a measure theoretic conceptualization of the fuzzy-mapping (previously studied in [1,5,7]). The membership-mappings allow a representation of data points through attribute values. This representation is motivated by fuzzy theory where the attributes are linguistic variables. A membership-mapping is characterized by a membership function that evaluates the degree-of-matching of data points to the attribute induced by a sequence of observations. The membership functions have been constrained to be satisfying the properties of a) nowhere vanishing, b) positive and bounded integrals, and c) consistency of induced probability measure. For a set of measurable functions, the membership function induces a probability measure (that is guaranteed by Kolmogorov extension theorem). The expectations w.r.t. the defined probability measure can be calculated via simply computing a weighted average with membership function as the weighting function. Finally, an analytical approach to the variational learning of a membership-mappings based data representation model is considered following [1,5,7].

2   Notations and Definitions

Let $n, N, p, M \in \mathbb{N}$. Let $\mathcal{B}(\mathbb{R}^N)$ denote the *Borel $\sigma-algebra$* on $\mathbb{R}^N$, and let λ^N denote the *Lebesgue measure* on $\mathcal{B}(\mathbb{R}^N)$. Let $(\mathcal{X}, \mathcal{A}, \rho)$ be a probability space with unknown probability measure ρ. Let $\mathcal{S}$ be the set of finite samples of data points drawn i.i.d. from ρ, i.e.,

$$\mathcal{S} := \{(x^i \sim \rho)_{i=1}^N \mid N \in \mathbb{N}\}. \tag{1}$$

For a sequence $\mathrm{x} = (x^1, \cdots, x^N) \in \mathcal{S}$, let $|\mathrm{x}|$ denote the cardinality i.e. $|\mathrm{x}| = N$. If $\mathrm{x} = (x^1, \cdots, x^N)$, $\mathrm{a} = (a^1, \cdots, a^M) \in \mathcal{S}$, then $\mathrm{x} \wedge \mathrm{a}$ denotes the concatenation of the sequences x and a, i.e., $\mathrm{x} \wedge \mathrm{a} = (x^1, \ldots, x^N, a^1, \ldots, a^M)$. $\mathbb{F}(\mathcal{X})$ denotes the set of $\mathcal{A}\text{-}\mathcal{B}(\mathbb{R})$ measurable functions $f : \mathcal{X} \to \mathbb{R}$, i.e.,

$$\mathbb{F}(\mathcal{X}) := \{f : \mathcal{X} \to \mathbb{R} \mid f \text{ is } \mathcal{A}\text{-}\mathcal{B}(\mathbb{R}) \text{ measurable}\}. \tag{2}$$

For convenience, the values of a function $f \in \mathbb{F}(\mathcal{X})$ at points in the collection $\mathrm{x} = (x^1, \cdots, x^N)$ are represented as $f(\mathrm{x}) = (f(x^1), \cdots, f(x^N))$. For a given $\mathrm{x} \in \mathcal{S}$ and $A \in \mathcal{B}(\mathbb{R}^{|\mathrm{x}|})$, the cylinder set $\mathcal{T}_{\mathrm{x}}(A)$ in $\mathbb{F}(\mathcal{X})$ is defined as

$$\mathcal{T}_{\mathrm{x}}(A) := \{f \in \mathbb{F}(\mathcal{X}) \mid f(\mathrm{x}) \in A\}. \tag{3}$$

Let $\mathcal{T}$ be the family of cylinder sets defined as

$$\mathcal{T} := \left\{ \mathcal{T}_{\mathrm{x}}(A) \mid A \in \mathcal{B}(\mathbb{R}^{|\mathrm{x}|}), \ \mathrm{x} \in \mathcal{S} \right\}. \tag{4}$$

Let $\sigma(\mathcal{T})$ be the σ-algebra generated by $\mathcal{T}$. Given two $\mathcal{B}(\mathbb{R}^N) - \mathcal{B}(\mathbb{R})$ measurable mappings, $g : \mathbb{R}^N \to \mathbb{R}$ and $\mu : \mathbb{R}^N \to \mathbb{R}$, the weighted average of $g(\mathrm{y})$ over all $\mathrm{y} \in \mathbb{R}^N$, with $\mu(\mathrm{y})$ as the weighting function, is computed as

$$\langle g \rangle_\mu := \frac{1}{\int_{\mathbb{R}^N} \mu(\mathrm{y}) \, \mathrm{d}\lambda^N(\mathrm{y})} \int_{\mathbb{R}^N} g(\mathrm{y}) \mu(\mathrm{y}) \, \mathrm{d}\lambda^N(\mathrm{y}). \tag{5}$$

3 Representation of Samples via Attribute Values

Let us consider a given observation $x \in \mathcal{X}$, a data point $\tilde{x} \in \mathcal{X}$, and a mapping $\mathbf{A}_x(\tilde{x}) : \tilde{x} \mapsto \mathbf{A}_x(\tilde{x}) \in [0, 1]$ such that $\mathbf{A}_x(\tilde{x})$ can be interpreted as evaluation of the degree to which the data point $\tilde{x}$ matches a given attribute induced by the observation x. $\mathbf{A}_x(\cdot)$ is called a membership function and this interpretation is motivated by fuzzy theory. In our approach we consider $\mathbf{A}_{x,f}(\tilde{x}) = (\zeta_x \circ f)(\tilde{x})$ to be composed of two mappings $f : \mathcal{X} \to \mathbb{R}$ and $\zeta_x : \mathbb{R} \to [0, 1]$. $f \in \mathbb{F}(\mathcal{X})$ can be interpreted as physical measurement (e.g., temperature), and $\zeta_x(f(\tilde{x}))$ as degree to which $\tilde{x}$ matches the attribute under consideration, e.g. "hot" where e.g. x is a representative sample of "hot". Next, we extend this concept to sequences of data points in order to evaluate how much a sequence $\tilde{\mathrm{x}} = (\tilde{x}^1, \ldots, \tilde{x}^N) \in \mathcal{S}$ matches to the attribute induced by observed sequence $\mathrm{x} = (x^1, \ldots, x^N) \in \mathcal{S}$ w.r.t. the feature f via defining

$$\mathbf{A}_{\mathrm{x},f}(\tilde{\mathrm{x}}) = (\zeta_{\mathrm{x}} \circ f)(\tilde{\mathrm{x}}) \tag{6}$$

$$= \zeta_{\mathrm{x}}(f(\tilde{x}^1), \ldots, f(\tilde{x}^N)), \tag{7}$$

where the membership functions $\zeta_{\mathrm{x}} : \mathbb{R}^{|\mathrm{x}|} \to [0, 1]$, $\mathrm{x} \in \mathcal{S}$, satisfy the following properties:

Nowhere Vanishing: $\zeta_x(y) > 0$ for all $y \in \mathbb{R}^{|x|}$, i.e.,

$$\text{supp}[\zeta_x] = \mathbb{R}^{|x|}. \tag{8}$$

Positive and Bounded Integrals: the functions ζ_x are absolutely continuous and Lebesgue integrable over the whole domain such that for all $x \in \mathcal{S}$ we have

$$0 < \int_{\mathbb{R}^{|x|}} \zeta_x \, d\lambda^{|x|} < \infty. \tag{9}$$

Consistency of Induced Probability Measure: The membership function induced probability measures $\mathbb{P}_{\zeta_x}$, defined on any $A \in \mathcal{B}(\mathbb{R}^{|x|})$, as

$$\mathbb{P}_{\zeta_x}(A) := \frac{1}{\int_{\mathbb{R}^{|x|}} \zeta_x \, d\lambda^{|x|}} \int_A \zeta_x \, d\lambda^{|x|} \tag{10}$$

are consistent in the sense that for all x, $a \in \mathcal{S}$:

$$\mathbb{P}_{\zeta_{x \wedge a}}(A \times \mathbb{R}^{|a|}) = \mathbb{P}_{\zeta_x}(A). \tag{11}$$

For convenience, let us denote the collection of membership functions satisfying aforementioned assumptions by

$$\Theta := \{\zeta_x : \mathbb{R}^{|x|} \to [0,1] \mid (8), (9), (11), \; x \in \mathcal{S}\}. \tag{12}$$

3.1   A Measure Space

Result 1 (A Probability Measure on $\mathbb{F}(\mathcal{X})$) $(\mathbb{F}(\mathcal{X}), \sigma(\mathcal{T}), \mathbf{p})$ *is a measure space and the probability measure* $\mathbf{p}$, *that was guaranteed by Kolmogorov extension theorem, is defined as*

$$\mathbf{p}(\mathcal{T}_x(A)) := \mathbb{P}_{\zeta_x}(A) \tag{13}$$

where $\zeta_x \in \Theta$, $x \in \mathcal{S}$, $A \in \mathcal{B}(\mathbb{R}^{|x|})$, *and* $\mathcal{T}_x(A) \in \mathcal{T}$.

Proof. Given a sequence of samples $(x^i)_{i=1}^N$, define $S(N) := (x^1, \cdots, x^N)$ i.e. $S(N+1) = S(N) \wedge (x^{N+1})$, $N \in \mathbb{N}$. For each $N \in \mathbb{N}$, let $\mathbb{P}_{\zeta_{S(N)}}$ be a probability measure induced by a membership function $\zeta_{S(N)} \in \Theta$. As per assumption (11), the measures, $(\mathbb{P}_{\zeta_{S(N)}})_{N=1}^N$, are consistent in the sense that $\mathbb{P}_{\zeta_{S(N+1)}}(A \times \mathbb{R}) = \mathbb{P}_{\zeta_{S(N)}}(A)$, for any $A \in \mathcal{B}(\mathbb{R}^N)$ and $N \in \mathbb{N}$. Then Kolmogorov extension theorem guarantees the existence of a probability measure $\mathbf{p}$ on $\mathbb{R}^\mathbb{N}$ satisfying $\mathbf{p}(A \times \mathbb{R}^\mathbb{N}) = \mathbb{P}_{\zeta_{S(N)}}(A)$, for any $A \in \mathcal{B}(\mathbb{R}^N)$. It can be observed that $\mathcal{T}$ forms an algebra of subsets of $\mathbb{F}(\mathcal{X})$. To see this, consider $x \in \mathcal{S}$, $A \in \mathcal{B}(\mathbb{R}^{|x|})$, $a \in \mathcal{S}$, and $B \in \mathcal{B}(\mathbb{R}^{|a|})$. Now, we have

$$\mathbb{F}(\mathcal{X}) = \mathcal{T}_{\mathrm{x}}(\mathbb{R}^{|\mathrm{x}|}) \in \mathcal{T} \tag{14}$$

$$(\mathcal{T}_{\mathrm{x}}(A))^{\complement} = \mathcal{T}_{\mathrm{x}}(\mathbb{R}^{|\mathrm{x}|} \setminus A) \in \mathcal{T} \tag{15}$$

$$\mathcal{T}_{\mathrm{x}}(A) \cap \mathcal{T}_{\mathrm{a}}(B) = \mathcal{T}_{\mathrm{x} \wedge \mathrm{a}}(A \times B) \in \mathcal{T}. \tag{16}$$

Thus, $\mathcal{T}$ is an algebra of subsets of $\mathbb{F}(\mathcal{X})$. Let $\tilde{\mathbf{p}} : \mathcal{T} \rightarrow [0,1]$ be a function defined as

$$\tilde{\mathbf{p}}(\mathcal{T}_{\mathrm{x}}(A)) := \mathbb{P}_{\zeta_{\mathrm{x}}}(A). \tag{17}$$

As $\zeta_{\mathrm{x}} \in \Theta$, (11) holds, and therefore (17) uniquely defines $\tilde{\mathbf{p}}$ over $\mathcal{T}$ without depending on the special representation of cylinder set $\mathcal{T}_{\mathrm{x}}(A)$. It follows from (17) that $\tilde{\mathbf{p}}$ is a σ−finite *pre-measure* (i.e. σ−additive) on algebra $\mathcal{T}$ of cylinder sets. Thus, according to *Carathéodory's extension theorem*, $\tilde{\mathbf{p}}$ can be extended in a unique way to a measure $\mathbf{p} : \sigma(\mathcal{T}) \rightarrow \mathbb{R}_{\geq 0}$ on the σ−algebra generated by $\mathcal{T}$. Hence, $(\mathbb{F}(\mathcal{X}), \sigma(\mathcal{T}), \mathbf{p})$ is measure space and a probabilistic measure $\mathbf{p}$, for a set $\mathcal{T}_{\mathrm{x}}(A) \in \mathcal{T}$, is defined as in (13). □

Result 2 (Expectations Over $\mathbb{F}(\mathcal{X})$). *For a given $\mathcal{B}(\mathbb{R}^{|\mathrm{x}|}) - \mathcal{B}(\mathbb{R})$ measurable mapping $g : \mathbb{R}^{|\mathrm{x}|} \rightarrow \mathbb{R}$, expectation of $(g \circ f)(\mathrm{x})$ over $f \in \mathbb{F}(\mathcal{X})$ w.r.t. probability measure $\mathbf{p}$ is given as*

$$\mathbb{E}_{\mathbf{p}}[(g \circ \cdot)(\mathrm{x})] = \langle g \rangle_{\zeta_{\mathrm{x}}}. \tag{18}$$

Proof. Given $\mathrm{x} \in \mathcal{S}$, define a projection from $\mathbb{F}(\mathcal{X})$ to $\mathbb{R}^{|\mathrm{x}|}$ as

$$\Pi_{\mathrm{x}}(f) := f(\mathrm{x}) \tag{19}$$

where $f \in \mathbb{F}(\mathcal{X})$. For any $A \in \mathcal{B}(\mathbb{R}^{|\mathrm{x}|})$,

$$\Pi_{\mathrm{x}}^{-1}(A) = \mathcal{T}_{\mathrm{x}}(A). \tag{20}$$

It follows from (13) and (20) that

$$\mathbb{P}_{\zeta_{\mathrm{x}}} = \mathbf{p} \circ \Pi_{\mathrm{x}}^{-1}. \tag{21}$$

For a $\mathcal{B}(\mathbb{R}^{|\mathrm{x}|}) - \mathcal{B}(\mathbb{R})$ measurable mapping $g : \mathbb{R}^{|\mathrm{x}|} \rightarrow \mathbb{R}$, the average value of $g(f(\mathrm{x}))$ over all real valued functions $f \in \mathbb{F}(\mathcal{X})$ can be calculated via taking expectation of $g(\Pi_{\mathrm{x}}(f))$ w.r.t. probabilistic measure $\mathbf{p}$. That is,

$$\mathbb{E}_{\mathbf{p}}[g(f(\mathrm{x}))] = \mathbb{E}_{\mathbf{p}}[g(\Pi_{\mathrm{x}}(f))] \tag{22}$$

$$= \int_{\mathbb{F}(\mathcal{X})} g \circ \Pi_{\mathrm{x}} \, d\mathbf{p} \tag{23}$$

$$= \int_{\mathbb{R}^{|\mathrm{x}|}} g \, d\mathbb{P}_{\zeta_{\mathrm{x}}} \tag{24}$$

$$= \langle g \rangle_{\zeta_{\mathrm{x}}}. \tag{25}$$

□

3.2   Student-t Membership-Mapping

Definition 1 (Student-t Membership-Mapping). *A Student-t membership-mapping, $\mathcal{F} \in \mathbb{F}(\mathcal{X})$, is a mapping with input space $\mathcal{X} = \mathbb{R}^n$ and a membership function $\zeta_x \in \Theta$ that is Student-t like:*

$$\zeta_x(y) = \left(1 + 1/(\nu - 2)(y - m_y)^T K_{xx}^{-1}(y - m_y)\right)^{-\frac{\nu + |x|}{2}} \tag{26}$$

where $x \in \mathcal{S}$, $y \in \mathbb{R}^{|x|}$, $\nu \in \mathbb{R}_+ \setminus [0, 2]$ is the degrees of freedom, $m_y \in \mathbb{R}^{|x|}$ is the mean vector, and $K_{xx} \in \mathbb{R}^{|x| \times |x|}$ is the covariance matrix with its $(i, j)-$th element given as

$$(K_{xx})_{i,j} = kr(x^i, x^j) \tag{27}$$

where $kr : \mathbb{R}^n \times \mathbb{R}^n \to \mathbb{R}$ is a positive definite kernel function defined as

$$kr(x^i, x^j) = \sigma^2 \exp\left(-0.5 \sum_{k=1}^{n} w_k \left| x_k^i - x_k^j \right|^2\right) \tag{28}$$

where x_k^i is the $k-$th element of x^i, σ^2 is the variance parameter, and $w = (w_1, \cdots, w_n)$ with $w_k \geq 0$.

Result 3. *Membership function as defined in (26) satisfies the consistency condition (11)*

Proof. It follows from (26) that

$$\int_{\mathbb{R}^{|x|}} \zeta_x(y) \, d\lambda^{|x|}(y) = \frac{\Gamma(\nu/2)}{\Gamma((\nu + |x|)/2)} (\text{pi})^{|x|/2}(\nu)^{|x|/2} \left(\frac{\nu - 2}{\nu}\right)^{1/2} |K_{xx}|^{1/2}, \tag{29}$$

$$\frac{\zeta_x(y)}{\int_{\mathbb{R}^{|x|}} \zeta_x(y) \, d\lambda^{|x|}(y)} = p_y(y; m_y, K_{xx}, \nu), \tag{30}$$

where $p_y(y; m_y, K_{xx}, \nu)$ is the density function of multivariate $t-$distribution with mean m_y, covariance K_{xx} (and scale matrix as equal to $((\nu - 2)/\nu)K_{xx})$, and degrees of freedom ν. Further, we have

$$\frac{\zeta_{x \wedge a}((y, u))}{\int_{\mathbb{R}^{|x|+|a|}} \zeta_{x \wedge a}((y, u)) \, d\lambda^{|x|+|a|}((y, u))} = p_{(y,u)}\left((y, u); (m_y, m_u), \begin{bmatrix} K_{xx} & K_{xa} \\ K_{ax} & K_{aa} \end{bmatrix}, \nu\right).$$

As the marginal distributions of multivariate $t-$distribution are also $t-$distributions [8] i.e.

$$\int_{\mathbb{R}^{|a|}} p_{(y,u)} \left((y,u); (m_y, m_u), \begin{bmatrix} K_{xx} & K_{xa} \\ K_{ax} & K_{aa} \end{bmatrix}, \nu \right) d\lambda^{|a|}(u) = p_y(y; m_y, K_{xx}, \nu),$$
(31)

we have

$$\frac{\int_{\mathbb{R}^{|a|}} \zeta_{x \wedge a}((y,u)) \, d\lambda^{|a|}(u)}{\int_{\mathbb{R}^{|x|+|a|}} \zeta_{x \wedge a}((y,u)) \, d\lambda^{|x|+|a|}((y,u))} = \frac{\zeta_x(y)}{\int_{\mathbb{R}^{|x|}} \zeta_x(y) \, d\lambda^{|x|}(y)}.$$
(32)

For any $A \in \mathcal{B}(\mathbb{R}^{|x|})$,

$$\frac{\int_{A \times \mathbb{R}^{|a|}} \zeta_{x \wedge a}((y,u)) \, d\lambda^{|x|+|a|}((y,u))}{\int_{\mathbb{R}^{|x|+|a|}} \zeta_{x \wedge a}((y,u)) \, d\lambda^{|x|+|a|}((y,u))} = \frac{\int_A \zeta_x(y) \, d\lambda^{|x|}(y)}{\int_{\mathbb{R}^{|x|}} \zeta_x(y) \, d\lambda^{|x|}(y)}.$$
(33)

Thus, (11) is satisfied.   □

3.3   Interpolation by Student-t Membership-Mapping

Let $\mathcal{F} \in \mathbb{F}(\mathbb{R}^n)$ be a zero-mean Student-t membership-mapping. Let $x = \{x^i \in \mathbb{R}^n \mid i \in \{1, \cdots, N\}\}$ be a given set of input points. The corresponding mapping outputs, represented by the vector $f := (\mathcal{F}(x^1), \cdots, \mathcal{F}(x^N))$, follow

$$\zeta_x(f) = \left(1 + (1/(\nu-2)) f^T K_{xx}^{-1} f\right)^{-\frac{\nu+N}{2}}.$$
(34)

Let $a = \{a^m \mid a^m \in \mathbb{R}^n, \, m \in \{1, \cdots, M\}\}$ be the set of auxiliary inducing points. The mapping outputs corresponding to auxiliary inducing inputs, represented by the vector $u := (\mathcal{F}(a^1), \cdots, \mathcal{F}(a^M))$, follow

$$\zeta_a(u) = \left(1 + (1/(\nu-2)) u^T K_{aa}^{-1} u\right)^{-\frac{\nu+M}{2}}$$
(35)

where $K_{aa} \in \mathbb{R}^{M \times M}$ is positive definite matrix with its $(i,j)-$th element given as

$$(K_{aa})_{i,j} = kr(a^i, a^j)$$
(36)

where $kr : \mathbb{R}^n \times \mathbb{R}^n \to \mathbb{R}$ is a positive definite kernel function defined as in (28). Similarly, the combined mapping outputs (f, u) follow

$$\zeta_{x \wedge a}((f,u)) = \left(1 + \frac{1}{\nu-2} \left(\begin{bmatrix} f \\ u \end{bmatrix} \right)^T \begin{bmatrix} K_{xx} & K_{xa} \\ K_{ax} & K_{aa} \end{bmatrix}^{-1} \begin{bmatrix} f \\ u \end{bmatrix} \right)^{-\frac{\nu+N+M}{2}}.$$
(37)

It can be verified using a standard result regarding the inverse of a partitioned symmetric matrix that

$$
\frac{\zeta_{x \wedge a}((f, u))}{|\zeta_a(u)|^{(\nu+N+M)/(\nu+M)}}
$$
$$
= \left(1 + \frac{(f - \bar{m}_f)^T \left(\frac{\nu + (u)^T (K_{aa})^{-1} u - 2}{\nu + M - 2} \bar{K}_{xx} \right)^{-1} (f - \bar{m}_f)}{\nu + M - 2} \right)^{-\frac{\nu+M+N}{2}}, \quad (38)
$$

$$
\bar{m}_f = K_{xa}(K_{aa})^{-1} u \tag{39}
$$
$$
\bar{K}_{xx} = K_{xx} - K_{xa}(K_{aa})^{-1} K_{xa}^T. \tag{40}
$$

The expression on the right hand side of equality (38) define a Student-t membership function with the mean $\bar{m}_f$. It is observed from (39) that $\bar{m}_f$ is an interpolation on the elements of u based on the closeness of points in x with that of a. Hence, f, based upon the interpolation on elements of u, could be represented by means of a membership function, $\mu_{f;u} : \mathbb{R}^N \to [0, 1]$, defined as r.h.s. of (38):

$$
\mu_{f;u}(\tilde{f}) := \left(1 + \frac{(\tilde{f} - \bar{m}_f)^T \left(\frac{\nu + (u)^T (K_{aa})^{-1} u - 2}{\nu + M - 2} \bar{K}_{xx} \right)^{-1} (\tilde{f} - \bar{m}_f)}{\nu + M - 2} \right)^{-\frac{\nu+M+N}{2}}. \quad (41)
$$

Here, the pair $(\mathbb{R}^N, \mu_{f;u})$ constitutes a fuzzy set and $\mu_{f;u}(\tilde{f})$ is interpreted as the degree to which $\tilde{f}$ matches an attribute induced by f for a given u.

3.4 Variational Learning of Membership-Mappings

Given a dataset $\{(x^i, y^i) \mid x^i \in \mathbb{R}^n, \ y^i \in \mathbb{R}^p, \ i \in \{1, \cdots, N\}\}$, it is assumed that there exist zero-mean Student-t membership-mappings $\mathcal{F}_1, \cdots, \mathcal{F}_p \in \mathbb{F}(\mathbb{R}^n)$ such that

$$
y^i \approx \left[\mathcal{F}_1(x^i) \cdots \mathcal{F}_p(x^i) \right]^T. \tag{42}
$$

Under modeling scenario (42), a variational learning solution can be derived via following an analytical approach as in [1,5,7]. Representing the variables associated to a membership-mapping model by means of membership functions, the mathematical expressions for membership functions are analytically derived using variational optimization such that the degree-of-belongingness of given data to the considered model is maximized. The analytical approach leads to the development of Algorithm 1 for learning. With reference to Algorithm 1,

- y_j, for $j \in \{1, 2, \cdots, p\}$, is defined as

$$y_j := \left[y_j^1 \cdots y_j^N \right]^T \in \mathbb{R}^N \tag{43}$$

where y_j^i denotes the j-th element of y^i.
- ξ is given as

$$\xi = N\sigma^2. \tag{44}$$

- $\Psi \in \mathbb{R}^{N \times M}$ is a matrix with its (i, m)-th element given as

$$\Psi_{i,m} = \frac{\sigma^2}{\prod_{k=1}^n \left(\sqrt{1 + w_k \sigma_x^2} \right)} \exp\left(-\frac{1}{2} \sum_{k=1}^n \frac{w_k |a_k^m - x_k^i|^2}{1 + w_k \sigma_x^2} \right) \tag{45}$$

where a_k^m and x_k^i denotes the k-th element of a^m and x^i respectively.
- $\Phi \in \mathbb{R}^{M \times M}$ is a matrix with its (m, m')-th element given as

$$\Phi_{m,m'} = \frac{\sigma^4}{\prod_{k=1}^n \left(\sqrt{1 + 2w_k \sigma_x^2} \right)} \sum_{i=1}^N \exp\left(-\frac{1}{4} \sum_{k=1}^n w_k (a_k^m - a_k^{m'})^2 \right.$$
$$\left. - \sum_{k=1}^n \frac{w_k |0.5(a_j^m + a_k^{m'}) - x_k^i|^2}{1 + 2w_k \sigma_x^2} \right). \tag{46}$$

- The quantities $(\hat{a}_\tau, \hat{b}_\tau, \hat{a}_z, \hat{b}_z, \hat{a}_r, \hat{b}_r, \hat{a}_s, \hat{b}_s)$ follow

$$\hat{a}_\tau = a_\tau + 0.5Np \tag{47}$$

$$\hat{b}_\tau(O) = b_\tau + \frac{\hat{a}_z}{2\hat{b}_z} O \tag{48}$$

$$\hat{a}_z = 1 + 0.5Np + \hat{a}_r / \hat{b}_r \tag{49}$$

$$\hat{b}_z(O) = \frac{\hat{a}_r}{\hat{b}_r} \frac{\hat{a}_s}{\hat{b}_s} + \frac{\hat{a}_\tau}{2\hat{b}_\tau} O \tag{50}$$

$$\hat{a}_r = a_r \tag{51}$$

$$\hat{b}_r = b_r + (\hat{a}_s / \hat{b}_s)(\hat{a}_z / \hat{b}_z) - \psi(\hat{a}_s) + \log\left(\hat{b}_s\right) - 1 - \psi(\hat{a}_z) + \log\left(\hat{b}_z\right) \tag{52}$$

$$\hat{a}_s = a_s + (\hat{a}_r / \hat{b}_r) \tag{53}$$

$$\hat{b}_s = b_s + (\hat{a}_r / \hat{b}_r)(\hat{a}_z / \hat{b}_z) \tag{54}$$

Algorithm 1. Variational learning of the membership-mappings

Require: Dataset $\{(x^i, y^i) \mid x^i \in \mathbb{R}^n, \, y^i \in \mathbb{R}^p, \, i \in \{1, \cdots, N\}\}$; number of auxiliary points $M \in \{1, 2, \cdots, N\}$; the degrees of freedom associated to the Student-t membership-mapping $\nu \in \mathbb{R}_+ \setminus [0, 2]$.

1: Choose free parameters as $\sigma^2 = 1$ and $\sigma_x^2 = 0.01$.
2: The auxiliary inducing points are suggested to be chosen as the cluster centroids:

$$\mathrm{a} = \{a^m\}_{m=1}^M = cluster\_centroid(\{x^i\}_{i=1}^N, M)$$

where $cluster\_centroid(\{x^i\}_{i=1}^N, M)$ represents the k-means clustering on $\{x^i\}_{i=1}^N$.

3: Define $w = (w_1, w_2, \cdots, w_n)$ such that w_k (for $k \in \{1, 2, \cdots, n\}$) is equal to the inverse of squared-distance between two most-distant points in the set: $\{x_k^1, x_k^2, \cdots, x_k^N\}$.

4: Compute K_{aa}, ξ, Ψ, and Φ using (36), (44), (45), and (46) respectively.
5: Choose $a_\tau = b_\tau = a_r = b_r = a_s = b_s = 1$.
6: Initialise $\hat{a}_\tau = \hat{b}_\tau = \hat{a}_z = \hat{b}_z = \hat{a}_r = \hat{b}_r = 1$.
7: Initialize $\hat{a}_s$ and $\hat{b}_s$ using (53) and (54).
8: **repeat**
9:    Update $\mathcal{E}(\hat{m}_{u_j}(y_j))$ as

$$\mathcal{E}(\hat{m}_{u_j}(y_j)) = K_{\mathrm{aa}} \left(\Phi + \frac{\xi - Tr((K_{\mathrm{aa}})^{-1}\Phi)}{\nu + M - 2} K_{\mathrm{aa}} + \frac{\hat{b}_\tau \hat{b}_z}{\hat{a}_\tau \hat{a}_z} K_{\mathrm{aa}} \right)^{-1} (\Psi)^T y_j. \quad (55)$$

10:    Update $\mathcal{E}(O)$ as

$$\begin{aligned}
\mathcal{E}(O) = \sum_{j=1}^p \Big(&\|y_j\|^2 - 2 \left(\mathcal{E}(\hat{m}_{u_j}(y_j))\right)^T (K_{\mathrm{aa}})^{-1} (\Psi)^T y_j \\
&+ \left(\mathcal{E}(\hat{m}_{u_j}(y_j))\right)^T (K_{\mathrm{aa}})^{-1} \Phi (K_{\mathrm{aa}})^{-1} \mathcal{E}(\hat{m}_{u_j}(y_j)) \\
&+ \left(\mathcal{E}(\hat{m}_{u_j}(y_j))\right)^T \frac{\xi - Tr((K_{\mathrm{aa}})^{-1}\Phi)}{\nu + M - 2} (K_{\mathrm{aa}})^{-1} \mathcal{E}(\hat{m}_{u_j}(y_j)) \Big). \quad (56)
\end{aligned}$$

11:    Update $\hat{a}_\tau, \hat{b}_\tau(\mathcal{E}(O)), \hat{a}_z, \hat{b}_z(\mathcal{E}(O)), \hat{a}_r, \hat{b}_r, \hat{a}_s, \hat{b}_s$ using (47), (48), (49), (50), (51), (52), (53), (54) respectively.
12:    Estimate β as

$$\beta = (\hat{a}_\tau / \hat{b}_\tau)(\hat{a}_z / \hat{b}_z). \quad (57)$$

13: **until** (β nearly converges)
14: Compute matrix B as

$$B = \left(\Phi + \frac{\xi - Tr((K_{\mathrm{aa}})^{-1}\Phi)}{\nu + M - 2} K_{\mathrm{aa}} + \frac{\hat{b}_\tau}{\hat{a}_\tau} \frac{\hat{b}_z}{\hat{a}_z} K_{\mathrm{aa}} \right)^{-1} (\Psi)^T. \quad (58)$$

Compute matrix $\alpha = \begin{bmatrix} \alpha_1 & \cdots & \alpha_p \end{bmatrix}$ with its j-th column defined as

$$\alpha_j := \left(\Phi + \frac{\xi - Tr((K_{\mathrm{aa}})^{-1}\Phi)}{\nu + M - 2} K_{\mathrm{aa}} + \frac{\hat{b}_\tau}{\hat{a}_\tau} \frac{\hat{b}_z}{\hat{a}_z} K_{\mathrm{aa}} \right)^{-1} (\Psi)^T y_j \quad (59)$$

15: **return** The parameters set $\mathbb{M} = \{\alpha, w, \mathrm{a}, \sigma^2, \sigma_x^2, B\}$.

3.5   Prediction by Membership-Mappings

Given the parameters set $\mathbb{M} = \{\alpha, w, \mathrm{a}, \sigma^2, \sigma_x^2, B\}$ returned by Algorithm 1, the learned membership-mappings could be used to predict output corresponding to any arbitrary input data point $x^* \in \mathbb{R}^n$ as

$$\hat{y}(x^*; \mathbb{M}) = \alpha^T (G(x^*; \mathbb{M}))^T. \tag{60}$$

Here, $G \in \mathbb{R}^{1 \times M}$ is a vector-valued function defined as

$$G(x; \mathbb{M}) := \begin{bmatrix} G_1(x; \mathbb{M}) \cdots G_M(x; \mathbb{M}) \end{bmatrix} \tag{61}$$

$$G_m(x; \mathbb{M}) := \frac{\sigma^2}{\prod_{k=1}^n \left(\sqrt{1 + w_k \sigma_x^2} \right)} \exp \left(-\frac{1}{2} \sum_{k=1}^n \frac{w_k |a_k^m - x_k|^2}{1 + w_k \sigma_x^2} \right), \tag{62}$$

where a_k^m and x_k are the k−th elements of x and a^m respectively.

4   Concluding Remarks

This paper has introduced the notion of membership-mapping using measure theoretic basis for representing data points through attribute values.

References

1. Kumar, M., Freudenthaler, B.: Fuzzy membership functional analysis for nonparametric deep models of image features. IEEE Trans. Fuzzy Syst. **28**(12), 3345–3359 (2020)
2. Kumar, M., Stoll, N., Stoll, R.: Variational Bayes for a mixed stochastic/deterministic fuzzy filter. IEEE Trans. Fuzzy Syst. **18**(4), 787–801 (2010)
3. Kumar, M., Stoll, N., Stoll, R.: Stationary fuzzy Fokker-Planck learning and stochastic fuzzy filtering. IEEE Trans. Fuzzy Syst. **19**(5), 873–889 (2011)
4. Kumar, M., Stoll, N., Stoll, R., Thurow, K.: A stochastic framework for robust fuzzy filtering and analysis of signals-part I. IEEE Tran. Cybern. **46**(5), 1118–1131 (2016)
5. Kumar, M., Zhang, W., Weippert, M., Freudenthaler, B.: An explainable fuzzy theoretic nonparametric deep model for stress assessment using heartbeat intervals analysis. IEEE Trans. Fuzzy Syst. (2020). https://doi.org/10.1109/TFUZZ.2020.3029284
6. Kumar, M., Mao, Y., Wang, Y., Qiu, T., Chenggen, Y., Zhang, W.: Fuzzy theoretic approach to signals and systems: static systems. Inf. Sci. **418**, 668–702 (2017)
7. Kumar, M., Singh, S., Freudenthaler, B.: Gaussian fuzzy theoretic analysis for variational learning of nested compositions. Int. J. Approx. Reasoning **131**, 1–29 (2021)
8. Nadarajah, S., Kotz, S.: Mathematical properties of the multivariate t distribution. Acta Applicandae Mathematica **89**(1), 53–84 (2005)
9. Zhang, W., Kumar, M., Zhou, Y., Yang, J., Mao, Y.: Analytically derived fuzzy membership functions. Cluster Comput. **22**(5), 11849–11876 (2017). https://doi.org/10.1007/s10586-017-1503-2

Membership-Mappings for Data Representation Learning: A Bregman Divergence Based Conditionally Deep Autoencoder

Mohit Kumar[1,2]([envelope]), Bernhard Moser[1], Lukas Fischer[1], and Bernhard Freudenthaler[1]

[1] Software Competence Center Hagenberg GmbH, 4232 Hagenberg, Austria
Mohit.Kumar@scch.at
[2] Institute of Automation, Faculty of Computer Science and Electrical Engineering, University of Rostock, Rostock, Germany

Abstract. This paper suggests to use membership-mapping as the building block of deep models. An alternative idea of deep autoencoder, referred to as *Bregman Divergence Based Conditionally Deep Autoencoder* (that consists of layers such that each layer learns data representation at certain abstraction level through a membership-mappings based autoencoder), is presented. A multi-class classifier is presented that employs a parallel composition of conditionally deep autoencoders to learn data representation for each class. Experiments are provided to demonstrate the competitive performance of the proposed framework in classifying high-dimensional feature vectors and in rendering robustness to the classification.

Keywords: Autoencoder · Bregman divergence · Variational learning

1 Introduction

An interest in applying fuzzy theory in deep learning arises not only from its interpretability potential but also from its capability of handling uncertainties in a rigorous mathematical manner. For a rigorous handling of uncertainties, stochastic fuzzy systems [3–6] have been introduced to integrate the concepts of randomness and fuzziness together. The current study is derived by the motivation of developing a framework (i.e. conceptualization, mathematical theory,

Supported by the Austrian Research Promotion Agency (FFG) Sub-Project PETAI (Privacy Secured Explainable and Transferable AI for Healthcare Systems); the Federal Ministry for Climate Action, Environment, Energy, Mobility, Innovation and Technology (BMK); the Federal Ministry for Digital and Economic Affairs (BMDW); and the Province of Upper Austria in the frame of the COMET - Competence Centers for Excellent Technologies Programme managed by Austrian Research Promotion Agency FFG.

ⓒ Springer Nature Switzerland AG 2021
G. Kotsis et al. (Eds.): DEXA 2021 Workshops, CCIS 1479, pp. 138–147, 2021.
https://doi.org/10.1007/978-3-030-87101-7_14

learning solution, and practical algorithms for applications) for fuzzy theoretic analytical deep models while addressing the issues related to optimal choice of model structure, small sized training data, and iterative time-consuming nature of numerical learning algorithms. Recent studies, reported in [2,7,11], have contributed to the development of a such framework via providing variational learning solutions based on the quantification of uncertainties on the variables and parameters associated to the deep model. Motivated by fuzzy theory to represent data points through attribute values, the notion of membership-mapping [8] has been introduced to provides a measure theoretic conceptualization of fuzzy theoretic analytical deep models. As the membership-mappings can be learned analytically using variational optimization, a motivation of designing deep models with the membership-mapping serving as deep model's building-block arises.

As a contribution to the fuzzy theoretic analytical deep models, this paper suggests a *Bregman divergence based conditionally deep autoencoder* for data representation learning. The classical deep autoencoder consists of two symmetrical networks of multiple layers such that first network represents the encoding and second network represents the decoding. However, the conditionally deep autoencoder considered in this study is composed of layers such that each layer learns data representation at certain abstraction level through a membership-mapping autoencoder. Also, a multi-class classifier is presented that employs a parallel composition of conditionally deep autoencoders to learn data representation for each class.

2   A Bregman Divergence Based Conditionally Deep Autoencoder

Definition 1 (Membership-Mapping Autoencoder).   *A membership-mapping autoencoder, $\mathcal{G} : \mathbb{R}^p \rightarrow \mathbb{R}^p$, maps an input vector $y \in \mathbb{R}^p$ to $\mathcal{G}(y) \in \mathbb{R}^p$ such that*

$$\mathcal{G}(y) \stackrel{\text{def}}{=} [\mathcal{F}_1(Py) \cdots \mathcal{F}_p(Py)]^T, \tag{1}$$

where $\mathcal{F}_j$ ($j \in \{1, 2, \cdots, p\}$) is a Student-t membership-mapping [8], $P \in \mathbb{R}^{n \times p}(n \leq p)$ is a matrix such that the product Py is a lower-dimensional encoding for y. That is, membership-mapping autoencoder first projects the input vector onto a lower dimensional subspace and then constructs the output vector through Student-t membership-mappings.

Definition 2 (Bregman divergence).   *The Bregman divergence $\mathcal{B}_F$, associated to a strictly convex twice differentiable function $F : \mathbb{R}^p \rightarrow \mathbb{R}$, is defined for any two vectors $y \in \mathbb{R}^p$ and $\hat{y} \in \mathbb{R}^p$ as*

$$\mathcal{B}_F(\hat{y}, y) := F(\hat{y}) - F(y) - (\hat{y} - y)^T \nabla F(y) \tag{2}$$

where ∇F denotes the gradient of F. Different choices of F leads to different forms of Bregman divergences. We are in-particularly interested in the following two forms:

Bregman divergence associated to squared Euclidean norm: *If we define* $F(y) = (1/2)\|y\|^2$, *then the corresponding Bregman divergence* $\mathcal{B}_{sE}(\hat{y}, y)$ *is defined as*

$$\mathcal{B}_{sE}(\hat{y}, y) := \frac{1}{2}\|\hat{y} - y\|^2. \tag{3}$$

Relative entropy: *For a vector* $y = [y_1 \cdots y_p]^T$ *(with* $y_j > 0$ *for all* $j \in \{1, \cdots, p\}$*), if we define* $F(y) = \sum_{j=1}^{p}(y_j \log(y_j) - y_j)$, *then the Bregman divergence* $\mathcal{B}_{re}(\hat{y}, y)$ *is the unnormalized relative entropy:*

$$\mathcal{B}_{re}(\hat{y}, y) := \sum_{j=1}^{p} \left(\hat{y}_j \log(\frac{\hat{y}_j}{y_j}) - \hat{y}_j + y_j \right). \tag{4}$$

We introduce a conditionally deep autoencoder such that the output of conditionally deep autoencoder is equal to the output of the layer re-constructing the given input vector as good as possible where re-construction error is measured in-terms of Bregman divergence. We consider the conditionally deep autoencoder based on two forms of Bregman divergence: squared Euclidean norm and relative entropy.

Definition 3 (Conditionally Deep Autoencoder (CDA)). *A conditionally deep autoencoder,* $\mathcal{D} : \mathbb{R}^p \to \mathbb{R}^p$, *maps a vector* $y \in \mathbb{R}^p$ *to* $\mathcal{D}(y) \in \mathbb{R}^p$ *through a nested composition of finite number of membership-mapping autoencoders such that*

$$\mathcal{D}(y) = \hat{y}^{l^*}, \tag{5}$$

$$\hat{y}^l = (\mathcal{G}_l \circ \cdots \circ \mathcal{G}_2 \circ \mathcal{G}_1)(y), \ \forall l \in \{1, 2, \cdots, L\}, \tag{6}$$

$$l^* = \begin{cases} \arg\min\limits_{l \in \{1,\cdots,L\}} \mathcal{B}_{sE}(\hat{y}^l, y), & choice\ 1 \\ \arg\min\limits_{l \in \{1,\cdots,L\}} \mathcal{B}_{re}\left([e^{\hat{y}_1^l} \cdots e^{\hat{y}_p^l}]^T, [e^{y_1} \cdots e^{y_p}]^T\right), & choice\ 2 \end{cases} \tag{7}$$

where $\mathcal{G}_l(\cdot)$ *is a membership-mapping autoencoder (Definition 1);* $\hat{y}^l$ *is the output of* $l-th$ *layer representing input vector* y *at certain abstraction level such that* $\hat{y}^1$ *is least abstract representation and* $\hat{y}^L$ *is most abstract representation of the input vector; and the autoencoder output* $\mathcal{D}(y)$ *is equal to the output of the layer re-constructing the given input vector as good as possible where re-construction error is measured in-terms of Bregman divergence. The Bregman divergence could be chosen either of squared Euclidean norm form or of relative entropy form. The structure of deep autoencoder is such that*

$$\hat{y}^l = \mathcal{G}_l(\hat{y}^{l-1}),$$

$$= \left[\mathcal{F}_1^l(P^l\hat{y}^{l-1}) \cdots \mathcal{F}_p^l(P^l\hat{y}^{l-1})\right]^T$$

where $\hat{y}^0 = y$, $P^l \in \mathbb{R}^{n_l \times p}$ *is a matrix with* $n_l \in \{1, \cdots, p\}$ *such that* $n_1 \geq n_2 \geq \cdots \geq n_L$, *and* $\mathcal{F}_j^l(\cdot)$ *is a Student-t membership-mapping.*

2.1   Variational Learning Algorithm

Given a set of N samples $\{y^1, \cdots, y^N\}$, the learning problem is of deriving an expression for the output of each layer of CDA under some optimality criterion. Since CDA consists of layers of membership-mappings, the algorithm for the variational learning of membership-mappings (as stated in [8]) could be directly applied for the variational learning of individual layers. Thus, Algorithm 1 is suggested for the variational learning of CDA.

Algorithm 1. Variational learning of conditionally deep autoencoder

---

Require: Data set $\mathbf{Y} = \{y^i \in \mathbb{R}^p \mid i \in \{1, \cdots, N\}\}$; the subspace dimension $n \in \{1, 2, \cdots, p\}$; number of auxiliary points $M \in \{1, 2, \cdots, N\}$; the number of layers $L \in \mathbb{Z}_+$.

1: Choose free parameters as $\nu^1 = 2.1, \nu^2 = \infty, \cdots, \nu^L = \infty$.
2: **for** $l = 1$ to L **do**
3:     Set subspace dimension associated to $l-$th layer as $n_l = \max(n - l + 1, 1)$.
4:     Define $P^l \in \mathbb{R}^{n_l \times p}$ such that $i-$th row of P^l is equal to transpose of eigenvector corresponding to $i-$th largest eigenvalue of sample covariance matrix of data set $\mathbf{Y}$.
5:     Define a latent variable $x^{l,i} \in \mathbb{R}^{n_l}$, for $i \in \{1, \cdots, N\}$, as

$$x^{l,i} = \begin{cases} P^l y^i & \text{if } l = 1, \\ P^l \hat{y}^{l-1}(x^{l-1,i}; \mathbb{M}^{l-1}) & \text{if } l > 1 \end{cases} \tag{8}$$

   where $\hat{y}^{l-1}$ is the estimated output of the $(l-1)-$th layer computed for the parameters set $\mathbb{M}^{l-1} = \{\alpha^{l-1}, w^{l-1}, a^{l-1}, \sigma^2, \sigma_x^2, B^{l-1}\}$.
6:     Compute parameters set $\mathbb{M}^l$ characterizing the membership-mappings associated to $l-$th layer by applying variational learning algorithm [8] on data set $\{(x^{l,i}, y^i) \mid i \in \{1, \cdots, N\}\}$ with number of auxiliary points M and degrees of freedom as ν^l.
7: **end for**
8: **return** The parameters set $\mathcal{M} = \{\{\mathbb{M}^1, \cdots, \mathbb{M}^L\}, \{P^1, \cdots, P^L\}\}$.

The salient features of Algorithm 1 are as follow:

- Following [2], the degree of freedom $\nu^l \in \mathbb{R}_+ \setminus [0, 2]$ for $l = 1$ (i.e. for the first layer) is sufficiently low for a robust filtering of high-dimensional data. As the uncertainties on input data have been filtered out by the first layer, ν^l for subsequent layers (i.e. for $l > 1$) is increased to ∞ so that the precision of disturbance model increases as high as possible.
- CDA discovers layers of increasingly abstract data representation as a result of letting $\{n_1, \cdots, n_L\}$ a monotonically decreasing sequence at step 3 of Algorithm 1. This will be illustrated in Fig. 1. As observed in Fig. 1, the first layer of CDA models the lowest level data-features while moving deep across the layer the higher level data-features are modeled.

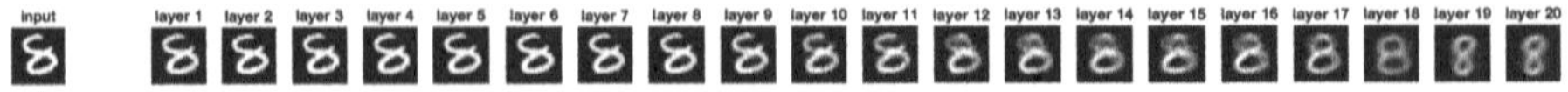

Fig. 1. A CDA was built using Algorithm 1 (taking $n = 20$; $M = 500$; $L = 20$) on a dataset consisting of 1000 randomly chosen samples of digit 8 from MNIST digits dataset. Corresponding to the input sample (shown at the extreme left of the figure), the estimated outputs of different layers of deep autoencoder are displayed. It is observed that CDA, as a result of letting $\{n_1, \cdots, n_L\}$ a monotonically decreasing sequence at step 3 of Algorithm 1, discover layers of increasingly abstract data representation with lowest-level data features being modeled by first layer and the highest-level by end layer.

Definition 4 (Filtering by CDA). *Given a CDA with its parameters being represented by a set $\mathcal{M} = \{\{M^1, \cdots, M^L\}, \{P^1, \cdots, P^L\}\}$, the autoencoder can be applied for filtering a given input vector $y \in \mathbb{R}^p$ as follows:*

$$x^l(y; \mathcal{M}) = \begin{cases} P^l y, & l = 1 \\ P^l \hat{y}^{l-1}(x^{l-1}; M^{l-1}) & l \geq 2 \end{cases} \tag{9}$$

Here, $\hat{y}^{l-1}$ is the output of the $(l-1)-th$ layer. Finally, CDA's output, $\mathcal{D}(y; \mathcal{M})$, is given as

$$\mathcal{D}(y; \mathcal{M}) = \hat{y}^{l^*}(x^{l^*}; M^{l^*}), \quad where \tag{10}$$

$$l^* = \begin{cases} \arg \min\limits_{l \in \{1, \cdots, L\}} \mathcal{B}_{sE}(\hat{y}^l(x^l, M^l), y), & choice\ 1 \\ \arg \min\limits_{l \in \{1, \cdots, L\}} \mathcal{B}_{re}\left([e^{\hat{y}_1^l(x^l, M^l)} \cdots e^{\hat{y}_p^l(x^l, M^l)}]^T, [e^{y_1} \cdots e^{y_p}]^T\right), & choice\ 2 \end{cases} \tag{11}$$

where $\hat{y}_j^l$ denotes the $j-th$ element of $\hat{y}^l$.

2.2 A Wide Conditionally Deep Autoencoder

For a big dataset i.e. N is large, Algorithm 1 may require a larger M. A higher value M would increase the computational time required by Algorithm 1 for learning. To circumvent the problem of large computation time for processing big data, it is suggested that data be partitioned into subsets and corresponding to each data-subset a separate CDA is learned. This motivates defining of a wide conditionally deep autoencoder as in Definition 5.

Definition 5 (A Wide CDA). *A wide CDA, $\mathcal{WD} : \mathbb{R}^p \to \mathbb{R}^p$, maps a vector $y \in \mathbb{R}^p$ to $\mathcal{WD}(y) \in \mathbb{R}^p$ through a parallel composition of S ($S \in \mathcal{Z}_+$) number of CDAs such that*

$$\mathcal{WD}(y; \mathcal{P} = \{\mathcal{M}^s\}_{s=1}^S) = \mathcal{D}(y; \mathcal{M}^{s^*}), \quad where \tag{12}$$

$$s^* = \begin{cases} \arg \min\limits_{s\in\{1,\cdots,S\}} \mathcal{B}_{sE}(\mathcal{D}(y;\mathcal{M}^s),y), & \text{choice 1} \\ \arg \min\limits_{s\in\{1,\cdots,S\}} \mathcal{B}_{re}\left(\exp[\mathcal{D}(y;\mathcal{M}^s)],\exp[y]\right), & \text{choice 2} \end{cases} \quad (13)$$

Here, $\mathcal{D}(y;\mathcal{M}^s)$ denotes the output of s−th CDA (that was characterized by parameters set $\mathcal{M}^s$) and $\exp[\cdot]$ denotes the element-wise exponential.

Algorithm 2 is suggested for the variational learning of wide CDA.

Algorithm 2. Variational learning of wide CDA

Require: Data set $\mathbf{Y} = \{y^i \in \mathbb{R}^p \mid i \in \{1,\cdots,N\}\}$; the subspace dimension $n \in \{1,2,\cdots,p\}$; ratio $M/N \in (0,1]$; the number of layers $L \in \mathbb{Z}_+$.

1: Apply k-means clustering to partition $\mathbf{Y}$ into S subsets, $\{\mathbf{Y}^1,\cdots,\mathbf{Y}^S\}$, where $S = \lceil N/1000 \rceil$.

2: **for** $s = 1$ to S **do**

3:    Build a CDA, $\mathcal{M}^s$, by applying Algorithm 1 on $\mathbf{Y}^s$ taking n as the subspace dimension; the number of auxiliary points as equal to $(M/N) \times \#\mathbf{Y}^s$ (where $\#\mathbf{Y}^s$ is the number of data points in $\mathbf{Y}^s$); and L as the number of layers.

4: **end for**

5: **return** the set of parameters sets: $\mathcal{P} = \{\mathcal{M}^s\}_{s=1}^S$.

---

3   Classification Applications

An application of deep autoencoder to classification follows via learning data representation for each class through a wide CDA. This motivates the defining of a classifier as in Definition 6.

Definition 6 (A Classifier). *A classifier, $\mathcal{C} : \mathbb{R}^p \rightarrow \{1,2,\cdots,C\}$, maps a vector $y \in \mathbb{R}^p$ to $\mathcal{C}(y) \in \{1,2,\cdots,C\}$ such that*

$$\mathcal{C}(y;\{\mathcal{P}_c\}_{c=1}^C) = \begin{cases} \arg \min\limits_{c\in\{1,\cdots,C\}} \mathcal{B}_{sE}(\mathcal{WD}(y;\mathcal{P}_c),y), & \text{choice 1} \\ \arg \min\limits_{c\in\{1,\cdots,C\}} \mathcal{B}_{re}\left(\exp[\mathcal{WD}(y;\mathcal{P}_c)],\exp[y]\right), & \text{choice 2} \end{cases}$$

$$(14)$$

where $\mathcal{WD}(y;\mathcal{P}_c)$, computed using (12), is the output of c−th wide CDA (that was characterized by parameters set $\mathcal{P}_c$) and $\exp[\cdot]$ denotes the element-wise exponential. The classifier assigns to an input vector the label of that class whose associated autoencoder best reconstructs the input vector where re-construction error is measured in-terms of Bregman divergence.

Finally, Algorithm 3 is provided for the learning of the classifier.

4   Experiments

4.1   Classification of High-Dimensional Image Features

The image category classification problem is considered using "Freiburg Groceries Dataset" [1] for comparing Algorithm 3 with classical machine learning algorithms. The dataset contains around 5000 labeled images of grocery products commonly sold in Germany and is freely available to download by the courtesy of authors of [1]. The images have been categorized into 25 different classes of grocery products. The dataset covers a wide range of real-world photographic conditions and represents a benchmark to evaluate machine learning algorithms.

Algorithm 3. Variational learning of the classifier

Require: Labeled data set $\mathbf{Y} = \left\{ \mathbf{Y}_c \mid \mathbf{Y}_c = \{ y^{i,c} \in \mathbb{R}^p \mid i \in \{1, \cdots, N_c\} \}, \ c \in \{1, \cdots, C\} \right\}$; the subspace dimension $n \in \{1, \cdots, p\}$; ratio $M/N \in (0,1]$; the number of layers $L \in \mathbb{Z}_+$.
1: **for** $c = 1$ to C **do**
2:     Build a wide CDA, $\mathcal{P}_c = \{\mathcal{M}_c^s\}_{s=1}^{S_c}$, by applying Algorithm 2 on $\mathbf{Y}_c$ for given n, M/N, and L.
3: **end for**
4: **return** the set of parameters sets $\{\mathcal{P}_c\}_{c=1}^C$.

A feature vector was created by extracting image features from "AlexNet" and "VGG-16" networks (which are pre-trained Convolutional Neural Networks). Both AlexNet and VGG-16 provide a rich feature representations for a wide range of images. The activations of the fully connected layer "fc6" in AlexNet constitute a $4096-$dimensional feature vector. Similarly, the activations of the fully connected layer "fc6" in VGG-16 constitute another $4096-$dimensional feature vector. The features extracted by both networks were joined together to form a $8192-$dimensional vector. The authors of [1] provide five different training-testing splits of images to evaluate the classification performance.

For each of the five training-testing data splits, Algorithm 3 was run on training images and the classification performance is evaluated on test images. Algorithm 3 was applied on the feature vectors (which were normalized to have zero-mean and unity-variance along each dimension) taking the subspace dimension $n = 20$, ratio $M/N = 0.5$, and the number of layers $L = 5$. To make a comparison of the proposed methodology (i.e. Algorithm 3) with the classical machine learning algorithms, following methods were considered:

- k-nearest neighbor with $k = 1$, $k = 2$, and $k = 4$ implemented using MATLAB function "*fitcknn*".
- Naive Bayes implemented using MATLAB function "*fitcnb*".
- Decision tree implemented using MATLAB function "*fitctree*".
- SVM implemented using MATLAB function "*fitcecoc*".
- Ensemble learning implemented using MATLAB function "*fitcensemble.*
- Random forest of 100 classification trees implemented using MATLAB function "*TreeBagger*".

Table 1. Results of experiments on Freiburg groceries dataset

Methods	Classification accuracy in %					
	Data 1	Data 2	Data 3	Data 4	Data 5	Average
Algorithm 3 (relative entropy)	87.82	87.06	85.88	85.63	86.19	**86.52**
Algorithm 3 (squared Euclidean norm)	87.92	87.16	85.16	85.73	85.99	86.39
SVM	77.90	79.54	77.17	76.98	76.98	77.71
1-NN	78.00	77.97	77.38	76.58	76.28	77.24
Back-propagation training of deep network	75.25	77.24	72.67	73.37	71.57	74.02
2-NN	73.48	73.38	70.11	70.05	70.57	71.52
4-NN	72.50	73.39	68.89	71.16	70.87	71.36
Random Forest	63.17	62.63	59.47	59.50	59.76	60.90
Naive Bayes	56.78	56.78	53.74	55.08	56.26	55.73
Ensemble Learning	38.31	39.35	38.89	37.69	38.34	38.51
Decision Tree	31.34	30.59	32.14	31.06	30.73	31.17

– The 8192−dimensional feature vector, formed by joining the outputs of fully connected layer "fc6" of AlexNet and VGG-16, can serve as input to another multi-layered feed-forward network to form a deep network. The so formed deep network with a soft max transfer function in the output layer can be used for classification. A network, processing the feature vector with a hidden layer consisting of 100 neurons followed by an output layer with 25 (= number of classes) neurons, is trained using scaled conjugate gradient back-propagation with cross-entropy as the performance function. It was experimentally observed that a single hidden layer with 100 neuron is sufficient and increasing the number of hidden layers in the network doesn't lead to any considerable improvement in the performance.

The performance of different classification algorithms on Freiburg groceries dataset is listed in Table 1. The discriminant analysis classifiers were not considered here as the image feature dimension is higher than the number of training samples. It is observed from Table 1 that Algorithm 3 performed best amongst all considered machine learning methods in each of the five training-testing data splits.

4.2   Robustness in Classification

The robust performance of Algorithm 3 is verified by considering a handwritten digits recognition problem with the widely used MNIST dataset. The dataset contains 28×28 sized images divided into training set of 60000 images and testing set of 10000 images. The images' pixel values were divided by 255 to normalize the values in the range from 0 to 1. The 28×28 normalized values of each image are flattened to an equivalent $784-$dimensional image-representing-vector. Algorithm 3 was applied on training data taking the subspace dimension $n = 20$, ratio $M/N = 0.5$, and the number of layers $L = 5$.

To study the robustness, the test images are contaminated by zero-mean Gaussian additive noise with varying level of standard deviation. The widely used Convolutional Neural Network (CNN) is taken as a reference for comparing the performance of Algorithm 3. A CNN with the patch size of 5×5, first convolutional layer of 32 features, second convolutional layer of 64 features, and densely connected layer of 1024 neurons is considered. The convolutions use a stride of one and are zero padded so that the output is the same size as the input. The pooling is max pooling over 2×2 blocks. The CNN was implemented using TensorFlow^{TM} which is an open-source software library for numerical computations and machine intelligence. The CNN was trained for 10000 iterations where each iteration uses 100 randomly chosen images from the training set.

Table 2. The performance in classifying noisy images of MNIST digits

Noise standard deviation	Classification accuracy on test images		
	Algorithm 3 (relative entropy)	Algorithm 3 (squared Euclidean norm)	**CNN**
0	0.9864	0.9866	**0.9897**
0.2	0.9814	**0.9826**	0.9608
0.4	0.9701	**0.9729**	0.8198
0.6	0.9233	**0.9274**	0.6227
0.8	0.8475	**0.8483**	0.4482

Table 2 clearly demonstrates the robustness of Algorithm 3 against noise in the test images. At zero noise level, both Algorithm 3 and CNN had nearly the same performance, however, with an increasing level of noise the decrease in classification accuracy is observed to be much slower in the case of Algorithm 3 than CNN. As the noise level increases, the improvement in the performance of Algorithm 3 than CNN becomes more and more significant.

5 Concluding Remarks

The capability of the conditionally deep autoencoder in effectively learning data representation can be used for classification applications. Experiments were provided to demonstrate the competitive performance of the proposed framework in classifying high-dimensional feature vectors and in rendering robustness to the classification. Bregman divergence based conditionally deep autoencoders could further facilitate explainable deep learning (following [7]) and privacy-preserving distributed deep learning (following [9, 10]).

References

1. Jund, P., Abdo, N., Eitel, A., Burgard, W.: The freiburg groceries dataset. CoRR abs/1611.05799 (2016). http://arxiv.org/abs/1611.05799

2. Kumar, M., Freudenthaler, B.: Fuzzy membership functional analysis for nonparametric deep models of image features. IEEE Trans. Fuzzy Syst. $28(12)$, 3345–3359 (2020)

3. Kumar, M., Insan, A., Stoll, N., Thurow, K., Stoll, R.: Stochastic fuzzy modeling for ear imaging based child identification. IEEE Trans. Syst. Man Cybern. Syst. $46(9)$, 1265–1278 (2016)

4. Kumar, M., et al.: Stress monitoring based on stochastic fuzzy analysis of heartbeat intervals. IEEE Trans. Fuzzy Syst. $20(4)$, 746–759 (2012)

5. Kumar, M., Stoll, N., Stoll, R.: Variational bayes for a mixed stochastic/deterministic fuzzy filter. IEEE Trans. Fuzzy Syst. $18(4)$, 787–801 (2010)

6. Kumar, M., Stoll, N., Stoll, R.: Stationary fuzzy Fokker-Planck learning and stochastic fuzzy filtering. IEEE Trans. Fuzzy Syst. $19(5)$, 873–889 (2011)

7. Kumar, M., Zhang, W., Weippert, M., Freudenthaler, B.: An explainable fuzzy theoretic nonparametric deep model for stress assessment using heartbeat intervals analysis. IEEE Trans. Fuzzy Syst. (2020). https://doi.org/10.1109/TFUZZ.2020.3029284

8. Kumar, M., Moser, B., Fischer, L., Freudenthaler, B.: Membership-mappings for data representation learning: measure theoretic conceptualization. In: Database and Expert Systems Applications (DEXA 2021). Springer, Cham (2021, in press)

9. Kumar, M., Rossbory, M., Moser, B.A., Freudenthaler, B.: Differentially private learning of distributed deep models. In: Adjunct Publication of the 28th ACM Conference on User Modeling, Adaptation and Personalization, UMAP 2020 Adjunct, pp. 193–200. Association for Computing Machinery, New York (2020)

10. Kumar, M., Rossbory, M., Moser, B.A., Freudenthaler, B.: An optimal $(\epsilon, \delta)-$differentially private learning of distributed deep fuzzy models. Inf. Sci. 546, 87–120 (2021)

11. Kumar, M., Singh, S., Freudenthaler, B.: Gaussian fuzzy theoretic analysis for variational learning of nested compositions. Int. J. Approximate Reasoning 131, 1–29 (2021)

Data Catalogs: A Systematic Literature Review and Guidelines to Implementation

Lisa Ehrlinger[1,2(✉)] ⓘ, Johannes Schrott[2], Martin Melichar[2],
Nicolas Kirchmayr[3], and Wolfram Wöß[2]

[1] Software Competence Center Hagenberg GmbH, Hagenberg, Austria
lisa.ehrlinger@scch.at
[2] Johannes Kepler University Linz, Linz, Austria
{lisa.ehrlinger,johannes.schrott,wolfram.woess}@jku.at
[3] KTM Innovation GmbH, Wels, Austria
nicolas.kirchmayr@ktm.com

Abstract. In enterprises, data is usually distributed across multiple data sources and stored in heterogeneous formats. The harmonization and integration of data is a prerequisite to leverage it for AI initiatives. Recently, data catalogs pose a promising solution to semantically classify and organize data sources across different environments and to enrich raw data with metadata. Data catalogs therefore allow to create a single, clear, and easy-accessible interface for training and testing computational models. Despite a lively discussion among practitioners, there is little research on data catalogs. In this paper, we systematically review existing literature and answer the following questions: (1) What are the conceptual components of a data catalog? and (2) Which guidelines can be recommended to implement a data catalog? The results benefit practitioners in implementing a data catalog to accelerate any AI initiative and researchers with a compilation of future research directions.

Keywords: Data catalog · Data integration · AI system engineering

1 Introduction

One of the key challenges of artificial intelligence (AI) system engineering is the integration and harmonization of data to enable high-quality analytics [5]. This paper investigates the extent to which data catalogs can address this challenge. The popularity of data catalogs is continuously increasing since 2016 and they are deemed to be "the new black in data management and analytics" [21] according to Gartner [21]. In 2020, Quimbert et al. [12] define data catalogs as tools to centrally "collect, create, and maintain metadata", allowing for easier findability and accessibility. Consequently, they do not only bear the potential to (virtually) integrate heterogeneous data sources, but also to semantically enrich data

The research in this paper has been funded by BMK, BMDW, and the Province of Upper Austria in the frame of the COMET Programme managed by FFG.

G. Kotsis et al. (Eds.): DEXA 2021 Workshops, CCIS 1479, pp. 148–158, 2021.
https://doi.org/10.1007/978-3-030-87101-7_15

with contextual information (i.e., metadata). Metadata is essential to support explainability in AI systems [5].

Case Study. The R&D department of motorbike manufacturer KTM, where heterogeneous data (e.g., sensor data from training runs with research prototype bikes) is stored in different formats and granularities. To enable deep insights into bike research and development with AI, KTM aims to deploy a data catalog to deliver high-quality data as basis for data science processes.

State of the Art. In recent years, several commercial data catalog tools have been developed, for example, Alation data catalog, Informatica enterprise data catalog, and Oracle cloud infrastructure data catalog [2,21]. However, despite a vital discussion among practitioners and several commercial tools, there is little research on data catalogs and to the best of our knowledge no other systematic literature review. In 2020, Labadie et al. [9] express the need for further research on data catalogs, specifically with respect to its implementation.

Contribution. In this paper, we contribute with a systematic literature review (SLR) on data catalogs to identify (1) necessary and optional conceptual components and (2) guidelines to implement a data catalog. The results offer a consolidated view on what constitutes a data catalog (with respect to its components) and consequently facilitate more research on the topic. For practitioners, this papers provides best practices on how to implement a data catalog.

Structure. This paper follows the classic IMRAD structure with Sect. 1 being the Introduction, Sect. 2 describing the research Method, Sect. 3 the Results of our study, and Sect. 4 concludes with a Discussion and future work.

2   Research Method

Our systematic literature review is based on Kitchenham [8]. First, we identified the need for a review on the topic of "data catalog", followed by the development of a review protocol including research questions and search criteria.

2.1   Research Questions

The two major aims of this survey are to identify the necessary and optional components of which a data catalog consists and to identify guidelines on how to implement a data catalog. According to these objectives, we formulated the following two research questions:

(RQ1) What are the conceptual components of a data catalog?
(RQ2) Which guidelines can be recommended to implement a data catalog?

2.2   Search Strategy

For the literature review, we queried the most common digital libraries as outlined in Table 1. Since literature on the topic of "data catalog" is rare, we added the term "data cataloging" to our search expression, which describes the process of creating a data catalog [15]. We also included the British and American English spelling for each term. Consequently, the following search expression

("data catalog" ∨ "data catalogue" ∨ "data cataloguing" ∨ "data cataloging")

has been applied to the scope of title and abstract, whenever setting the scope was possible. We filtered all papers published before 2000 since according to Gartner [21], data catalogs gained their popularity in 2016 and it continuously increased since then. The exact search expression applied to each of the digital library is shown in Table 1. For Google Scholar, the restriction "-VizieR"[1] was added, since a lot of results about the VizieR data catalog were delivered, which were of no relevance, e.g., information about astronomical data.

Table 1. Overview on digital libraries with exact search expressions

Source	Search expression	Scope	Additional restrictions
ACM Digital Library[a]	acmdlTitle: (+("data catalog" "data catalogue" "data cataloguing" "data cataloging")) OR recordAbstract: (+("data catalog" "data catalogue" "data cataloguing" "data cataloging")	Title, abstract	–
Google Scholar[b]	allintitle: "data catalog" OR "data catalogue" OR "data cataloguing" OR "data cataloging"	Title	-VizieR
IEEE Xplore[c]	"data catalog" OR "data catalogue" OR "data cataloguing" OR "data cataloging"	All metadata	–
ResearchGate[d]	"data catalog" OR "data catalogue" OR "data cataloguing" OR "data cataloging"	–	–
Science Direct[e]	"data catalog" OR "data catalogue" OR "data cataloguing" OR "data cataloging"	Title, abstract, keyword	–
Springer Link[f]	"data catalog" OR "data catalogue" OR "data cataloguing" OR "data cataloging"	Full text	Discipline computer science + availability filter

[a] https://dl.acm.org
[b] https://scholar.google.com
[c] https://ieeexplore.ieee.org/Xplore/home.jsp
[d] https://www.researchgate.net/search/publication
[e] https://www.sciencedirect.com
[f] https://link.springer.com

---

[1] VizieR is an online data catalog for astronomical data: http://vizier.u-strasbg.fr.

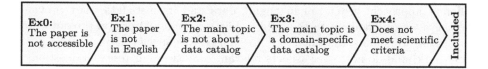

Fig. 1. Overview and order of exclusion criteria

Table 2. Number of found, excluded, and included publications

Source	No. of papers	Exclusion criteria					Included	
		Ex0	Ex1	Ex2	Ex3	Ex4	All	Uniques
ACM Digital Library	241	1	0	228	10	0	2	
Google Scholar	218	14	14	163	20	0	7	
IEEE Xplore	78	4	0	62	7	0	5	
ResearchGate	100	73	3	14	3	4	3	
Science Direct	54	4	0	46	4	0	0	
Springer Link	468	0[a]	0	464	3	0	1	
Total	1,159	96	17	977	47	4	18	**11**

[a]As seen in Table 1, not accessible results have been filtered when querying Springer.

2.3 Paper Selection Process

To select papers that are suitable to answer our research questions, we reduced the total number of identified papers with five predefined exclusion criteria (Ex), which were checked sequentially as shown in Fig. 1. All result records that were not removed by any of the exclusion criteria were included in the search result.

3 Results from the Literature Review

Across all libraries, 1,159 publications (including duplicates) were found on Feb. 16, 2021 using the search terms from Table 1. Table 2 shows the number of papers excluded and those that were selected to answer our research questions.

Our research questions can be answered based on the content of the eleven papers that remain in the SLR. In addition to the two research questions, Sect. 3.1 provides an overview on the domains in which data catalogs are currently used, compiled from all papers filtered by Ex3.

3.1 Overview on Data Catalog Implementations in Practice

From the 47 papers filtered by Ex3, 27 discuss data catalogs that provide open data of various domains. Most papers deal with government data, scientific research data, or geospatial data, but also educational or biological/medical data can be found. Although these systems are called "data catalog", they follow a different approach: instead of managing data and its metadata, they provide data of a specific domain to the public. The remaining 20 papers present data catalogs as we understand them, but are limited to a specific application (e.g., a wind park) and do not cover aspects relevant to answer our research questions.

3.2   Components of a Data Catalog

None of the investigated papers clearly lists the conceptual parts of a data catalog. Thus, in accordance to Aristotle's "the whole is greater than the sum of its parts", we identified the following components as most relevant by investigating all of the eleven papers: (1) metadata management, (2) business context, (3) data responsibility roles, and (4) the FAIR principles. We describe these components and their appearance in the single papers in the following paragraphs.

Metadata Management. Data catalogs "collect, create and maintain metadata" [12], which is why, metadata management is the quintessence of a data catalog. Metadata is "data that defines or describes other data" [6], e.g., data quality constraints, usage statistics, or access control [15]. Metadata can be created manually or automatically (e.g., information about data lineage) [15]. While Quimbert et al. [12] classify metadata into three general categories (as originally proposed by Riley [14]), Seshadri and Shanmugam [15] distinguish between eight types of metadata, which can be mapped to the categories as shown in Table 3.

Table 3. Classification of metadata by Quimbert et al. and Seshadri and Shanmugam

Metadata catagories by Quimbert et al. [12]	Data context variables and data attributes by Seshadri and Shanmugam [15]
Descriptive metadata like title, description, or information about the authors support a user in finding and classifying resources	Despite data quality ratings, a *data quality* attribute can contain subcategories like data formats or data ranges as an example The reliability of a dataset is represented by *reliability* attributes
Administrative metadata (also termed "technical information") like file format, text encoding as well as information about access rights and data provenance	*Data lineage* represents the dataflow through the entire organization or company *Technical context* variables provide technical details of a given data set *Data sensitivity and accessibility* attributes mark sensitive data as such and also provides access restrictions
Structural metadata describes how files or parts of resources relate to each other	*Data system relationships* context variables hold information about the data origin *Data linkage and relationships* context variables describe relationships among the data *Business context* variables represent relationships between data and business domains

To enable the linkage of data across different (heterogeneous) data sources, a metadata schema (also: metadata standard or data documentation) is required [1,16], which is defined by "a *set of elements* connected by some *structure*" [13]. For interoperability, also metadata standards from external institutions can be used to enhance a corporate-built metadata schema [12]. In this respect, also data provenance plays a crucial role since it contains information about the source of the data and all transformations it went through [17].

Early approaches to cataloging metadata are often based on XML, e.g., the work by Jensen et al. [7] from 2006, which implements a domain-specific schema based on XML. Since traditional data models are often too less expressive to model the complexity of metdata for a specific domain, ontologies (as the most expressive data model [4]) are recommended by different papers for the implementation of the metadata schema (cf. [2,12]). There exist several public ontologies, which address specific aspects of the data catalog metadata, e.g., the DCPAC (Data Catalog Provenance, and Access Control) ontology for data lineage and accessibility, which utilizes several other ontologies including DCAT (Data Catalog Vocabulary)[2] and PROV-O (PROV Ontology)[3], both being W3C recommendations [2]. Other ontologies commonly used for data catalogs are ISO9115, DataCite, Dublin Core Metadata Initiative, CERIF, and schema.org.

Business Context. As indicated by [9] and [18], the actual target group of a data catalog are typically business users and not just data or IT specialists. To achieve better workflows and data usage, one of the main foci of building a data catalog lies in the business context of the data. There are two different suggestions how to achieve the implementation of business context: it is either possible to enrich the metadata (cf. Table 3 classification by [15]) with additional business context attributes (cf. [15]), or to choose the more general path by establishing a company-wide *business glossary* [9]. A business glossary can be defined as "a central repository that contains key business terms whose names and definitions have been agreed upon by cross-functional subject matter experts" [20].

Data Responsibility Roles. There is a wide agreement that data is only as useful as its quality or reliability [15,22]. One of the main reasons for poor data quality is the lack of responsibility employees feel they have for a specific data set (i.e., unclear role assignment between IT and domain experts) [22]. Barbosa and Sena [1] go one step further and state that the success of a data catalog depends on the people maintaining it. Thus, one crucial aspect for the implementation of a data catalog is the assignment of responsible persons to the data [9]. Despite the traditional data expert roles (e.g., data architects), which are responsible for modeling the data, new less specialized roles that use the data to reach company goals are assigned in the context of data catalogs [9]. Labadie et al. [9] identify the *data steward* as most important data catalog role for companies. For Kurth et al. [11], establishing responsibility rules, particularly data stewardship, is one of the main tools for successful metadata maintenance and governance.

---

[2] https://www.w3.org/TR/vocab-dcat (Apr. 2021).
[3] https://www.w3.org/TR/prov-o (Apr. 2021).

FAIR Principles. The FAIR Principles[4] have been proposed in 2016 by Wilkinson et al. [19] and gained recent popularity in the enterprise context through the term "data democratization" [9]. The acronym FAIR stands for Findability, Accessibility, Interopability, and Re-use. Each term represents a category of guiding principles, where each principle defines specific characteristics of the data to fulfill FAIR [19]. The principles are designed to be "concise, domain-independent, high-level" [19] considerations for the publishing of data.

As described in [19], the connection between metadata, data management, and the FAIR principles is tight: each of the principles provides guidelines for desired characteristics of data, metadata, or both of them. Therefore, the quality of data as well as metadata directly affects the fulfillment of the FAIR principles.

The market analysis of data catalogs by Labadie et al. [9] identifies nine different function groups of data catalogs, which implement specific aspects of FAIR. For example, the "data search and tagging" group relate to the "findable" principle, whereas the data "analytics and workflows" group make use of the "accessible" and "reusable" [9]. Due to brevity, we refer to [9] for details on the function groups and the extent to which they address the FAIR principles.

3.3 Guidelines to Implement a Data Catalog

From the small number of scientific papers on data catalogs in general, we identified only three papers that were dedicated to implementation suggestions (this lack was already outlined in [9]). Wang [18] point out that the *definition of a metadata schema* is the first necessary step towards implementing a data catalog. A company should decide whether (partly) reusing an existing public metadata schema is possible, and only develop a completely new schema if none is available [18]. Seshadri and Shanmugam [15] recommend the following 8-step solution for implementing a data catalog, where step 1–5 effectively refer to the definition of a metadata schema:

1. Initially, a company/organization *defines data context variables*, which contain data-system relationships, business context, technical context, data lineage as well as linkage information.
2. The second step covers the *definition of data attributes*, which represent the quality, sensitivity, accessibility, and reliability of data.
3. Third, the authors suggest the *tagging of data*, where it is decided which metadata (i.e., data attributes and context variables) is attached to data at a particular level, e.g., column-level, entity-level, or data-set-level.
4. Next, *rules should be defined*, which regulate the data access or audits. For more flexibility, external business rule engines could be used and the rules can also be applied on multiple hierarchy-levels in analogy to the metadata.
5. After the previous steps have been accomplished, the *final data catalog schema* can be assembled into one enterprise data model, i.e., ontology.
6. Eventually, the data *catalog can be populated* with data.

---

[4] https://www.go-fair.org/fair-principles (Apr. 2021).

7. After the catalog is populated, it can be *exposed to the users*.
8. The final and ideally ongoing step is to take all the *feedback, revisions, and reviews* to improve the data catalog.

On a more general level, Labadie et al. [9] distinguish between two different approaches for the creation of a metadata schema: the *top-down approach*, where the structure is defined first, and the data imported in a second step, and the *bottom-up approach*, in which the schema is developed according to the analysis of imported data [9]. In terms of practical implementation, Labadie et al. [9] again distinguish between two contrasting approaches: the *data supply-driven approach* (also input-oriented approach), in which the requirements of the users who will provide and maintain data in the data catalog are prioritized, and the *data demand approach*, where the focus is on the output of the data catalog and prioritizes the requirements of end users who consume data from the data catalog. Three case studies in [9] show the connection between the two modeling approaches (top-down and bottom-up) and the two implementation approaches (data supply-driven and data demand). The top-down approach is typically conducted by users who maintain the data catalog, and therefore combined with the data supply-driven implementation approach, whereas the bottom-up modeling approach first considers the available data as it is used and therefore combined naturally with the data demand approach. It is pointed out that a combination of both sides and an agile iterative approach is also possible [9].

Lee and Sohn [10] propose a semi-automated method to create the metadata schema: the tag-based dynamic data catalog (DaDDCat). With DaDDCat, users are requested to annotate web resources (e.g., web pages, images, videos) with tags (i.e., a set of words) that are then used to automatically built an ontology.

One of the main challenges in the implementation of a data catalog is metadata interoperability across an entire organization. Kurth et al. [11] recommend the following two measures to address this challenge: (1) establish an enterprise-wide consensus on metadata mapping decisions, which prevents duplicate work by different teams, and (2) establish data stewardship to govern the data.

4   Discussion and Outlook

In this paper, we performed a SLR to (1) identify the main conceptual components of a data catalog and to (2) provide guidelines for its implementation.

(RQ1) Main Components. We answer (RQ1) by compiling the main conceptual components for a data catalog, which are: (1) effective metadata management, (2) the incorporation of business context either to the metadata or as separate business glossary, (3) the assignment of dedicated data responsibility roles, and (4) the adherence to the FAIR principles. We conclude that the major distinction of data catalogs to traditional data management or integration projects is on the one hand the commitment to use ontologies for describing the metadata, and on the other hand, the dedicated incorporation of business users with newly defined roles, such as the data steward.

(RQ2) Data Catalog Implementation. Sect. 3 indicates that the definition of a metadata schema (or ontology) is the key challenge in implementing a data catalog. In addition to fitting organizational needs, the metadata schema should fulfill the FAIR principles and adhere to common standards. Interestingly, none of the existing implementation suggestions incorporates the assignment of data responsibility roles. Due to the inherent importance of this conceptual component, we promote the following high-level process to implement a data catalog:

1. Assignment of data responsibility roles to stakeholders that contribute to the definition of the metadata schema or ontology.
2. Definition of a metadata schema (cf. steps 1–5 by [15]).
3. Population of data catalog schema with data (cf. step 6 by [15]).
4. Assignment of data responsibility roles to technical and business users for updates and continuous maintenance of the metadata.
5. Continuous improvement according to revisions and reviews (cf. step 8 by [15]).

We claim that it is necessary to divide the role assignment: in step (1), responsibility roles are assigned for the metadata schema modeling phase, and in step (4), responsibility roles are assigned for the daily use and maintenance of the metadata. Although these role assignments may overlap, they are often disjoint in practice, e.g., IT people are more involved in the data modeling phase, whereas business users without a global view on the data might maintain specific parts of the data on a daily basis.

Open Issues for Practitioners. According to Dibowski et al. [2], main data catalog vendors do not support the usage of existing public ontologies, but restrict the use to proprietary metadata schemas. In order to enhance interopability and adhere to the FAIR principles, existing data catalogs should allow the incorporation of standardized public ontologies, such as DCAT or schema.org.

Open Issues for Researchers. In our SLR, we identified the following three topics for future research: (1) automated data catalog creation, (2) data stewardship in data catalog literature, and (3) data quality in data catalogs.

We did not find any attempt to automatically create the metadata schema of a data catalog, which would be specifically interesting with for bottom-up approaches. Most use cases with bottom-up approaches are restricted to the manual analysis of existing data sources [9] and do not address automated schema extraction, as, e.g., suggested in [3]. Barbosa and Sena [1] even state that this step cannot be automated. Considering the high human effort of schema modeling (cf. [9]), we claim that a scientific evaluation of this statement is needed.

As already pointed out in the discussion of (RQ2), current data catalog implementation approaches do not address the topic of data stewardship sufficiently. Considering the importance of the topic for organizational needs as shown in [9], the lack of data stewardship in data catalog literature indicates a gap between real-world business needs and research, which should be closed in future work.

Seshadri and Shanmugam [15] highlight the importance of data quality for data catalog projects. Metadata can be used to determine the quality of data in aggregated metrics. In our ongoing research, we plan to integrate the concept of automated data quality monitoring [3] with tools like DQ-MeeRKat[5] into an existing data catalog implementation at KTM Innovations GmbH.

References

1. Barbosa, E.B.d.M., Sena, G.d.: Scientific data dissemination a data catalogue to assist research organizations. Ciência da Informação **37**, 19–25 (04 2008)
2. Dibowski, H., et al.: Using semantic technologies to manage a data lake: data catalog, provenance and access control, p. 17 (2020)
3. Ehrlinger, L., Wöß, W.: Automated data quality monitoring. In: Talburt, J.R. (ed.) Proceedings of the 22nd MIT International Conference on Information Quality (ICIQ 2017), Little Rock, AR, USA, pp. 15.1–15.9 (2017)
4. Feilmayr, C., Wöß, W.: An analysis of ontologies and their success factors for application to business. Data Knowl. Eng. **101**, 1–23 (2016)
5. Fischer, L., et al.: AI system engineering-key challenges and lessons learned. Mach. Learn. Knowl. Extr. **3**(1), 56–83 (2021)
6. Data Quality - Part 8: Information and Data Quality Concepts and Measuring. Standard, International Organization for Standardization, Switzerland (2015)
7. Jensen, S., et al.: A hybrid XML-relational grid metadata catalog. In: International Conference on Parallel Processing Workshops (ICPPW 2006), pp. 8–24 (2006)
8. Kitchenham, B.: Procedures for performing systematic reviews, p. 33 (2004)
9. Labadie, C., et al.: Fair enough? Enhancing the usage of enterprise data with data catalogs. In: 2020 IEEE 22nd Conference on Business Informatics (CBI), vol. 1, pp. 201–210, June 2020
10. Lee, H.J., Sohn, M.: Construction of tag-based dynamic data catalog (TaDDCaT) using ontology. In: 2012 15th International Conference on Network-Based Information Systems, pp. 697–702 (2012). https://doi.org/10.1109/NBiS.2012.116
11. Martin Kurth, David Ruddy, N.R.: Repurposing MARC metadata: using digital project experience to develop a metadata management design. Library Hi Tech **22**(2), 153–165 (2004). https://doi.org/10.1108/07378830410524585
12. Quimbert, E., Jeffery, K., Martens, C., Martin, P., Zhao, Z.: Data cataloguing. In: Zhao, Z., Hellström, M. (eds.) Towards Interoperable Research Infrastructures for Environmental and Earth Sciences. LNCS, vol. 12003, pp. 140–161. Springer, Cham (2020). https://doi.org/10.1007/978-3-030-52829-4_8
13. Rahm, E., Bernstein, P.A.: A survey of approaches to automatic schema matching. VLDB J. **10**(4), 334–350 (2001)
14. Riley, J.: Understanding metadata: what is metadata, and what is it for? National Information Standards Organization (NISO) (2017). https://groups.niso.org/apps/group_public/download.php/17446/Understanding%20Met%E2%80%A6
15. Shanmugam, S., Seshadri, G.: Aspects of data cataloguing for enterprise data platforms. In: IEEE 2nd International Conference on Big Data Security on Cloud (BigDataSecurity), IEEE International Conference on High Performance and Smart Computing (HPSC), and IEEE International Conference on Intelligent Data and Security (IDS), pp. 134–139 (2016)

---

[5] https://github.com/lisehr/dq-meerkat.

16. Skopal, T., et al.: Improving findability of open data beyond data catalogs. In: Proceedings of the 21st International Conference on Information Integration and Web-based Applications & Services, pp. 413–417. ACM (2019)

17. Vicknair, C.: Research issues in data provenance. In: Proceedings of the 48th Annual Southeast Regional Conference. ACM SE 2010, Association for Computing Machinery, New York (2010). https://doi.org/10.1145/1900008.1900037

18. Wang, X.: An analysis of the benefits and issues in the development of an enterprise data catalogue. Master's thesis, School of Information Management, Victoria Business School, Victoria University of Wellington (2014)

19. Wilkinson, M.D., et al.: The FAIR guiding principles for scientific data management and stewardship. Sci. Data **3**(1), 160018 (2016)

20. Winningham, S.: Knowledge nugget: business glossary vs. data dictionaries (2019). https://web.stanford.edu/dept/pres-provost/cgi-bin/dg/wordpress/knowledge-nugget-business-glossary-vs-data-dictionaries

21. Zaidi, E., et al.: Data catalogs are the new black in data management and analytics (2017). https://www.gartner.com/en/documents/3837968/data-catalogs-are-the-new-black-in-data-management-and-a

22. Zhu, H., et al.: Data and information quality research: its evolution and future. In: Computing Handbook: Information Systems and Information Technology, pp. 16.1–16.20. Chapman and Hall/CRC, London (2014)

Task-Specific Automation in Deep Learning Processes

Georg Buchgeher[1], Gerald Czech[1(✉)], Adriano Souza Ribeiro[2], Werner Kloihofer[2], Paolo Meloni[3], Paola Busia[3], Gianfranco Deriu[3], Maura Pintor[3,4], Battista Biggio[3,4], Cristina Chesta[5], Luca Rinelli[5], David Solans[6], and Manuel Portela[6]

[1] Software Competence Center Hagenberg, Softwarepark 32a, 4232 Hagenberg, Austria
{georg.buchgeher,gerald.czech}@scch.at
[2] PKE Holding AG, Computerstr. 6, 1100 Wien, Austria
{a.ribeiro,w.kloihofer}@pke.at
[3] University of Cagliari, Via Università, 40, 09124 Cagliari, CA, Italy
{paolo.meloni,paola.busia,gianfranco.deriu,maura.pintor,
battista.biggio}@unica.it
[4] Pluribus One S.R.L., Via Vincenzo Bellini, 9, 09128 Cagliari, CA, Italy
{maura.pintor,battista.biggio}@pluribus-one.it
[5] Concept Reply, Via Cardinal Massaia 83, 10147 Torino, TO, Italy
{c.chesta,l.rinelli}@reply.it
[6] University Pompeu Fabra, Carrer de Tànger, 122-140, 08012 Barcelona, Spain
{david.solans,manuel.portela}@upf.edu

Abstract. Recent advances in deep learning facilitate the training, testing, and deployment of models through so-called pipelines. Those pipelines are typically orchestrated with general-purpose machine learning frameworks (e.g., Tensorflow Extended), where developers manually call the single steps for each task-specific application. The diversity of task- and technology-specific requirements in deep learning projects increases the orchestration effort. There are recent advances to automate the orchestration with machine learning, which are however, still immature and do not support task-specific applications. Hence, we claim that partial automation of pipeline orchestration with respect to specific tasks and technologies decreases the overall development effort. We verify this claim with the ALOHA tool flow, where task-specific glue code is automated. The gains of the ALOHA tool flow pipeline are evaluated with respect to human effort, computing performance, and security.

Keywords: Deep learning · Software engineering · Process · Pipeline

1 Introduction

Deep learning (DL) has become an important player in software business, far surpassing the traditional rule-based approaches in fields such as computer vision [1] or autonomous driving [2].

© Springer Nature Switzerland AG 2021
G. Kotsis et al. (Eds.): DEXA 2021 Workshops, CCIS 1479, pp. 159–169, 2021.
https://doi.org/10.1007/978-3-030-87101-7_16

The increasing integration of DL and other machine learning (ML) capabilities into software and services throughout the information technology sector has forced organizations to evolve their development processes [4]. This leads to a growing number of newly defined processes in research [4, 6] and practice [3, 7, 8]. These processes differ largely in respect to the range and detail of phases and targeted technologies.

Another engineering challenge compared to traditional software engineering (SE) are new project roles. Data engineers and data scientists extend existing software development teams and increase communication effort to align different views on engineering projects and processes. This increases the communication effort between manual process steps. As processes are typically iterative, the need for automation similar to continuous integration/delivery (see [3]) and for adequate tooling rises.

This paper is organized as follows: The remainder of the Introduction discusses related work on the need of automated tool support, focusing on ML pipelines. Section 2 gives an overview of the ALOHA tool flow (https://www.aloha-h2020.eu/) as one example for automation of tool support for a DL process. Section 3 evaluates the gains of the ALOHA tool flow. Section 4 concludes this work.

1.1 Related Work

Due to the novelty and rapid change in the field of ML there is a still a huge lack of well-functioning tools (e.g. see [13]). The authors of [13] identified 12 challenges in the categories development, production and organization in seven deep-learning projects. With respect to the automation of tool support in the ALOHA tool flow, we want to stress the challenges 'Glue Code and Supporting Systems', and 'Privacy and Safety'. The prominent paper of Scully et al. [16] state that ML-Systems contain 5% ML-code and 95% glue code and identify data preparation as source for complex pipeline jungles.

1.2 Machine Learning Pipelines

To overcome time consuming and error prone data related tasks the ML community tries to automate process steps, for example management of data quality [11], retraining on data change, labeling, and experimentation [10]. That is where ML pipelines come into focus. To the best of our knowledge, we could not find a unique definition for a ML pipeline. For our needs we make a distinction between a ML process, which we define as a sequence of process steps, and a ML pipeline, which we define as the executable automation of the sequence. Note, that although the pipeline is automatically executable the process itself is defined manually, e.g. by a data scientist.

First steps towards automating ML pipelines were hardcoded implementations of manually designed processes. State-of-the-art orchestrators (e.g. https://www.tensorflo w.org, and https://mlflow.org/) enable engineers to define the execution sequence of process steps in a user interface. Once defined, the pipeline can be executed automatically. Such orchestrations are for any kind of pipeline steps.

1.3 Automatic ML

Automatic machine learning (Auto ML) automates pipeline creation, by applying ML to replace the manual work of the data scientist. Auto ML aims to "learn how to learn"

[15]. For example in [15]. Drorie et al. use a single-player game to discover a model for pipeline synthesis. The aim is to learn the intuition of a data scientist executing process steps to get a valid pipeline for a given ML task on a specific dataset.

1.4 Task Specific Pipelines

Auto ML still has to go a far way until it can be applied from end to end for industrial solutions. ML pipeline orchestrators are of great help but task and technology specific projects still demand the implementation of much glue code and even more often the duplication of slightly different glue code for each slightly different experiment.

We believe that between general-purpose orchestration of pipelines and Auto ML is much room for task and technology specific automation of certain parts of the ML process. We argue that task and technology specific ML pipelines are a promising and for industry projects feasible way to enhance automation. In addition to general purpose ML pipelines, task specific pipelines automate use case specific glue code generation by utilizing automatic ML and SE techniques (e.g. code generation).

2 ALOHA Tool Flow

The ALOHA tool flow is one example for a task and technology specific automation. Figure 1 gives an overview which parts of the ML process are automated by the ALOHA tool flow. We choose the probably most known ML process [4] to enable the reader to match the ALOHA tool flow's steps to generalized process phases.

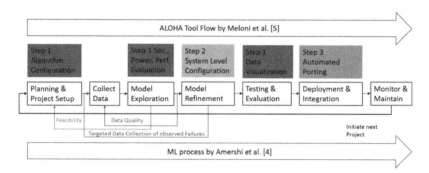

Fig. 1. The ALOHA tool flow [5] (colored boxes) compared to the ML process defined in [4]

Meloni et al. [5] describe the ALOHA tool flow as follows: "It essentially automates three different steps: algorithm selection, application partitioning and mapping, and deployment on target hardware."

The overall goal is to automatically find a neural network architecture specific to a certain deep learning task (dataset) and a certain hardware platform by meeting user specified constraints (i.e. security, performance, power). The ALOHA tool flow reaches this goal in three steps (see Fig. 2).

Step 1: the Design Space Exploration (DSE) engine applies a genetic algorithm with an initial population of different network configurations, trains these networks to achieve applicable accuracy and further adjusts the configurations according to computational workload, security, performance, memory, IO bandwidth, and power consumption of the inference task on the specified hardware. This leads to a new set of different network configurations used as input for the next iteration of the algorithm. The process repeats until it meets all constraints or a certain threshold. For training and evaluation, the DSE utilizes different tools.

Step 2: the System-level DSE engine follows the same design of a genetic algorithm and usage of different tools for evaluations. Here the task is to find the best partitioning of the algorithm configuration found in step 1 into sub-tasks. Then it finds the optimal mapping scheme for these sub-tasks on the target hardware platform taking further user constraints (i.e. throughput, latency and power) into account. Further, tools in this step

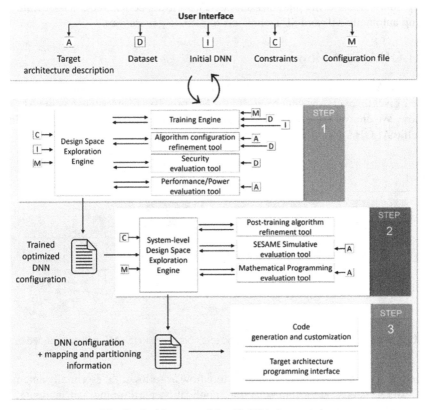

Fig. 2. Architecture of the ALOHA framework

adapt the deep neural network (DNN) algorithm graph and reduce the computational workload to optimize usage of hardware resources.

Step 3: ports the network configuration to the target hardware architecture. Partitioning and mapping information from step 2 is translated to computing and communication primitives of the hardware. This generated platform-specific code is optimized to minimize power consumption and improve performance.

3   Evaluation and Results

To evaluate the benefits of the ALOHA tool flow three different use cases of the ALOHA project were observed. These are a Surveillance Use Case, a Smart Industry (Audio) Use Case, and a Medical Application Use Case. Although they are different in nature, they all benefit from the ALOHA tool flow.

3.1   Surveillance Use Case

The goal of the Surveillance Use Case is to recognize objects from video frames and subsequently identify malicious behaviors or actions (e.g. access to a restricted areas in critical infrastructure). Any surveillance system has to deal with the tradeoff between having a sensible system, capable of detecting all security relevant events but with false alarms and a system without false alarms that is not able to detect all relevant events. To use smart cameras with Deep Learning capabilities the ALOHA tool flow is used to generate optimized solutions regarding accuracy, security and power consumption.

3.2   Smart Industry Use Case

The Smart Industry Use Case uses DL for voice control of collaborative robots and machinery in an industrial environment, without relying on a cloud backend. Challenges for speech recognition in industry are noisy environments, impaired speech, and users demanding high accuracy because they do several things in parallel. To avoid concerns about response latency, data security, access control, user privacy and legal risk the voice control is required to run at the edge and not in the cloud.

Google Speech Commands are used for training. These commands are one-second.wav files containing single spoken English words like 'up', 'down', 'yes', 'no', etc. There are several implementations, including different keywords and so a different number of classes. To improve the performance of the models in a real scenario, where noise and other people talking are present, two specific classes are introduced to identify respectively silence/noise and unknown words, which are all the other words in the dataset that are not used in another class.

3.3   Medical Use Case

The Medical Use Case uses DL for automatic medical diagnosis of Brain computer tomography (CT) scans. One application is an intra-cranial (IC) hemorrhage detection tool. The results are automatically annotated images which can be utilized as a 'second read' by the physicians as stroke decision support, to identify areas of suspected bleeds.

Similar to the surveillance use case medical image diagnosis deals with a tradeoff. In the medical use case, it is between having a sensible system, capable of diagnosing all acute care disease, and the specificity for every medical problem, to correctly mitigate false positive errors (i.e., wrong diagnoses of pathologies in healthy patients). The ALOHA tool flow targets the requirements of energy efficiency, system security and robustness. Energy efficiency is needed in energy-starved field operations in military environment and mobile stroke units in developing countries. Concerning security and robustness, high regulatory standards in the medical device industry demand reduction of classification errors, dealing with inputs that can be anomalously corrupted by worst-case noise, and to avoid comprising medical imaging artifacts.

3.4   Evaluation Method

The impact of the ALOHA tool flow on the three use cases will be studied in a qualitative and a quantitative way. The ALOHA project is still ongoing and final evaluation will be reported at the end of the project by means of Key Performance Indicators (KPIs). Those KPIs where defined to assess the tool flow in different aspects, as for instance energy efficiency, accuracy, security and especially productivity gains. Table 1 shows examples of three KPIs for the Smart Industry use case.

Table 1. Example KPI definitions

	KPI1_1 - Time spent in algorithm design	KPI1_4 - Time spent for security evaluation	KPI1_6 – Performance/power evaluation accuracy
Without adoption of ALOHA	Not available - limited experience in DL development – Estimated time for a new speech-processing project: months	No framework available. Required integration with existing open-source/commercial support tools to create adversarial/perturbed audio samples. Need of a pervasive evaluation in the transformed space of the spectrogram Estimated time: weeks	Considers only number of operations or memory footprint as a method for estimating performance and power consumption
With ALOHA	Custom tuned topology - Estimated time for a new design: days	Automatic creation of adversarial/perturbed examples. Reproducible tests and reporting Possibility of performing slow/fast evaluations Estimated time: minutes/hours	Relies on detailed architecture model to estimate performance and power consumption Expected less than 20% inaccuracy

3.5 Preliminary Results

After setting up a pipeline project using the ALOHA Graphical User Interface [12], the tool flow will automatically run all needed tools to complete the pipeline. This includes for instance training of different design points, security evaluation and evaluation of the performance expected on the target hardware platform. Below we show a few examples of the execution of some of those tasks.

Algorithm Selection and Improvement
First, we analyze an application of the Smart Industry use case where CNN based Key Word Spotting (KWS) is used to control a robot driven by a SensorTile board (see https://www.aloha-h2020.eu/use-cases/speech-recognition).

To try to assess the time required to traverse the different steps of the process, we performed a simple exploration considering 24 models undergoing training, pruning and quantization steps. The whole exploration required approximately 40 h, on Azure cluster exploiting NVIDIA Tesla GPU and six virtual CPUs. Training and quantization time were optimized through parallel execution on four threads. The chart below shows the time required for each task and the number of epochs.

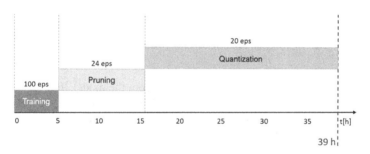

Fig. 3. Training and quantization time

Clearly, if we consider more complex networks, such as YOLO and UNET, additional effort is needed in minimizing the runtime. In the ALOHA project, several solutions are evaluated such as dataset sampling, approaches complying with the One-Fits-All methodology described in [9] and selective application of pruning and quantization.

The execution of the complete tool flow on a KWS example used for the Kaggle competition (https://www.kaggle.com/c/tensorflow-speech-recognition-challenge), shows how the KPI1_1 is met, as well as similar productivity KPIs for step 2 and 3 (see Table 2). The timeline for the competition was 60 days and the best model had an accuracy of 91.6% while with ALOHA we obtained a model with accuracy of 87.7% in only about 10 days.

Security Evaluation
In this example related to the Surveillance use case, we show that a small perturbation applied to the input image can allow the depicted person to stay undetected. The added perturbation is obtained with the use of adversarial techniques that aim to find small

Table 2. Productivity on a KWS example

ALOHA step	Tasks	Target effort	Effort with ALOHA
Step 1 Algorithm Configuration	Plan experiments; Model exploration Tune & debug	Days	9 days
Step 2 System Level Configuration	Model Refinement	Hours	5 h
Step 3 Automated porting	Deployment and integration	Hours	2 h

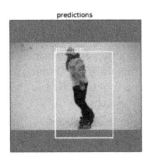

Fig. 4. Adversarial perturbation for video surveillance use case.

perturbations in order to produce a specific output from the model. This perturbation is computed by targeting and reducing the "objectness" score of the bounding box estimated by the given network model (TinyYOLO). This value corresponds to the probability that the box contains an object from the classes detectable by the model. The perturbed image (right side of Fig. 4. Adversarial perturbation for video surveillance use case.) is not visually different from the source image, but the person remains undetected in the perturbed image.

This highlights another important aspect related to design time: the contribution to the overall effort dedicated to the evaluation and improvement of the security of neural networks to adversarial attacks. Within ALOHA, we aim to automatize and systematize the evaluation of the impact of such attacks on deep neural networks under a consistent, unifying framework.

In Fig. 5, we show how the accuracy of a model decreases under adversarial (worst-case) input perturbations (solid lines) and under random perturbations (dashed lines) and how model security can be improved via a properly designed robust training procedure, at the expense of a small decrease of the classification accuracy on the unperturbed data.

The Algorithm Selection and Security Evaluation experiments above strongly suggest the capability of the integrated tool flow to provide optimized deployed designs in a matter of days, as expected according to KPIs outlined in Table 1.

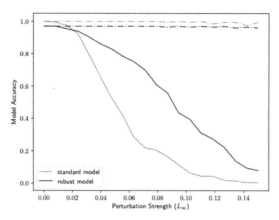

Fig. 5. Accuracy for different perturbation examples with security evaluation improvements

ALOHA Performance Modeling on NEURAghe

Within the project, to the aim of reducing workload and enabling performance optimization through design space exploration, accurately modeling the architecture to pre-estimate parameters is extremely important. We have defined and developed an architecture modeling methodology that details much more characteristics of the target architecture with respect to other approaches used at the state-of-the-art.

We have measured the execution time of 840 different CNN layers on NEURAghe [12], one of the project reference architectures. We have compared the on-hardware measurements with pre-estimates obtained using the ALOHA detailed methodology and a classic widely used roofline model. The plots below represent the error obtained using the two methods.

As may be noticed in Fig. 6, while the roofline model provides just a rough estimation, giving a general idea of the execution time order of magnitude, our estimation is much more precise, with average error around 7%.

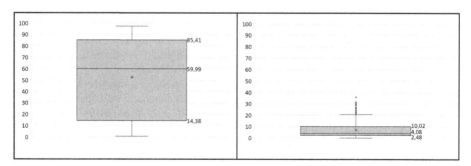

Fig. 6. Pre-estimation error with roofline model (left) vs. using ALOHA methodology (right)

This experiment also strongly suggests that the results will be aligned with the expectations reported in Table 1.

4 Conclusion

In this paper, we looked on the challenges of AI system development from a SE point of view. These challenges lead to new ML processes automated in general purpose ML pipelines. These pipelines still lack the ability to support the huge diversity of task and technology specific requirements of ML solutions. Automatic ML ('learn how to learn') aiming at full end-to-end pipeline synthesis is promising but still not mature enough for large scale application in industry projects. We argued task and technology specific automation taking advantage from both approaches are the next steps towards better ML pipelines.

As an example we presented the ALOHA tool flow automating the steps of algorithm selection, application partitioning and mapping and deployment on target hardware. We presented the evaluation method, based on real world industry relevant use cases. Although the ALOHA project is still ongoing, examples based on already implemented components strongly suggest the capability of the ALOHA tool flow to provide designs optimized for specific hardware platforms in a matter of days, compared to common industry practices that can take weeks to complete similar tasks.

Acknowledgement. This project has received funding from the European Union's Horizon 2020 Research and Innovation program under grant agreement No. 780788.

We want to thank the ALOHA Team Members for their contribution of their results and comments. Further, we want to thank Lisa Ehrlinger from SCCH for her critical eye to enforce scientific correctness and understandability.

References

1. Krizhevsky, A., Sutskever, I., Hinton, G.E.: ImageNet classification with deep convolutional neural networks. In: Advances in Neural Information Processing Systems, pp. 1097–1105 (2012)
2. Huang, Y., Chen, Y.: Autonomous driving with deep learning: a survey of state-of-art technologies CoRR, abs/2006.06091(2020)
3. https://martinfowler.com/articles/cd4ml.html. Accessed 16 Apr 2021
4. Amershi, S., et al. (eds.): Software engineering for machine learning: a case study. In: Proceedings of the 41st International Conference on Software Engineering, Montreal, QC, Canada, May 25–31 2019, pp. 291–300. IEEE/ACM (2019)
5. Meloni, P., et al. (eds.): Optimization and deployment of CNNs at the edge: the ALOHA experience. In: Proceedings of the 16th ACM International Conference on Computing Frontiers (CF 2019), Alghero, Italy, April 30—May 2 2019, pp. 326–332. ACM (2019)
6. John, M.M., Olsson, H.H., Bosch, J.: Developing ML/DL models : a design framework. In: International Conference on Software and Systems Process, Seoul, Republic of Korea (2020)
7. https://www.jeremyjordan.me/ml-projects-guide, Accessed 16 Apr 2021
8. https://towardsdatascience.com/the-7-steps-of-machine-learning-2877d7e5548e. Accessed 16 Apr 2021
9. Cai, H., Gan, C., Han, S.: Once for all: train one network and specialize it for efficient deployment. ArXiv, abs/1908.09791 (2020)
10. Bosch, J., Crnkovic, I., Olsson, H.: Engineering AI systems: a research Agenda (2020)

11. Ehrlinger, L., Wöß, W.: Automated Data Quality Monitoring. In: Proceedings of the 22nd MIT International Conference on Information Quality. Little Rock, AR (2017)

12. Meloni, P., et al.: NEURAghe: exploiting CPU-FPGA synergies for efficient and flexible CNN inference acceleration on Zynq SoCs. ACM Trans. Reconfigurable Tech. Syst. **11**(18), 1–18:24 (2018)

13. Arpteg, A., Brinne, B., Crnkovic-Friis, L., Bosch, J.: Software engineering challenges of deep learning. In: Proceedings of the 44th Euromicro Conference on Software Engineering and Advanced Applications, IEEE. abs/1810.12034 (2018)

14. https://www.aloha-h2020.eu/images/Deliverables/D12.pdf. Accessed 23 Apr 2021

15. Drori, I., et al.: Machine learning pipeline synthesis. In: Proceedings of AutoML Workshop at ICML (2018)

16. Sculley, D., et al. (eds.): Hidden technical debt in machine learning systems. In: Advances in Neural Information Processing Systems 28: Annual Conference on Neural Information Processing Systems, Montreal, Quebec, Canada (2015)

Time Ordered Data

Approximate Fault Tolerance for Edge Stream Processing

Daiki Takao[✉], Kento Sugiura, and Yoshiharu Ishikawa

Graduate School of Informatics, Nagoya University, Aichi, Japan
takao@db.is.i.nagoya-u.ac.jp, {sugiura,ishikawa}@i.nagoya-u.ac.jp

Abstract. Existing distributed stream processing systems generally guarantee fault tolerance by switching to standby machines and reprocessing lost data. In edge computing environments, however, we have to duplicate each edge for this conventional approach. This duplication cost increases sharply with expansion in the system scale. To solve this problem, we propose an approach to support *approximate fault tolerance* without edge duplication. We focus on environmental monitoring applications and utilize the correlation between sensors. In this paper, we assume that each edge estimates missing data from the observed data and aggregates them approximately. We provide a method to estimate the outputs of failed edges taking care of the uncertainty of the processing results at each edge. Our method allows the server to continue processing without waiting for the recovery of failed edges. We also show that the validity of our method by experiments using synthetic data.

Keywords: Data stream processing · Edge computing · Fault tolerance

1 Introduction

Fault tolerance is an essential requirement for distributed data stream processing systems. Existing systems, such as Flink [2], process dynamically generated data in real-time by pipeline processing. Each task distributed to multiple servers receives inputs from the previous one and sends the processing results to the next one. This processing model enables efficient data processing, but a failure in one task affects the entire system. Since many applications, such as environmental monitoring, require high availability and low latency, processing systems need a mechanism to continue processing even if each server fails.

Existing systems generally guarantee fault tolerance by switching to standby nodes and reprocessing lost data [2,3,6,12]. When the manager detects a worker failure, a newly launched worker takes over the processing of the failed one.

This paper is based on results obtained from a project, JPNP16007, commissioned by the New Energy and Industrial Technology Development Organization (NEDO). Also, This work was partly supported by KAKENHI (16H01722 and 20K19804).

© Springer Nature Switzerland AG 2021
G. Kotsis et al. (Eds.): DEXA 2021 Workshops, CCIS 1479, pp. 173–183, 2021.
https://doi.org/10.1007/978-3-030-87101-7_17

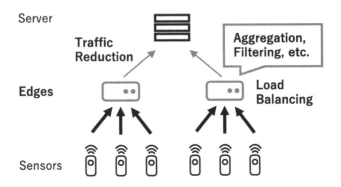

Fig. 1. Overview of the edge computing

Besides, some systems can recover from the failure without error by reprocessing only the lost data. This approach is suitable for cluster environments where the system can manage all resources centrally and assign the input data management task to the message queue.

In edge computing environments, however, we need a different approach to guarantee fault tolerance. Edge computing is a new processing model for traffic reduction and load balancing [15]. Each edge performs simple data processing such as aggregation and filtering, as shown in Fig. 1. For example, consider environmental sensing applications in a smart city. Environmental sensors widely installed in various places send measurements to the nearby edge by radio. Edges aggregate the inputs at regular intervals and send the result to the server. When an edge fails, another one at a distance cannot receive the measurements and therefore cannot take over the processing instead. That is, we have to duplicate each edge for the conventional approach: switching to standby nodes and reprocessing lost data. This duplication cost increases sharply with expansion in the system scale, unlike the cloud environment, which can manage all resources centrally.

To solve this problem, we focus on environmental monitoring applications and propose an approach to guarantee *approximate fault tolerance* without edge duplication. We deal with various failures by estimating missing data using the *correlation* between sensors rather than reprocessing. This approach guarantees the error bounds for a user-specified confidence threshold and allows the server to continue subsequent processing without waiting for the inputs from failed edges.

In this paper, we focus on aggregation queries and assume that some measurements are lost due to sensor/communication failures. Edges can handle these failures by estimating missing data from observed data and aggregating them approximately [8]. For example, if sensor D fails in Fig. 2, edge 2 estimates missing data from the measurements of sensor C and continues aggregation without waiting for the inputs from sensor D.

We extend this approach to the problem of edge failures. That is, the server estimates the outputs of failed edges from the others to continue processing. In Fig. 2, aggregation results for sensors A and B are lost due to the failure of edge 1. The server estimates them from the results for sensors C and D obtained from edge 2 and continues the subsequent processing without waiting for the recovery of edge 1.

In our approach, due to the approximate aggregation at each edge, the server has to take care of the uncertainty of the aggregation results to predict the error bounds accurately. There are various techniques to estimate missing values, such as mean imputation [10] and Gaussian process regression [14]. However, these techniques cannot take care of the uncertainty of the estimation in each edge, which causes the lack of reliability. On the other hand, our method handles the uncertainty as a probability distribution and guarantees the error bounds appropriately.

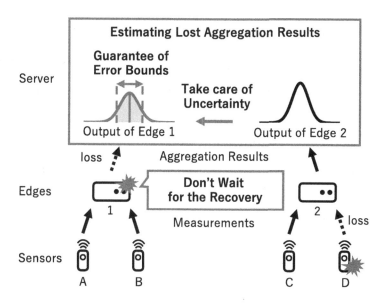

Fig. 2. Overview of the proposed approach

The rest of this paper is organized as follows. In Sect. 2, we discuss related work on fault tolerance in data stream processing systems. In Sect. 3, we explain the approximate aggregation at edges, which is the basis of our approach. In Sect. 4, we propose an approach to support approximate fault tolerance and provide a method to estimate the missing aggregation results taking care of the uncertainty. We evaluate the validity of our approach by experiments in Sect. 5, and we conclude the paper in Sect. 6.

2   Related Work

Many systems guarantee *at-most-once* semantics and *at-least-once* semantics [3, 13]. A system that guarantees at-most-once semantics only switches processing to the standby machines to recover from failures, but this approach can result in data loss. On the other hand, a system that guarantees at-least-once semantics reprocesses the lost data to recover from failures, but the same data can be processed multiple times. That is, these systems cannot guarantee the error bounds caused by failures.

Some stream processing systems, such as Flink [2] and Spark Streaming [6], guarantee *exactly-once* semantics. These systems recover from failure without error by restoring the last checkpoint of the internal states and reprocessing only lost data. This approach is suitable for cluster environments where the system can manage all resources centrally and assign the input data management task to the message queue.

However, for edge computing, there is a problem that the conventional approach needs to duplicate each edge. This duplication cost increases sharply with expansion in the system scale, unlike the cloud environment, which can manage all resources centrally. Besides, reprocessing lost data causes a delay because new inputs are generated one after another even during the reprocessing. We can suppress the delay by parallelizing failure recovery [16], but this approach also needs duplication.

AF-Stream supports approximate fault tolerance to address the trade-off between performance and accuracy [11]. This system mitigates the overhead by adaptively checkpointing while guarantees that the error upon failure is within the user-specified threshold. However, this system also requires duplication and is not suitable for edge computing environments.

3   Preliminaries

In this section, we explain the idea of approximate aggregation at edges [8], which is the basis of our approach.

In this paper, we assume that all n sensors $\boldsymbol{X} = \{X_1, X_2, \ldots, X_n\}$ send measurements periodically and synchronously to the nearby edge. Let $\boldsymbol{x}^t = \langle x_1^t, x_2^t, \ldots, x_n^t \rangle$ be the true value of $\boldsymbol{X}$ at time $t \in \mathbb{N}^+$ and let $\boldsymbol{X}_i \subseteq \boldsymbol{X}$ be the sensor set assigned to edge i. If sensor failures or communication failures occur, edges cannot receive measurements from some sensors. In other word, at time t, edge i only obtains the measurements $\boldsymbol{o}_i^t$ from sensors $\boldsymbol{O}_i^t \subseteq \boldsymbol{X}_i$. We assume that each sensor is assigned to only one edge, and the observed values are always equal to the true ones.

Edges divide the series of observations by time windows and aggregate them approximately for each time window. In this paper, we deal with two aggregation queries: *sum* and *average*. Let t' be the start point of a time window and let w be the window width. Edge i calculates the aggregation result $\boldsymbol{Y}_X$ for each sensor $X \in \boldsymbol{X}_i$ from the series of observations $\boldsymbol{o}_i^{[t', t'+w)} = \langle \boldsymbol{o}_i^{t'}, \boldsymbol{o}_i^{t'+1}, \ldots, \boldsymbol{o}_i^{t'+w-1} \rangle$.

However what we really want is the aggregation result for $x_i^{[t',t'+w)}$ not for $o_i^{[t',t'+w)}$. It indicates that simply aggregating $o_i^{[t',t'+w)}$ causes errors due to missing data and has no theoretical guarantee of the error bounds.

To solve this problem, we estimate missing data from observations. We utilize the correlation between sensors X modeled by a *multivariate Gaussian distribution* (hereafter, just Gaussian) $\mathcal{N}(\mu, \Sigma)$. Suppose that μ and Σ denote the mean vector and the covariance matrix of X, respectively. For the measurements o_i^t of sensors O_i^t, edge i calculates the *posterior distribution* $\mathcal{N}(\mu_{X_i^t|o_i^t}, \Sigma_{X_i^t|o_i^t})$ for sensors $X_i^t = X_i \setminus O_i^t$ [7]:

$$\mu_{X_i^t|o_i^t} = \mu_{X_i^t} + \Sigma_{X_i^t O_i^t} \Sigma_{O_i^t O_i^t}^{-1} \left(o_i^t - \mu_{O_i^t} \right) \text{ and} \tag{1}$$

$$\Sigma_{X_i^t|o_i^t} = \Sigma_{X_i^t X_i^t} - \Sigma_{X_i^t O_i^t} \Sigma_{O_i^t O_i^t}^{-1} \Sigma_{O_i^t X_i^t}. \tag{2}$$

The subscripts of each symbol indicate corresponding rows/columns in μ and Σ. For instance, $\Sigma_{X_i^t O_i^t}$ is a sub matrix of Σ formed by rows X_i^t and columns O_i^t, which represents the covariance between X_i^t and O_i^t.

Finally, we aggregate the estimated distributions in the window. In the following, we focus on the average query but we can handle the sum query in the same way. Since Gaussians are in the family of *stable distributions*, without temporal correlation, a Gaussian $\mathcal{N}(\mu_{Y_{X_i}}, \Sigma_{Y_{X_i}})$ for the average Y_{X_i} of sensors X_i is represented as follows [8]:

$$\mu_{Y_{X_i}} = \frac{1}{w} \left(\sum_{t \in [t',t'+w)} \mu_{X_i|o_i^t} \right) \text{ and} \tag{3}$$

$$\Sigma_{Y_{X_i}} = \frac{1}{w^2} \left(\sum_{t \in [t',t'+w)} \Sigma_{X_i|o_i^t} \right). \tag{4}$$

Note that, for sensors O_i^t, the mean vector is its measurements o_i^t and all the elements of the covariance matrix are 0.

This method theoretically guarantees the error bounds. Let $f(x \mid \mu, \Sigma)$ be the probability density function for $\mathcal{N}(\mu, \Sigma)$. For an error bound e, we can calculate the probability that the average Y_X of the sensor $X \in X_i$ is within e of the mean μ_{Y_X}:

$$P\left(Y_X \in [\mu_{Y_X} - e, \mu_{Y_X} + e]\right) = \int_{\mu_{Y_X}-e}^{\mu_{Y_X}+e} f\left(y \mid \mu_{Y_X}, \Sigma_{Y_X}\right) dy. \tag{5}$$

That is, for a user-specified *confidence threshold* δ, we can calculate the minimum error bound e' that satisfies δ by solving:

$$P(Y_X \in [\mu_{Y_X} - e', \mu_{Y_X} + e']) = \delta. \tag{6}$$

This guarantees that the true value of Y_X is within $\mu_{Y_X} \pm e'$ with the probability of δ. Note that $\Sigma_{Y_X} = 0$ means that all data of X are observed in the time window and the aggregation result has no error (i.e. $e' = 0$).

4   Proposed Approach

In this section, we propose our approach to support low-latency and high-availability fault tolerance without edge duplication. First, we explain how to guarantee approximate fault tolerance in our approach. Next, we provide a method to estimate the outputs of failed edges taking care of the uncertainty of the processing results.

4.1   Overview

We assume that we have m edges that send the aggregation results to the server periodically and synchronously. Note that edge i sends a Gaussian $\mathcal{N}(\mu_{Y_{X_i}}, \Sigma_{Y_{X_i}})$ as the aggregation result. For example, in Fig. 2, edge 2 calculates a bivariate Gaussian as the aggregation result for sensors C and D and sends it to the server. Then the server proceeds with the subsequent processing as soon as the processing results of all edges are available.

If a non-duplicated edge fails, the server cannot obtain the processing results during that time. In Fig. 2, due to the failure of edge 1, the server cannot obtain the aggregation result for sensors A and B and cannot proceed with the subsequent processing.

We solve this problem by estimating missing results using the correlation between sensors. Let $X' \subseteq X$ be the sensors assigned to failed edges (hereafter, referred to as *missing sensors*) and let $O = X \setminus X'$ be the sensors assigned to remaining edges (hereafter, referred to as *observed sensors*). The server obtains a distribution $\mathcal{N}(\mu_{Y_O}, \Sigma_{Y_O})$ as the aggregation results Y_O for observed sensors and estimates a distribution $\mathcal{N}(\mu_{Y_{X'}}, \Sigma_{Y_{X'}})$ as the aggregation results $Y_{X'}$ for the missing sensors. Then the server continues the subsequent processing without waiting for the recovery of failed edges.

For example, in Fig. 2, the missing sensors are $X' = X_1 = \{X_A, X_B\}$ and the observed sensors are $O = X_2 = \{X_C, X_D\}$. The server can filter those whose aggregation result Y_X for sensor $X \in X'$ is less than a threshold θ in two steps: First, the server calculates the probability $P(Y_X < \theta)$ from the Gaussian $\mathcal{N}(\mu_{Y_X}, \Sigma_{Y_X})$. Then the server checks whether this is greater than or equal to δ.

In our approach, it is essential to take care of the uncertainty of processing results to estimate the outputs of failed edges accurately. For example, when estimating the output $\mathcal{N}(\mu_{Y_{X_1}}, \Sigma_{Y_{X_1}})$ of edge 1 from the output $\mathcal{N}(\mu_{Y_{X_2}}, \Sigma_{Y_{X_2}})$ of edge 2 in Fig. 2, we can consider a method that uses the posterior probability distribution given the mean vector $\mu_{Y_{X_2}}$ as described in Sect. 3. However, this method does not use the covariance matrix $\Sigma_{Y_{X_2}}$, which represents the uncertainty of the output of edge 2, and results in an underestimation of the error bounds.

4.2   Aggregation Result Estimation

If we can model the correlation between sensors X by a Gaussian $\mathcal{N}(\mu, \Sigma)$, we can also model the correlation between the aggregation results Y_X by a Gaussian.

Consider an average query for a time window with the window width w. From the reproductive property of Gaussian, we can model the correlation between Y_X by a Gaussian $\mathcal{N}(\mu', \Sigma')$, whose mean vector and covariance matrix are:

$$\mu' = \frac{1}{w} \left(\sum_{t \in [t', t'+w)} \mu^t \right) = \mu \text{ and} \tag{7}$$

$$\Sigma' = \frac{1}{w^2} \left(\sum_{t \in [t', t'+w)} \Sigma^t \right) = \frac{1}{w} \Sigma. \tag{8}$$

If the server knows that the aggregation results Y_O are equal to y, the server can calculate the posterior probability distribution $\mathcal{N}(\mu_{Y_{X'}|y}, \Sigma_{Y_{X'}|y})$ as the estimated aggregation results $Y_{X'}$:

$$\mu_{Y_{X'}|y} = \mu'_{X'} + \Sigma'_{X'O} \left(\Sigma'_{OO} \right)^{-1} (y - \mu'_O) \text{ and} \tag{9}$$

$$\Sigma_{Y_{X'}|y} = \Sigma'_{X'X'} - \Sigma'_{X'O} \left(\Sigma'_{OO} \right)^{-1} \Sigma'_{OX'}. \tag{10}$$

However, the server cannot know the exact value y because edges aggregate sensor data approximately.

In our method, the server estimates the aggregation results $Y_{X'}$ using the Gaussian $\mathcal{N}(\mu_{Y_O}, \Sigma_{Y_O})$ that represents the uncertainty of Y_O. That is, the server calculates the probability that Y_O is equal to y from $\mathcal{N}(\mu_{Y_O}, \Sigma_{Y_O})$ and marginalizes it:

$$P(Y_{X'}) = \int P(Y_O = y) P(Y_{X'} \mid Y_O = y) \, dy \tag{11}$$

$$= \int f(y \mid \mu_{Y_O}, \Sigma_{Y_O}) f(y' \mid \mu_{Y_{X'}|y}, \Sigma_{Y_{X'}|y}) \, dy. \tag{12}$$

Note that, some edges aggregate measurements of a part of sensors O separately, so that the distribution $\mathcal{N}(\mu_{Y_O}, \Sigma_{Y_O})$ of Y_O is a combination of their outputs. In this paper, since edge i cannot get the observations of sensors X_j assigned to another edge j, we consider all of the covariances between Y_{X_i} and Y_{X_j} in Σ_{Y_O} as 0.

Calculating Eq. (12), we get a Gaussian $\mathcal{N}(\mu'_{Y_{X'}}, \Sigma'_{Y_{X'}})$, whose mean vector and covariance matrix are:

$$\mu'_{Y_{X'}} = \mu'_{X'} + \Sigma'_{X'O} \left(\Sigma'_{OO} \right)^{-1} (\mu_{Y_O} - \mu'_O) \text{ and} \tag{13}$$

$$\Sigma'_{Y_{X'}} = \Sigma'_{X'X'} - \Sigma'_{X'O} \left(\Sigma'_{OO} \right)^{-1} \Sigma'_{OX'} + \Sigma'_{X'O} \left(\Sigma'_{OO} \right)^{-1} \Sigma_{Y_O} \left(\Sigma'_{OO} \right)^{-1} \Sigma'_{OX'}. \tag{14}$$

Note that these are similar to the posterior probability distribution given the mean vector μ_{Y_O} as the aggregation results: the mean vector is equal to Eq. (13) and the covariance matrix is equal to the first and second terms of Eq. (14).

The difference is the third term of Eq. (14) which is the correction term of the covariance matrix based on the uncertainty of processing results. It indicates that, unlike simply estimating the result of $Y_{X'}$ from the mean vector μ_{Y_O}, our method corrects the covariance matrix Σ'_{Y_X}, taking care of the uncertainty to predict the error bounds accurately.

5   Experimental Evaluation

In this section, we demonstrate the validity of the proposed method by experiments. We explain the experimental settings and then describe the experimental results in detail. Note that we omit the results of the sum query because it has the same tendency as the average query.

5.1   Experimental Settings

We use the following two datasets to evaluate the validity of our method.

Real. We measure the temperature in our laboratory with 24 environmental sensors 2JCIE-BL [1]. This dataset has tuples for 24 days at 1-minute intervals. We use the data for the first 16 days for model training and the rest for the evaluation. Note that pre-test using mvnormtest [4] revealed that this data does not follow the multivariate Gaussian.

Synthetic. We prepare synthetic data to verify the validity of the theoretical error guarantee in our method. The dataset has 11520 tuples correspond to 8 days, which follow the Gaussian obtained from the training data. We use rmvnorm function [5] that generates an n-dimensional random number vector that follows the n-dimensional Gaussian given as input. Note that each tuple has no temporal correlation because we generate tuples independently.

In this experiment, we assume a simple failure scenario and prepare test data in three steps: First, we randomly delete part of the measurements at the drop rate r as data lost due to temporary communication failures between sensors and edges. Next, we split this partially deleted data by the window width w and calculate the multivariate Gaussian for the aggregation results as described in Sect. 3. Finally, we randomly select m failed edges and delete these aggregation results as data lost due to edge failures.

5.2   Methodology

We evaluate the validity of our approach from the perspective of theoretical error guarantee. In our approach, the server estimates the missing aggregation result Y_X for sensor X as a Gaussian $\mathcal{N}(\mu_{Y_X}, \Sigma_{Y_X})$ and guarantees its error bounds e' for a user-specified confidence threshold δ. It indicates that the true value of Y_X is theoretically within $\mu_{Y_X} \pm e'$ with the probability of δ. Therefore, we consider the aggregation result for the lossless dataset as the true value and define the

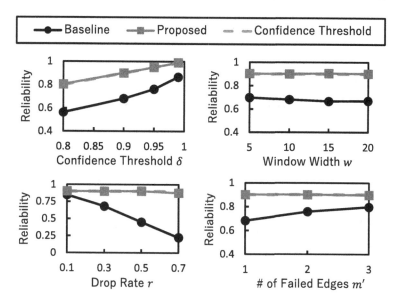

Fig. 3. Experimental results for synthetic data

reliability as the probability that the true value exists within $\mu_{Y_X} \pm e'$. When the reliability satisfies δ, we can consider the error guarantee of our approach to be valid.

We evaluate the reliability by varying each parameter: confidence threshold δ, window width w, drop rate r, and the number of failed edges m'. Note that these default values are $\delta = 0.9$, $w = 10$, $r = 0.3$, and $m' = 1$, respectively. We compare our method with a method that estimates missing results not taking care of the uncertainty (i.e. calculating Eq. (9) and Eq. (10) with $y = \mu_{Y_O}$). We refer to this method as *baseline*.

5.3 Results

We show the experimental results for the synthetic data in Fig. 3. The dotted lines in the figures show the confidence threshold δ. The reliability of the baseline is always below δ, whereas our method satisfies δ for all parameter settings. These graphs show that the uncertainty of aggregation results affects the estimation of error bounds and our method can recover missing aggregation results reliably from partial observations.

Consider the tendency of reliability change for each parameter. We see that the difference in reliability between the baseline and our method increases as the error rate r increases. It is considered that an increase in missing tuples causes an increase in the uncertainty of processing results of each edge, which results in a lack of reliability of the baseline. The difference also increases as the number of failed edges m' decreases. A decrease in failed edges means an increase in the observed processing results with uncertainty. We find that our method

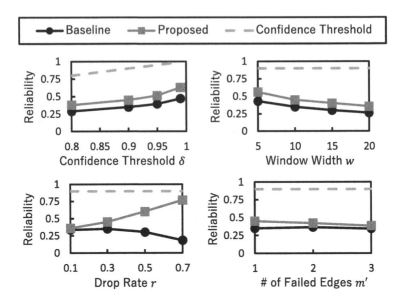

Fig. 4. Experimental results for real data

is particularly effective in these scenarios where the impact of the uncertainty increases.

On the other hand, as shown in Fig. 4, our method does not satisfy the confidence threshold for real data. We found that this is due to temperature changes over time. To solve this problem, we have to extend our method to handle temporal correlations. We are currently considering an approach to update the model by applying the Kalman filter [9]. Also, we should pay attention to the difference in daily trends due to human activity. For example, the temperature is kept by the air conditioner when someone is in the room, whereas the temperature decreases gradually when the room is vacant. We can address this problem by simply learning a different model for each situation.

6   Conclusions

We proposed an approach to guarantee approximate fault tolerance for edge computing environments. In our approach, the server estimates missing aggregation results using the correlation between sensors to continue the processing without waiting for the recovery of failed edges. We also provided a method to estimate missing aggregation results taking care of the uncertainty of observed processing results. The experimental results demonstrated that the importance of handling uncertainty and the validity of our method. However, our method could not estimate error bounds accurately for real data. To solve this problem, we are currently considering extending our method to handle temporal correlations.

References

1. 2JCIE-BL Environment Sensor | OMRON - Americas. https://components.omron.com/product-detail?partId=73064. Accessed 20 Apr 2021
2. Apache Flink: Stateful Computations over Data Streams. https://flink.apache.org/. Accessed 20 Apr 2021
3. Apache Storm. https://storm.apache.org/. Accessed 20 Apr 2021
4. CRAN - package mvnormtest. https://CRAN.R-project.org/package=mvnormtest. Accessed 20 Apr 2021
5. Mvnorm function | R Documentation. https://www.rdocumentation.org/packages/mvtnorm/versions/1.0-11/topics/Mvnorm. Accessed 20 Apr 2021
6. Spark Streaming | Apache Spark. https://spark.apache.org/streaming/. Accessed 20 Apr 2021
7. Bishop, C.M.: Pattern Recognition and Machine Learning. Springer, New York (2006). https://doi.org/10.1007/978-0-387-45528-0
8. Daiki, T., Kento, S., Yoshiharu, I.: Approximate streaming aggregation with low-latency and high-reliability for edge computing. IEICE Trans. Inf. Syst. **J104-D**(5), 463–475 (2021). (in Japanese)
9. Deshpande, A., Guestrin, C., Madden, S.R., Hellerstein, J.M., Hong, W.: Model-based approximate querying in sensor networks. VLDB J. **14**(4), 417–443 (2005)
10. Enders, C.K.: Applied Missing Data Analysis. Guilford Press, New York (2010)
11. Huang, Q., Lee, P.P.C.: Toward high-performance distributed stream processing via approximate fault tolerance. Proc. VLDB **10**(3), 73–84 (2016)
12. Hwang, J.H., Balazinska, M., Rasin, A., Çetintemel, U., Stonebraker, M., Zdonik, S.: High-availability algorithms for distributed stream processing. In: Proceedings of ICDE, pp. 779–790, April 2005
13. Neumeyer, L., Robbins, B., Nair, A., Kesari, A.: S4: Distributed stream computing platform. In: 2010 IEEE International Conference on Data Mining Workshops, pp. 170–177, January 2010
14. Rasmussen, E., Williams, C.K.I.: Gaussian Processes for Machine Learning. The MIT Press, Cambridge (2006)
15. Shi, W., Cao, J., Zhang, Q., Li, Y., Xu, L.: Edge computing: vision and challenges. IEEE Internet Things J. **3**(5), 637–646 (2016)
16. Zaharia, M., Das, T., Li, H., Hunter, T., Shenker, S., Stoica, I.: Discretized streams: a fault-tolerant model for scalable stream processing. Technical report, California University of Berkeley, Department of Electrical Engineering and Computer Science, (2012)

Deep Learning Rule for Efficient Changepoint Detection in the Presence of Non-Linear Trends

Salma Mahmoud[1], Jorge Martinez-Gil[1(✉)], Patrick Praher[1],
Bernhard Freudenthaler[1], and Alexander Girkinger[2]

[1] Software Competence Center Hagenberg GmbH,
Softwarepark 32a, 4232 Hagenberg, Austria
{salma.mahmoud,jorge.Martinez-Gil}@scch.at
[2] ISW Industriesoftware GmbH, Wolfernstrasse 20b, 4400 Steyr, Austria

Abstract. This study presents our ongoing research on designing new methods for changepoint detection in industrial environments using a CUSUM method variant. The changepoint detection refers to identifying the location of change of some aspect in a given time series. The significant difference concerning a state-of-the-art time series prediction technique (using an LSTM) is that our method can handle anomalies masked by non-trivial trends. We have evaluated our proposal with a systematic series of test data and an example set with wear-induced anomalies.

Keywords: Anomaly detection · Time series · Changepoint detection · CUSUM · LSTM

1 Introduction

In manufacturing, time-series data anomaly detection is usually related to finding untypical patterns for a flawless production mode in the presence of strong noise [12]. Among the first successful anomaly detection routines were Wald's SPRT [17], Page's CUSUM [13], Barnard's V-mask [3], and Hinkley's test [9]. Over the decades, a vast amount of literature has been accumulated about the optimal design of detectors - for a discussion see for example Basseville [4], Killick et al. [11], Tartakovsky et al. [16], in which average run lengths are considered, and the discipline of Statistical Process Control and Control Charts is developed - see Sharma et al. [15] for a review. See also [6,18] for structural changes in terms of the properties of linear regression. For the standard metric for cumulative sum tests, the average run length (ARL) see [7], and the literature discussed.

The original paper [13] about CUSUM takes the sequential point of view [17]: A hypothesis is either assumed or rejected, or more data is collected until a decision can be made. This extra data comes from the most recent observations of a stream of continuously collected time series data.

© Springer Nature Switzerland AG 2021
G. Kotsis et al. (Eds.): DEXA 2021 Workshops, CCIS 1479, pp. 184–191, 2021.
https://doi.org/10.1007/978-3-030-87101-7_18

The test's sensitivity versus the step size $\delta = \mu_1 - \mu_0$ between the means μ_0, μ_1 of two stationary sequences is discussed in manifold ways in the literature, first notably by [9] for in the context of the asymptotic form of the test for large sequence lengths. If μ_1 is unknown, the maximum likelihood estimator turns out to be the running mean across the later part of the sample, starting at the estimated jump time r (see discussion in [5], Sect. 2). It is here that our approach sets in: Instead of a running mean estimator, we use a time-series predictive model for estimating the mean after the anomaly. Thus, the fluctuations from more sophisticated trend predictions than arithmetic means may be detected.

When an abrupt change in the behavior of a time series occurs, it is usually due to a significant alteration in the data generation process. Naturally, detecting such moments is of great importance in practical applications because it allows getting more profound insights into the underlying data generation process's current state. Therefore, an accurate method is needed to calculate such changes, even in the presence of (non-anomalous) trends.

To date, many of the widely used methods for this purpose use the classical CUSUM rule, which is based on likelihood-ratio statistics. The heuristics in most of these techniques is accumulating differences of observations to a running estimate of the corresponding location parameter ('quality number' [13]). Usually, the CUSUM method is proved to discover single-step anomalies in either the mean or the variance. This rule is adapted to discover untypical deviations from the quality number represented by more sophisticated, non-linear trends in the present approach. In particular, a frequency-modulated sinusoidal trend is studied.

Instead of undertaking a separate trend removal procedure as a pre-processing step, we apply the CUSUM rule directly to the fluctuations from a quality number defined by predicting a learning model. A predictive model we could use involving periodic trends is the s-ARIMA [2] mode. However, for more sophisticated oscillating trends, it is necessary to use the so-called Long Short Term Memory deep learning method (LSTM, [10]) as they are not relying on constant auto-regressive modeling. What is identified as 'anomalous' then corresponds to the deviation from the trend discovered by these predictive models.

The advantage of our approach lies in not having to rely on the 'off-line' nature of the pre-processing trend-removal and subsequent application of CUSUM. The detection of the trend happens simultaneously with the detection of the anomaly. Also, lack of accuracy in the trend-detection and restrictions to the online applicability are the main conceptual advantages of our method. Therefore, our study consists of the following:

- We present a variant of the traditional CUSUM in which the quality number is the one-step-ahead prediction of a predictive model.
- In an empirical study, we investigate how the new method performs for cases with anomalies and specific additional trends.

The paper is structured as follows: Sect. 2 discusses related work, Sect. 3 presents our method for changepoint detection in the presence of noise and a non-trivial trend. Section 4 provides an empirical study of the behavior of this new method using different benchmark datasets. Finally, we discuss the improvements obtained using time series predictive models to replace the quality number in CUSUM.

2   The Problem: Anomalies in the Presence of Trends

When trends can be removed easily, pre-processing yields a process for which anomalies can be represented as departures from stationarity (standard reference about ARIMA). However, the trends may be challenging to detect online in the presence of anomalies. Therefore, the method presented here allows their sequential detection by accumulating unbalanced deviations from an online one-step-ahead prediction of the trend.

The detection of changepoints falls within the scope of time series analysis. This is because a change point usually means an abrupt change in the underlying point generation process. Moreover, although there is an extensive body of literature on this topic [1], little attention has been paid to its application in the domain of anomaly detection. However, due to the importance of the industrial sector in general and manufacturing and production industries, techniques are needed to facilitate the human operator to detect and correct faults to minimize resource consumption in the form of time and money.

Some of the most popular methods for identifying industrial systems' incorrect behavior are Anomaly Detection (AD) and Root Cause Analysis (RCA). The main difference between them is that AD focuses on identifying events that do not conform to a particular pattern. At the same time, RCA tries to provide clues to the human operator to help him identify and understand the natural causes of the problems. Therefore, in the frame of this work, we will work with methods for AD.

If we pay attention to the literature, the methods for changepoint detection can be usually classified as follows: (1) online vs. offline, (2) univariate vs. multivariate, and (3) model-based vs. non-parametric.

- Regarding the first one, online changepoint detection is used on live-streaming time series. It is usually performed for constant monitoring or immediate anomaly detection. In contrast, changepoint detection approaches are considered offline when they do not use live streaming data.
- Regarding the second one, univariate changepoint detection involves working with only one variable, whereas univariate changepoint detection consists of working with more than one variable simultaneously.
- Finally, model-based modeling assumes the design of a model whose parameters can be learned and even optimized. In contrast, non-parametric methods are usually based on explicit hypothesis testing, where a changepoint is considered to occur when a statistical test exceeds a certain threshold.

However, one feature that seems to be familiar to all possible ways of calculating changepoints is that its proper detection can be viewed as partitioning a time series into an indeterminate number of segments [14]. Our proposition can be viewed as an *online*, *uni-variate*, *parametric* version of such a partitioning scheme.

3   Description of the Experiment

Since we want to discover patterns that do not conform to expected behavior, one of the first steps is determining the typical behavior and which observations do not conform to that behavior. However, defining a region that covers the expected behavior is often difficult, especially when we do not know exactly the difference between ordinary and anomalous behavior.

Definition: We compare the following three methods: Given the time-series (x_n), and the CUSUM-rule

$$S_n := S_{n-1} + x_n - \theta_n,$$

define the following 3 methods, by taking θ_n to be the

1. global mean $\mu = \frac{1}{n} \sum_{i=1}^{n} x_i$

2. running mean $\mu_k = \frac{1}{k} \sum_{i=n-k+1}^{n} x_i,$

3. one-step-ahead prediction Z_n of a single layer LSTM.

   For all three methods, we apply the termination rule $S_n - \min_{k<n} S_k > \lambda$ (for some value $\lambda > 0$) from the original paper [13] (see the discussion in [8]). This corresponds to checking if the height of the 'steepest' part in recent history ending with the time-index of the present exceeds the critical value in magnitude. This is the same (see (6) in [5]) as checking for $\max_r S_n(r) > \lambda$ over an interval with starting point r. We start by comparing the performance of the three CUSUM-rules, applied to a few time series data examples with different degrees of noise and frequency-modulated sinusoidal trends, which are present in addition to a peak-shaped anomaly.

   The LSTM network has a single layer of 10 nodes, a 50% drop-out layer, in addition to the dense output layer. The input data is shaped with lag 4 (since it is univariate, it is a tensor of size $n \times 4 \times 1$). The activation function is the tanh function, we use the Adam-optimizer, and the accuracy measure is mean absolute error, instead of the mean square error, not to be over-influenced by outliers. The network is used as a regression method, and the number of epochs during the training has been chosen to be 80 (by inspection of convergence of the MAE).

4   Discussion

4.1   Application to Synthetic Data

Figures 1 and 3 show that the oscillating trend, which has a periodicity on the scale of the anomaly to be detected, has a strong influence on the performance of the detector. In particular, the precision, calculated here by the 'delay before detection' (DBD) of finds (red) inside the interval of the support of the anomaly, is reduced significantly and non-monotonically. The latter is due to the trend

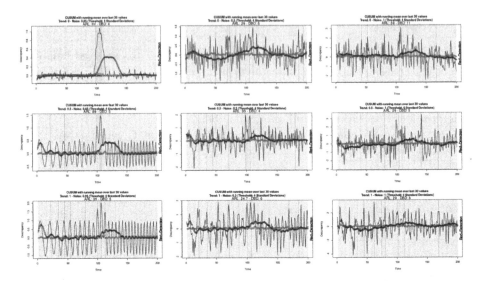

Fig. 1. Three different amplitudes of noise cross-multiplied with three different amplitudes of oscillating trend, with a (modulated) wavelength comparable to the support of the anomaly. The spike anomaly itself is well visible in the upper left diagram (equally present in all other cases). Data: black, S_n: Green. Red (as opposed to green) marked background indicates anomaly finds. The parameter λ used here is 4.0 times the standard deviation of x_n (found from optimal precision/recall pair in the case with lowest noise and trend). With increasing trend-dominance (downward), the CUSUM-rule performance decreases. Also, the peaks of the oscillating trend are recognised as anomalies. (Color figure online)

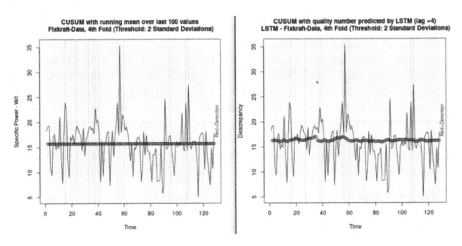

Fig. 2. Detailed comparison of the two methods (1. and 3.) to the same input time series data. The reduction of the number of false positives due to the adaption of the indicator (Green) to the local structure is clearly visible. (Color figure online)

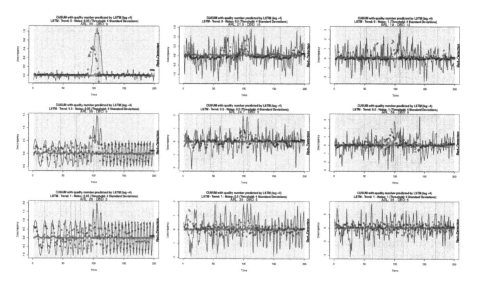

Fig. 3. Same cases considered, as in Fig. 1, with method predicting the quality number changed to LSTM. In the case of high and medium noise and strong and medium presence of the oscillating trend, the number of false positives is reduced, seen by the increase in the ARL. (Color figure online)

being able to either amplify or lessen the dominance of the anomaly, and at the same time, increase the variance of the overall signal (Fig. 2).

Furthermore, a clear improvement is seen at the simultaneous presence of noise and trend with at least intermediate intensity: Here, the number of false positives (measured by the reciprocal of the average run length between such false positives: ARL) is drastically reduced. In particular, the method doesn't interpret all the peaks of the oscillation as anomalies.

4.2 Empirical Study: Application to Food Production Data

In Fig. 4 a typical times series of recorded processing power per unit weight is displayed with the vertical lines representing maintenance instances: Here an essential part subject to strong wear is replaced. Figure 5 shows a single such interval between two replacements. Evidently, for the LSTM-assisted method, there is higher sensitivity to high lying outlier accumulations occurring before the maintenance than for the standard (mean-assisted) CUSUM methods.

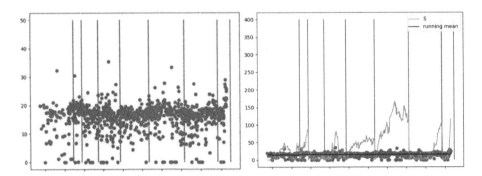

Fig. 4. Left: Real time-series example from food processing plant with part replacement-incidents indicated at the vertical lines. In addition to local accumulations of outliers, there is an oscillating trend pattern. Right: Classical CUSUM-Rule applied to data, with resets at replacements.

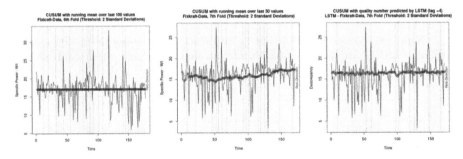

Fig. 5. The CUSUM-test applied to the food processing data for a single interval between two instances of maintenance (exchange of parts). The standard CUSUM method with a constant (global) mean (Left) and the running mean over the last 30 time-steps (Middle) both show a uniform distribution of alarms (anomaly 'finds'), while LSTM-assisted method recognises an increase in high lying outliers, which are responsible for an increase of alarms towards the end of the interval. (Color figure online)

5   Conclusions

We conclude that a generalization of the classical CUSUM-rule is well possible by replacing the usual choice of the running mean with the one-step-ahead prediction of a predictive model. The method is superior to the simple CUSUM rule even if only a single layer LSTM-based predictive model is used in terms of the average run length between false positives and before detection.

As this work is only a documentation of the feasibility in principle of the approach, more detailed studies focusing on the optimal choice of deep learning model given a particular type of time series data will follow. It is particularly interesting for the data management point of view to be able to 'pick the right neural network' for the type of stochastic process underlying the data in question.

Acknowledgements. We thank the anonymous reviewers for theil helpful comments to improve the manuscript. This work has been supported by the project AutoDetect (Project No. 862019; Innovative Upper Austria 2020 (call Digitalization)) as well as the Austrian Ministry for Transport, Innovation and Technology, the Federal Ministry of Science, Research and Economy, and the Province of Upper Austria in the frame of the COMET center SCCH.

References

1. Aminikhanghahi, S., Cook, D.J.: A survey of methods for time series change point detection. Knowl. Inf. Syst. **51**(2), 339–367 (2016). https://doi.org/10.1007/s10115-016-0987-z

2. Athanasopoulos, R.J., George, H.: Forecasting: Principles and Practice. 2nd edn. (2018)

3. Barnard, G.A.: Control charts and stochastic processes. J. R. Stat. Soc. Ser. B (Methodol.) **21**(2), 239–257 (1959)

4. Basseville, M., Nikiforov, I.V., et al.: Detection of Abrupt Changes: Theory and Application, vol. 104. Prentice Hall Englewood Cliffs, Englewood Cliffs (1993)

5. Benveniste, A.: On-line detection of jumps in mean. Lect. Notes Control Inf. Sci. **77**, 567 (1984)

6. Brown, R.L., Durbin, J., Evans, J.M.: Techniques for testing the constancy of regression relationships over time. J. R. Stat. Soc. Ser. B (Methodol.) **37**(2), 149–163 (1975)

7. Graves, S., et al.: A new approximation for the average run length of a cusum. In: Joint Statistical Meeting, Indianapolis (2000)

8. Hawkins, D.M., Olwell, D.H.: Statistics for engineering and physical science-cumulative sum charts and charting for quality improvement (1998)

9. Hinkley, D.V.: Inference about the change-point in a sequence of random variables (1970)

10. Hochreiter, S., Schmidhuber, J.: Long short-term memory. Neural Comput. **9**(8), 1735–1780 (1997)

11. Killick, R., Fearnhead, P., Eckley, I.A.: Optimal detection of changepoints with a linear computational cost. J. Am. Stat. Assoc. **107**(500), 1590–1598 (2012)

12. Mahmoud, S., Sobieczky, F., Martinez-Gil, J., Praher, P., Freudenthaler, B.: Decay-parameter diagnosis in industrial domains by robustness through isotonic regression. Procedia Comput. Sci. **180**, 466–475 (2021)

13. Page, E.S.: Continuous inspection schemes. Biometrika **41**(1/2), 100–115 (1954)

14. Pettitt, A.N.: A non-parametric approach to the change-point problem. J. R. Stat. Soc. Ser. C (Appl. Stat.) **28**(2), 126–135 (1979)

15. Sharma, S., Swayne, D.A., Obimbo, C.: Trend analysis and change point techniques: a survey. Energy Ecol. Environ. **1**(3), 123–130 (2016)

16. Tartakovsky, A., Nikiforov, I., Basseville, M.: Sequential Analysis: Hypothesis Testing and Changepoint Detection, 1st edn. Chapman Hall/CRC, Boca Raton (2014)

17. Wald, A.: Sequential Analysis, 1st edn. John Wiley and Sons, New York (1947)

18. Zeileis, A., Leisch, F., Hornik, K., Kleiber, C.: strucchange: an r package for testing for structural change in linear regression models. J. Stat. Softw. Articles **7**(2), 1–38 (2002)

Time Series Pattern Discovery by Deep Learning and Graph Mining

Alex Romanova$^{(\boxtimes)}$ (iD)

Melenar, LLC, McLean, VA 22101, USA
http://sparklingdataocean.com/

Abstract. Outstanding success of CNN image classification affected using it as an instrument for time series classification. Powerful graph clustering methods have capabilities to come across entity relationships. In this study we propose time series pattern discovery approach as a hybrid of independent CNN image classification and graph mining. Our experiments are based on Electroencephalography (EEG) channel signals data from research of Alcoholic and Control person behaviors. For image classification we used techniques of transforming vectors to images on Gramian Angular Fields (GAF) and for graph mining we built time series graphs on pairs of vectors with high cosine similarities. We unlocked EEG time series patterns that not just validate differences in stimuli reactions of persons from Alcoholic or Control groups but also indicate similarities or dissimilarities between EEG channel signals located in different scalp landscape positions.

Keywords: Time series · Deep learning · Graph mining · Image classification

1 Introduction

In the last few years deep learning demonstrated great success outperforming previous state-of-the-art machine learning techniques in various domains [1]. In particular, after the evolutionary model AlexNet was created in 2012, deep learning techniques became very powerful in Convolutional Neural Network (CNN) image classification [2].

CNN image classification methods are getting high accuracies but being based on supervised machine learning, they require labeling of huge volumes of data. One of the solution of this challenge is transfer learning. Fine-tuning a network with transfer learning usually works much faster and has higher accuracy than training CNN image classification models from scratch [3].

Success stories of ImageNet transfer learning influenced usage of CNN image classification as an instrument for techniques such as time series classification. We were inspired by practice suggested by Ignacio Oguiza as a method of encoding time series as images by Gramian Angular Field (GAF) - a polar coordinate transformation that allow machines to recognize and classify the time series [4].

© Springer Nature Switzerland AG 2021
G. Kotsis et al. (Eds.): DEXA 2021 Workshops, CCIS 1479, pp. 192–201, 2021.
https://doi.org/10.1007/978-3-030-87101-7_19

In his study author translated Olive Oil time series data to images and demonstrated how CNN transfer learning works for time series classification.

Deep learning techniques achieved success in many areas, but they come with drawbacks because deep learning algorithms are still far from human brain abilities such as reasoning and inference. These drawbacks were discussed on Knowledge Representation and Reasoning Meets Machine Learning (KR2ML), interdisciplinary workshop on NeurIPS 2020 conference [5,6]. On this workshop several presentations including an invited talk [7] were about graphs that by acting like human brains perform cognitive inferences.

Our experiments for this study explored Electroencephalography (EEG) data that was used to distinguish between Alcoholic and Control group person behaviors. We selected EEG channel time series data for our study because EEG is applicable to variety of healthcare and research applications, and EEG data is very difficult for pattern recognition and interpretation even by specialists [8]. One of the reasons why EEG is so complex is that it is a combination of time series and spatial data: EEG channel signal patterns have to reflect recording electrode locations on two-dimensional scalp landscape.

Our solution for time series pattern discovery:

- Convert EEG channel signal time series to GAF images.
- Classify images using CNN transfer learning.
- Evaluate impact of transformation methods on classification accuracy.
- Illustrate a view of EEG channel signal images projected on two-dimensional scalp landscape.
- Build time series graphs on EEG channel signal pairs with high cosine similarities.
- Examine relationships between EEG signals and find graph clusters to detect hidden patterns.
- Project graph clusters to scalp landscape and compare patterns with EEG channel positions.

In the pages that follow, we will show:

- Studies about CNN image classification and graph mining methods that were applied to time series.
- Process of converting time series data to GAF images.
- Comparison of model accuracy metrics for different types of trials and different vector to image transformation methods.
- Process of building time series graph on pairs with high cosine similarities.
- Pattern discovery method by graph clustering and visualization.

2   Related Work

In the recent years deep learning techniques such as Long-Short Term Memory (LSTM) were successfully applied to time series forecasting applications [9,10].

CNN image classification techniques are very useful for time series classification especially when one-dimensional time series signals are transformed into two-dimensional matrices. In study [11] authors suggest time series transformation to Recurrence Plots (RP) and in studies [12,13] to Gramian Angular Fields (GAF) and Markov Transition Fields (MTF) images. Techniques of transforming vectors to two-dimensional matrices allow machines to "visually" recognize signals and improve time series classification.

Based on our research, some studies suggest to use graph mining techniques like Spectral Temporal Graph Neural Network (StemGNN) for multivariate time-series forecasting [14]. However we could not find studies for graphs mining techniques applied to time series classifications. In the same time, graph mining can be used for classification of embeddable entities such as semantic graph mining methods [15–17].

The automatic classification of EEG signals is widely used in research involving neural engineering, neuroscience, sleep analysis, and biomedical engineering. Recently, deep learning techniques such as CNN, RNN, LSTM has shown great promise in EEG signal analysis due to its capacity to learn good feature representations from raw data [18–20].

3   Methods

Steps that we used for data processing, training and interpreting the results:

- Converted time series to embedded vectors and transformed vectors to GAF images.
- Trained CNN image classification model based on fast.ai transfer learning.
- Evaluated the impact of GAF transformation method in comparison with plot images.
- Created graphs on pairs of vectors with high cosine similarity.
- Created and analyzed graph clusters.

3.1   Transform Time Series Data to Embedded Vectors

As the first step of time series data processing we transformed data to embedded vectors that were used as basis for both methods of this study: image classification and graph clustering. Code of transforming raw data to vectors is described in our blog [21].

3.2   Transform Vectors to Images

As a method of vector to image translation we used Gramian Angular Field (GAF) - a polar coordinate transformation based techniques [12,13].

3.3   Train CNN Image Classification Model

For this study we used fast.ai CNN transfer learning image classification. To deal with comparatively small set of training data, instead of training the model from scratch, we followed ResNet-50 transfer learning: loaded the results of model trained on images from the ImageNet database and fine tuned it with data of interest [22, 23]. Python code for transforming vectors to GAF images and fine tuning ResNet-50 is described in fast.ai forum [24].

3.4   Graph Mining of Time Series Data

We applied graph mining approach to identify more implicit time series patterns and uncover hidden patters. We used graph mining procedures from Spark GraphFrame library [25, 26]. Graph was built on pairs of embedded vectors with high cosine similarities and graph clusters were found using Spark GraphFrame Connected Components function.

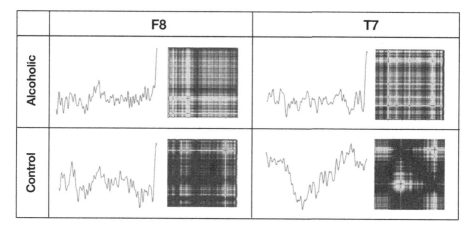

Fig. 1. Alcoholic group and Control group EEG channel signal images on F8 and T7 positions: traditional plot pictures and Gramian Angular Field images.

For graph visualization we transformed graph edges data to graph description language (DOT) and used Gephi, graph visualization tool. Spark code for graph mining and visualization is described in our blog [21].

4   Experiments

4.1   Data Source

As a data source we used 'EEG-Alcohol' dataset from kaggle.com [27] - publicly available information about EEG channel time series data taken from a large study of examining EEG correlates of genetic predisposition to alcoholism.

The amount of subjects in each dataset group was 8. The 64 electrodes were placed on subject's scalps to measure the electrical activity of the brain. The response values were sampled 256 Hz (3.9-ms epoch) for 1 s. Each subject was exposed to pictures from the 1980 Snodgrass and Vanderwart picture set [28] as a single stimulus and two stimuli in matched or non-matched conditions.

4.2 Data Transformation: From Raw Data to Embedding Space

The EEG dataset about Alcoholic vs. Control groups analysis is published on kaggle.com [29] and slightly modified Python code is described in our blog [21].

4.3 Data Transformation: From Vectors to Images

To illustrate vector to GAF image transformation, as examples on Fig. 1 we show traditional plot pictures and GAF images for EEG channels on F8 and T7 positions of one person from Alcoholic group and one person from Control group. All time series were taken from "two stimuli - match" trial. EEG channel positions are described in [8].

Observations:

- Alcoholic person's time series in positions F8 and T7 are more similar to each other than Control person's time series in these positions.
- There are more differences between Alcoholic and Control person's time series located on the same positions than between any person time series located on F8 and T7 positions.

Table 1. Error rate and accuracy metric (100% - error rate) of EEG channel signal time series image classification: Alcoholic or Control group person.

	Error rate	Accuracy
All data - plot images	**19.8%**	**80.2%**
All data - Gramian Angular Field images	**17.5%**	**82.5%**
Single stimulus	**12.4%**	**87.6%**
Two stimuli - matched	**11.0%**	**89.0%**
Two stimuli - non-matched	**8.2%**	**91.8%**

4.4 CNN Image Classification

We prepared several sets of training data to distinguish between Alcoholic and Control person behaviors.

- All data on plot images.
- All data on GAF images.
- Single stimulus data on GAF images.
- Two stimuli - matched data on GAF images.
- Two stimuli - non-matched data on GAF images.

For vector to image transformation we followed the code provided on fast.ai forum [30] and for CNN classification we used fast.ai transfer learning method [23]. To estimate the results we calculated accuracy metrics as the proportion of the total number of predictions that were correct.

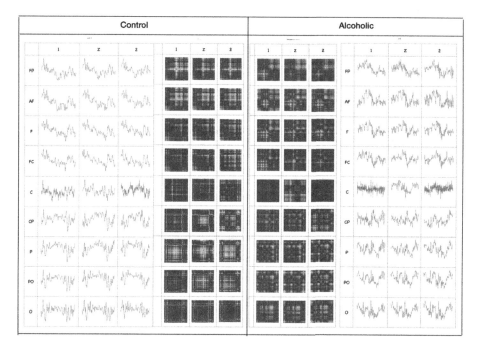

Fig. 2. Control group vs. Alcoholic group EEG channel signals for "two stimuli, non-matched" patterns. EEG time series were taken from positions of lines '1', 'Z', '2' where 'Z' is a middle line of scalp, and lines '1' and '2' stay next to line 'Z' from left and right sides.

Based on classification metrics (Table 1) GAF image classification accuracy, 82.5% is higher than 80.2% accuracy for traditional graph plot picture classification. Accuracy metrics for data separated by different types of stimulus are higher than for all data classifying together. The highest accuracy metric - 91.8% was received for "two non-matched stimuli" trial therefore such trial is the most effective to find a difference between Alcoholic and Control group behaviors.

4.5   EEG Channel Positions

By using CNN image classification model we were able to classify EEG time series only on Alcoholic vs. Control category level. To uncover patterns on lower level, we projected images to EEG channel positions on two-dimensional scalp landscape (Fig. 2). We selected plot pictures and GAF images for "two non-matched stimuli" trial for locations on lines '1', 'Z', '2'. For EEG channel positions [8] subscript 'Z' (zero) refers to electrodes placed on the middle of scalp between left and right hemispheres; the odd numbers are used for points over the left hemisphere and even number for points over the right hemisphere.

Observations:

– GAF images provide an additional view to plot pictures to recognize distinctions and similarities between time series.
– Images located at scalp landscape demonstrate how EEG channel signal positions differentiate between Alcoholic and Control groups.

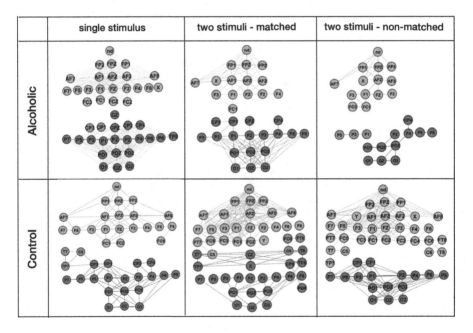

Fig. 3. Graph patterns of EEG channel signal time series for Alcoholic and Control persons by stimuli types.

4.6   Build Time Series Graph and Find Hidden Patterns

We built graphs for EEG channel signals of one person from Alcoholic group and one person from Control group. For each {person, trial type} data set we did the following:

- calculated cosine similarities between pairs of vectors
- selected pairs with cosine similarities higher than 0.9
- built a graph and calculated graph clusters as connected components

4.7   Graph Cluster Illustration

For graph visualization we used Gephi tool. To compare patterns, we defined different colors to differentiate connected components within graphs (Fig. 3). Full Spark code with description for graph mining and translating graph edges to DOT language with colors can be checked in our blog [21].

Observations:

- All graphs have separate clusters for front (orange) and back (blue) scalp regions.
- The "single stimulus" patterns are very similar for Alcoholic and Control group persons and therefore such trials are not useful for predisposition to alcoholism.
- The biggest difference between Alcoholic and Control person patterns is in the "two stimuli, non-matched" trial patterns. This observation corresponds with image classifier metrics: "two stimuli, non-matched" trial has the highest accuracy in classifying Alcoholic verses Control group behaviors.
- Graph clusters for Control group person in both "two stimuli" trials have much higher tightness than for Alcoholic group person, therefore, EEG channel signals of Alcoholic group have much weaker connections than EEG signals of Control group.

5   Conclusion

In this study we introduced time series pattern discovery approach as a hybrid of independent techniques: CNN transfer learning image classification and graph mining.

We demonstrated that CNN image classification model with vector to GAF image transformation data gets higher accuracy metrics than model with plot pictures.

Transforming time series to images and drawing images on top of spatial data, allowed us to uncover patterns not only on categorical level (Alcoholic group vs Control group), but also on fine-grain level of EEG channel positions on two-dimensional scalp landscape.

To examine relationships between EEG channel signals we built time series graphs on pairs of vectors with high cosine similarities. Graph clusters visualization allowed us to uncover patterns that not only confirmed differences in behaviors of persons from Alcoholic or Control groups but also exhibited similarities or dissimilarities between EEG channel signals located in different scalp landscape positions.

6   Broader Impact

The pattern discovery approach of this study, a hybrid of independent techniques - deep learning image classification and graph mining - is implemented through transforming time series to embedded vectors. In addition to time series, this process can be applied to a variety of embeddable entities such as words, documents, images, videos, and many other [31].

EEG time series data that we used in this study, has spatial data information about EEG channel locations on scalp landscape. Projecting time series images to channel locations allowed us to detect fine-grained patterns. This practise is applicable to a variety of data mining scenarios such as climate change where data is a combination of spatial data and embedded vectors.

References

1. LeCun, Y., Bengio, Y., Hinton, G.: Deep learning. Nature **521**(7553), 436–444 (2015)
2. Krizhevsky, A., Sutskever, I., Hinton, G.E.: ImageNet classification with deep convolutional neural networks. In: Advances in Neural Information Processing Systems, pp. 1097–1105 (2012)
3. Yosinski, J., Clune, J., Bengio, Y., Lipson, H.: How transferable are features in deep neural networks? In: Advances in Neural Information Processing Systems, pp. 3320–3328 (2014)
4. Howard, J., Gugger, S.: Chapter 1. Your deep learning journey. In: Deep Learning for Coders with Fastai and PyTorch. https://www.oreilly.com/library/view/deep-learning-for/9781492045519/ch01.html
5. KR2ML Workshop at NeurIPS'20 (2020). https://kr2ml.github.io/2020/papers/
6. Workshop: KR2ML - Knowledge Representation and Reasoning Meets Machine Learning (2020). https://kr2ml.github.io/2020/
7. Leskovec, J., Ren, R., Ying, J., You, J.: Reasoning in knowledge graphs using embeddings (2020). https://slideslive.com/38938119/reasoning-in-knowledge-graphs-using-embeddings
8. Farnsworth, B.: EEG (Electroencephalography): The Complete Pocket Guide (2019). https://imotions.com/blog/eeg/
9. Fawaz, H.I., Forestier, G., Weber, J., Idoumghar, L., Muller, P.-A.: Deep learning for time series classification: a review. Data Min. Knowl. Disc **33**, 917–963 (2019)
10. Sezera, O.B., Ugur Gudeleka, M., Ozbayoglua, A.M.: Financial time series forecasting with deep learning : a systematic literature review: 2005–2019 (2019). https://arxiv.org/pdf/1911.13288.pdf
11. Hatami, N., Gavet, Y., Debayle, J.: Classification of time-series images using deep convolutional neural networks. In: Tenth International Conference on Machine Vision (ICMV 2017) (2017)
12. Wang, Z., Oates, T.: Encoding time series as images for visual inspection and classification using tiled convolutional neural networks. Association for the Advancement of Artificial Intelligence (2015). (www.aaai.org)
13. Wang, Z., Yan, M., Oates, T.: Time series classification from scratch with deep neural networks: a strong baseline. In: International Joint Conference on Neural Networks (IJCNN) (2017)

14. Cao1, D., et al.: Spectral temporal graph neural network for multivariate time-series forecasting. In: 34th Conference on Neural Information Processing Systems (NeurIPS 2020) (2020)
15. Chen, L., Jose, J.M., Yu, H., Yuan, F.: A semantic graph-based approach for mining common topics from multiple asynchronous text streams. In: 2017 International World Wide Web Conference Committee (IW3C2) (2017)
16. Zuckerman, M., Last, M.: Using graphs for word embedding with enhanced semantic relations In: Proceedings of the Thirteenth Workshop on Graph-Based Methods for Natural Language Processing (TextGraphs-13) (2019)
17. Romanova, A.: Detect text topics by semantics graphs. In: Proceedings of the 2nd International Conference on Blockchain and Internet of Things (BIoT 2021), vol. 11 (2021)
18. Craik, A., He, Y., Contreras-Vidal, J.L.: Deep learning for electroencephalogram (EEG) classification tasks: a review. J. Neural Eng. **16**, 031001 (2019)
19. Lukas, A.W.: Gemein: machine-learning-based diagnostics of EEG pathology (2020). https://www.sciencedirect.com/science/article/pii/S1053811920305073
20. Roy, Y., Banville, H., Albuquerque, J., Fauber, J.: Deep learning-based electroencephalography analysis: a systematic review (2019). https://arxiv.org/pdf/1901.05498
21. EEG Patterns by Deep Learning and Graph Mining (2020). http://sparklingdataocean.com/2020/08/19/brainGraphEeg/
22. Howard, J., Gugger, S.: Deep Learning for Coders with fastai and PyTorch. O'Reilly Media, Inc., Sebastopol (2020)
23. Practical Deep Learning for Coders (2010). https://course.fast.ai/
24. Time series/ sequential data study group (2019). https://forums.fast.ai/t/time-series-sequential-data-study-group/29686
25. Chambers, B., Zaharia, M.: Spark: The Definitive Guide: Big Data Processing Made Simple. O'Reilly Media, Inc., Sebastopol (2018)
26. GraphFrames User Guide (2020). https://graphframes.github.io/graphframes/docs/_site/user-guide.html
27. EEG-Alcohol (2017). https://www.kaggle.com/nnair25/Alcoholics
28. Snodgrass, J.G., Vanderwart, M.: A standardized set of 260 pictures: norms for name agreement, image agreement, familiarity, and visual complexity (1980). https://pubmed.ncbi.nlm.nih.gov/7373248/
29. EEG Data Analysis (2019). https://www.kaggle.com/ruslankl/eeg-data-analysis
30. Oguiza, I.: Time series - Olive oil country (2019). https://gist.github.com/oguiza/c9c373aec07b96047d1ba484f23b7b47
31. Something 2 vec (2016). https://gist.github.com/nzw0301/333afc00bd508501268fa7bf40cafe4e

Biological Knowledge Discovery
from Big Data

Integrating Gene Ontology Based Grouping and Ranking into the Machine Learning Algorithm for Gene Expression Data Analysis

Malik Yousef[1,2]([⊠]), Ahmet Sayıcı[3], and Burcu Bakir-Gungor[3]

[1] Department of Information Systems, Zefat Academic College, 13206 Zefat, Israel
[2] Galilee Digital Health Research Center (GDH), Zefat Academic College, Safed, Israel
[3] Department of Computer Engineering, Faculty of Engineering, Abdullah Gul University, Kayseri, Turkey
{ahmet.sayici,burcu.gungor}@agu.edu.tr

Abstract. Recent advances in the high throughput technologies resulted in the production of large gene expression data sets for several phenotypes. Via comparing the gene expression levels under different conditions, such as disease vs. control, treated vs. not treated, drug A vs. drug B, etc., one could identify biomarkers. As opposed to traditional gene selection approaches, integrative gene selection approaches incorporate domain knowledge from external biological resources during gene selection, which improves interpretability and predictive performance. In this respect, Gene Ontology provides cellular component, molecular function and biological process terms for the products of each gene. In this study, we present Gene Ontology based feature selection approach for gene expression data analysis. In our approach, we used the ontology information as grouping (term) information and embedded this information into a machine learning algorithm for selecting the most significant groups (terms) of ontology. Those groups are used to build the machine learning model in order to perform the classification task. The output of the tool is a significant ontology group for the task of 2-class classification applied on the gene expression data. This knowledge allows the researcher to perform more advanced gene expression analyses. We tested our approach on 8 different gene expression datasets. In our experiments, we observed that the tool successfully found the significant Ontology terms that would be used as a classification model. We believe that our tool will help the geneticists to identify affected genes in transcriptomic data and this information could enable the design of platforms to assist diagnosis, to assess patients' prognoses, and to create patient treatment plans.

1 Introduction

Data generated from genome-wide gene expression analyzes help scientists and physicians to better understand the molecular mechanisms of disease development. The gene expression data reflects gene activities and physiological status in a biological system at the transcriptome level. But it includes small sample sizes, high dimensions and noise. For each sample, while a single gene chip or next generation sequencing technology can

© Springer Nature Switzerland AG 2021
G. Kotsis et al. (Eds.): DEXA 2021 Workshops, CCIS 1479, pp. 205–214, 2021.
https://doi.org/10.1007/978-3-030-87101-7_20

detect at least tens of thousands of genes, only a few groups of genes are associated with disease development. Hence, one of the most popular methods to identify such genes is feature selection. However, computational feature selection and other machine learning methods do not consider the biological background of genes. On the other hand, the integrated gene selection takes into account biological knowledge. In this regard, many traditional filtration techniques, such as Information Gain and ReliEF, can obtain benefits from integrative gene selection [1]. Gene Ontology (GO), Kyoto Encyclopedia of Genes and Genomes (KEGG) and DisGeNET are the most popular biological knowledge resources used in integrative gene selection [2]. Qi and Tang show that using GO as a biological knowledge outperforms traditional gene selection methods [3]. Another approach used KEGG terms in order to filter genes more accurately [4]. A recent survey by Yousef et al. [2] has reviewed different approaches that perform biological integration for gene expression data analysis. maTE [5], cogNet [6], SVM-RCE-R [7, 8] and miRcorrNet [9] applies grouping and ranking based machine learning concepts. In another study, Gene Ontology (GO) terms have been used to address the limitations of network-based annotations in disease-causing gene prediction [10].

Gene Ontology aims to assemble a detailed standardized vocabulary that defines various components of molecular biology shared amongst life forms. It provides tools for searching these vocabularies and explaining biological terms using that vocabulary [12]. Gene Ontology is created as a collaborative project by The Gene Ontology (GO) Consortium. The goal of the Consortium is to generate an organized, precisely defined, regulated vocabulary to explain the functions of genes and gene products in every organism [11]. Initially, three model organism databases (FlyBase, Mouse Genome Informatics (MGI) and Saccharomyces Genome Database (SGD)) are used by The GO Consortium and later it is extended to several organisms. Currently, more than 45 000 terms exist in ontology, which are connected by almost 134 000 links. Three distinct aspects of genes are covered by ontology, i.e., molecular function, cellular component, and biological process. GO annotations, which are generated by connecting particular gene products (from species around the tree of life) to terms in ontology, are also included in the GO knowledgebase. Each annotation contains the proof information such as based on a peer-reviewed paper, using the evidence codes from the Evidence and Conclusion Ontology (ECO). In total, there are 45,000 terms in GO, where 29,698 terms belong to biological processes; 11,147 terms belong to molecular functions; and 4201 terms belong to cellular components. These terms are connected by approximately 134,000 relationships. Additionally, over 7 million annotations on genes/gene products for more than 3,200 organisms are included in the GO knowledgebase. More than 10% of these annotations are provided by scientific data included in research papers. Nearly half of that 10% experimental annotations are related with relatively small number of model organisms [12].

In this paper, using Gene Ontology as an external biological information, an innovative algorithm is proposed for selecting informative and relevant genes from microarray data sets, which helps to improve classification performance. The novelty of our approach stems from its ability to search the space of groups of ontologies in order to rank and find the most significant groups. To this end, it is different from the traditional approaches where the search is performed by considering individual genes.

2 Materials and Methods

2.1 Gene Expression Data

Gene Expression Omnibus is the main source of gene expression data [13]. In this study, we used 8 different gene expression datasets. The GEO accession numbers, titles, number of samples, number of genes and positive & negative classes of gene expression datasets are given in Table 1.

Table 1. Details of the 8 gene expression datasets used in this study.

GEO accession	Title	#Samples	Classes	#Genes
GDS1962	Glioma-derived stem cell factor effect on angiogenesis in the brain	180	Negative = 23, Positive = 157	54675
GDS2519	Early-stage Parkinson's disease: whole blood	105	Negative = 55, Positive = 50	22283
GDS2547	Metastatic prostate cancer (HG-U95C)	164	Negative = 75, Positive = 89	12646
GDS3268	Colon epithelial biopsies of ulcerative colitis patients	202	Negative = 73, Positive = 129	44290
GDS3646	Celiac disease: primary leukocytes	132	Negative = 22, Positive = 110	22185
GDS3874	Diabetic children: peripheral blood mononuclear cells (U133A)	117	Negative = 24, Positive = 93	22283
GDS5037	Severe asthma: bronchial epithelial cell	108	Negative = 20, Positive = 88	41108
GDS5499	Pulmonary hypertensions: PBMCs	140	Negative = 41, Positive = 99	49576

2.2 Gene Ontology Data

The biological background is provided by Gene Ontology and the data is downloaded from Molecular Signatures Database [14, 15]. Three subsets of Gene Ontology, i.e., Biological Process, Molecular Functions and Cellular Components, are used in this study. Additionally, gene sets have been filtered for inter-set redundancy in each subset. The numbers of the groups or terms which belong to each subset are presented in Table 2. The general format of the Gene Sets is shown in Table 3. Each group has a title and its related genes.

Table 2. Summary table of Gene Ontology subsets. Second column represents the number of terms associated with each GO subset shown in the first column.

Subset of gene ontology	#Ontology groups (Terms)
Biological process	7573
Molecular functions	1001
Cellular component	1697

Table 3. An example of grouping the genes into gene sets based on their biological process

Ontology groups (Terms)	Genes
Mitochondrial genome maintenance	AKT3, PPARGC1A, POLG2, PARP1, DNA2, TYMP, FLCN, PRIMPOL, STOX1, SLC25A4, LIG3, MEF2A, MPV17, OPA1, MSTO1, SLC25A36, TOP3A, TP53, PIF1, SESN2, SLC25A33, MGME1, LONP1
Single strand break repair	AP002495.1, ERCC8, PARP1, APLF, ERCC6, SIRT1, LIG4, APTX, TDP1, TERF2, TNP1, XRCC1
Small nucleolar ribonucleoprotein complex assembly	RUVBL2, PIH1D2, NUFIP1, SNU13, ZNHIT6, PIH1D1, SHQ1, TAF9, RUVBL1, NAF1, ZNHIT3
Regulation of mitotic recombination	RAD50, ZSCAN4, ERCC2, MLH1, MRE11, TERF2
Ribosomal large subunit assembly	RPL10L, RPLP0P6, FASTKD2, DHX30, MDN1, RRS1, BOP1, NOP53, NOP2, MRTO4, RSL24D1, NLE1, MRPL20, BRIX1, DDX28, PPAN, RPL3, RPL3L, RPL5, RPL6, RPL10, RPL11, RPL12, RPL23A, RPL24, RPL38, RPLP0, MRPL11, RPF2, TRAF7

3   Methods

3.1   Algorithm

Our proposed algorithm consists of two main components as illustrated in Table 4. The first component is CreateGroups (D) that takes gene expression data D with two-class labels as an input. The CreateGroups () uses the biological knowledge of Ontology in order to generate all the groups. The output of this component is a list of k groups. Each group is a list of genes.

Our algorithm evaluates the gene expressions and the corresponding genes of Gene Ontology terms in terms of two conditions, i.e., negative (control) and positive (cases, having the disease). Gene expression values represent the corresponding conditions for

Table 4. The pseudo code of our main algorithm

Group and Rank (D)

Input: D Gene Expression Data with two-class labels

CreateGroups (D)
  G= run Ontology grouping function on D
  [G = {groups$_i$ = [gene$_{i1}$, gene$_{i2}$, ..., gene$_{ik}$]}, i = 1,...,n$_t$
  return G

RankGroups(G)
  For each group t in G
    R = {rank (t)}
  [R is the collection of the groups and its ranks]

---

the machine learning step. There is not a prior knowledge about Gene Ontology and disease relations. The machine learning algorithm, Random Forest (RF) in our case, will learn the disease related terms. The main component of the algorithm is RankGroups (G). Each Gene Ontology term and their related genes are ranked by this component. Each gene has gene expression values in the gene expression data. The values represent features, and the features are grouped by Gene Ontology terms. Examples of Gene Ontology terms are given in Table 3.

Covariate samples and n number of genes create two-class gene expression datasets. While the classes are control and disease in our case, in other settings they may be any condition versus a control. The Gene Ontology terms may have different numbers of genes and they all create one group. Iterating over all groups, the RankGroups (G) ranks the Gene Ontology terms according to their results of differentiating for two classes by training a random forest classifier using 80% training and 20% test data. At the end, RankGroups (G) returns the average accuracy.

The best j terms (we set j to 2) are chosen after the ranking stage for each term in Gene Ontology, and their groups are combined. The best j terms are used to train an RF model. The model is tested, and performance measures are reported.

We performed the full protocol 10 times using Monte Carlo Cross Validation (MCCV). The input is stratified, sampled equally for each fold, and grouped into training and testing sets. The training set conducts a t-test analysis. A number of 2000 differentially expressed genes are selected with a P-value of less than 0.05. The extracted genes are then used to filter the reference dataset, meaning that all reference datasets will contain the same genes. Gene Ontology terms are ranked first within each iteration and then the best j terms are used to train an RF classifier that combines the best j terms.

3.2 Implementation

In order to test our approach and provide a user interface, we implement our algorithm in KNIME Analytics Platform [16]. KNIME is a data analysis, reporting and integration tool under GNU General Public License.

3.3 Model Performance Evaluation

To evaluate model efficiency, we measured a range of statistical measures such as sensitivity, specificity, and accuracy for each created model. In order to calculate the statistics, the following formulations were used:

$$Sensitivity(Recall) = \frac{True\ Positive}{(True\ Positive + False\ Negative)}$$

$$Specificity = \frac{True\ Negative}{(True\ Negative + False\ Positive)}$$

$$Accuracy = \frac{(True\ Positive + True\ Negative)}{(True\ Positive + True\ Negative + False\ Positive + False\ Negative)}$$

Additionally, in order to approximate the probability of a classifier which would score a randomly selected positive instance higher than a randomly selected negative instance, the Area Under the Receiver Operating Characteristic (ROC) Curve (AUC) is used [17].

The average of 10-fold Monte Carlo Cross Validation (MCCV) is used by all reported performance measures.

In order to deal with the imbalanced dataset problem, we have applied an under-sampling approach. This approach decreases the number of samples in the majority class to the number of samples in the minority class. By this, we would be able to reduce the bias in the size distribution of data sets and overcome the imbalanced class distribution problem. The under-sampling ratio is chosen as 1:2.

4 Results and Discussions

We have tested our algorithm over 8 data sets and compare it with the results of maTE. Although maTE and our methodology generate different output tables, they have a common table, which shows the performance of the tool. Table 4 presents an example output of our tool for a specific dataset. The performance is calculated over the top ranked group and then over the top two groups to reach the 10 ranked groups cumulatively. The results are the mean of the 10 iterations, performed by the cross-validation procedure.

For each group, our method records the size, which is the number of genes included in the group. #Genes (Mean) column reports the mean of this size over 10 iterations. For example, the top group at the last row is 12.3 genes on average. The number of genes for the top 2 groups is 21.8 which is associated with the #Groups with value 2. This value is the aggregate of the size of the top and top 2 groups. According to Table 4, one could consider that the model created from the top 2 groups will perform 0.97 AUC and the

Table 5. An example performance output of our tool.

#Groups	#Genes (Mean)	Accuracy (Mean)	Sensitivity (Mean)	Specificity (Mean)	Area under curve (Mean)
10	107.1	0.96	0.98	0.9	0.99
9	100	0.96	0.96	0.95	0.99
8	85.9	0.93	0.96	0.85	0.99
7	68.3	0.94	0.96	0.9	0.99
6	55.8	0.94	0.96	0.9	0.99
5	44.7	0.96	0.96	0.95	0.985
4	36	0.93	0.94	0.90	0.98
3	29.8	0.91	0.94	0.85	0.98
2	21.8	0.90	0.92	0.85	0.97
1	12.3	0.87	0.90	0.80	0.945

number of genes is 21.8. However, no dramatic improvement is obtained when more groups are included. Thus, one is able to build a simple model with a low number of genes that contribute to better understanding of the model.

For the current study, we have considered the "Biological Process" ontology information and the results are presented in Table 6. Table 6 consists of two parts. While the upper part shows the mean of 10 cross-validation, the lower part displays the mean of number of genes. We comparatively present the AUC performance metric for maTE tool and our current tool for 8 different datasets.

The results shown on Table 6 indicates that the tool is able to find the most significant ontology groups that are able to serve as a marker for distinguishing the two classes for each dataset.

Considering the level 2 of the results which is the top first group, we observed that for most of the results, our current tool outperforms maTE tool with a range of 1% to 22%. For only one dataset, maTE is over our current tool about 13%.

5   Conclusion

The recent advances in DNA gene expression technology makes it feasible to obtain gene expression profiles of tissue samples at relatively low costs. As the high-throughput technologies advance, several gene expression datasets became publicly available and extracting knowledge from lists of differentially expressed genes became a major challenge. In this study, we have presented a computational tool that benefits from gene ontology as the biological knowledge, which is integrated into the machine learning algorithm in terms of gene selection. Since our proposed method searches the space of groups of ontologies in order to rank and find the most significant groups, it is different from traditional approaches where the search is performed by considering individual genes. We compare the performance of our current tool to maTE, which is similar

Table 6. Comparison results between our current tool and maTE over 8 datasets.

	maTE-microRNA targets								Our ontology approach							
#Groups	GDS1962	GDS2519	GDS2547	GDS3268	GDS3646	GDS3874	GDS5037	GDS5499	GDS1962	GDS2519	GDS2547	GDS3268	GDS3646	GDS3874	GDS5037	GDS5499
	AUC	AUC	AUC	AUC	AUC	AUC	AUC	AUC	AUC	AUC	AUC	AUC	AUC	AUC	AUC	AUC
10	0.98	0.54	0.82	0.79	0.66	0.87	0.74	0.88	0.99	0.64	0.81	0.79	0.70	0.75	0.86	0.97
9	0.97	0.57	0.82	0.79	0.68	0.84	0.73	0.89	0.99	0.65	0.81	0.78	0.67	0.75	0.85	0.98
8	0.98	0.56	0.83	0.76	0.70	0.86	0.74	0.90	0.99	0.61	0.80	0.77	0.66	0.74	0.85	0.98
7	0.95	0.59	0.81	0.77	0.62	0.87	0.78	0.89	0.99	0.57	0.81	0.8	0.64	0.78	0.81	0.98
6	0.96	0.54	0.78	0.74	0.66	0.84	0.77	0.89	0.99	0.67	0.81	0.77	0.74	0.8	0.79	0.97
5	0.95	0.58	0.78	0.76	0.63	0.86	0.70	0.89	0.98	0.61	0.81	0.75	0.70	0.78	0.84	0.98
4	0.97	0.54	0.78	0.73	0.65	0.87	0.66	0.89	0.98	0.63	0.82	0.79	0.73	0.76	0.83	0.97
3	0.96	0.55	0.78	0.73	0.62	0.86	0.70	0.88	0.98	0.62	0.80	0.77	0.72	0.75	0.84	0.96
2	**0.96**	**0.51**	**0.77**	**0.75**	**0.58**	**0.89**	**0.64**	**0.85**	**0.97**	**0.58**	**0.80**	**0.81**	**0.69**	**0.77**	**0.86**	**0.95**
1	0.94	0.51	0.72	0.63	0.49	0.88	0.62	0.81	0.94	0.56	0.76	0.75	0.68	0.76	0.71	0.93
#Groups	#G	#G	#G	#G	#G	#G	#G	#G	#G	#G	#G	#G	#G	#G	#G	#G
10	24.7	24	20.4	24.1	26.6	24.7	16.9	25.6	107.1	224.5	126.3	145.9	135.2	195.7	173.1	229.9
9	22.9	22.6	19.2	22.7	23.7	22.4	15.7	23.5	100	213.5	122.7	136.9	117.6	189.4	164.2	222
8	20.8	20.7	18.1	21.2	22	19.3	13.9	21.4	85.9	201.8	116.1	126	108.5	176.5	153.2	201.4
7	18.2	17.7	16.7	19.6	19.2	17	12.6	19.7	68.3	188.4	108.7	118.2	99.5	167.3	136.7	179.6
6	16.5	16.3	15.1	18.4	17.4	14	11.5	17.6	55.8	168	95.9	108.5	73.2	148.6	123.8	156.2
5	14.5	13.3	13.5	16.1	14.7	12	10.1	15.2	44.7	148.8	85.5	91.8	68.9	136.2	108.7	141
4	12	11.3	12.4	13.7	12	10.2	8.3	12.7	36	127.7	71.7	76.4	53.8	109.8	91.3	114.2
3	9.7	8.2	9.7	11.2	9.8	8.5	6.9	9.2	29.8	100.5	59.2	59.4	42.6	94.5	74.9	96.6
2	7.5	5.6	6.6	8.6	5.5	6.7	4.9	6.8	21.8	74.9	42.6	47.2	31.2	76.4	44	62.3
1	3.8	3.6	3.3	3.5	2.7	3.1	3.1	3.5	12.3	45.9	23.1	25.5	20.7	50	24.5	32.6

in its merit. The results show that in most cases, our current tool outperforms maTE. We hope that our tool will help scientists and physicians to deeply analyze their gene expression datasets and hence to better understand disease development and progression mechanisms.

References

1. Perscheid, C., Grasnick, B., Uflacker, M.: Integrative gene selection on gene expression data: providing biological context to traditional approaches. J. Integr. Bioinform. **2018**, 16 (2018). https://doi.org/10.1515/jib-2018-0064
2. Yousef, M., Kumar, A., Bakir-Gungor, B.: Application of biological domain knowledge based feature selection on gene expression data. Entropy **23**, 2 (2020). https://doi.org/10.3390/e23010002
3. Qi, J., Tang, J.: Integrating gene ontology into discriminative powers of genes for feature selection in microarray data. In: Proceedings of the Proceedings of the 2007 ACM Symposium on Applied Computing – (SAC 2007), p. 430. ACM Press: Seoul, Korea (2007)
4. Fang, O.H., Mustapha, N., Sulaiman, M.: An Integrative gene selection with association analysis for microarray data classification. IDA **18**, 739–758 (2014). https://doi.org/10.3233/IDA-140666
5. Yousef, M., Abdallah, L., Allmer, J.: MaTE: Discovering expressed interactions between micrornas and their targets. Bioinformatics **35**, 4020–4028 (2019). https://doi.org/10.1093/bioinformatics/btz204
6. Yousef, M., Ülgen, E., Sezerman, O.U.: CogNet: classification of gene expression data based on ranked active-subnetwork-oriented KEGG pathway enrichment analysis. Peer J. (2020)
7. Yousef, M., Jung, S., Showe, L.C., Showe, M.K.: Recursive cluster elimination (RCE) for classification and feature selection from gene expression data. BMC Bioinformatics **8**, 144 (2007). https://doi.org/10.1186/1471-2105-8-144
8. Yousef, M., Bakir-Gungor, B., Jabeer, A., Goy, G., Qureshi, R.C., Showe, L.: Recursive cluster elimination based rank function (SVM-RCE-R) implemented in KNIME. F1000 Res. **9**, 1255 (2020). https://doi.org/10.12688/f1000research.26880.1
9. Yousef, M., Goy, G., Mitra, R., Eischen, C.M., Jabeer, A., Bakir-Gungor, B.: MiRcorrNet: machine learning-based integration of miRNA and mRNA expression profiles, combined with feature grouping and ranking. PeerJ. 9:e11458 (2021). https://doi.org/10.7717/peerj.11458. PMID: 34055490. PMCID: PMC8140596
10. Asif, M., Martiniano, H.F.M.C.M., Vicente, A.M., Couto, F.M.: Identifying disease genes using machine learning and gene functional similarities, assessed through gene ontology. PLoS ONE 13, e0208626 (2018). https://doi.org/10.1371/journal.pone.0208626
11. Ashburner, M., et al.: Gene ontology: tool for the unification of biology. Nat. Genet. **25**, 25–29 (2000). https://doi.org/10.1038/75556
12. The gene ontology consortium the gene ontology resource: 20 years and still going strong. Nucleic Acids Res. **47**, D330–D338 (2019). https://doi.org/10.1093/nar/gky1055
13. Barrett, T., et al.: NCBI GEO: archive for functional genomics data sets—update. Nucleic Acids Res. **41**, D991–D995 (2012). https://doi.org/10.1093/nar/gks1193
14. Subramanian, A., et al.: Gene set enrichment analysis: a knowledge-based approach for interpreting genome-wide expression profiles. Proc. Natl. Acad. Sci. **102**, 15545–15550 (2005). https://doi.org/10.1073/pnas.0506580102
15. Mootha, V.K., et al.: PGC-1α-responsive genes involved in oxidative phosphorylation are coordinately downregulated in human diabetes. Nat Genet **34**, 267–273 (2003). https://doi.org/10.1038/ng1180

16. Berthold, M.R., et al.: KNIME - the Konstanz Information Miner: Version 2.0 and Beyond. SIGKDD Explor. Newsl. **11**, 26–31 (2009). https://doi.org/10.1145/1656274.1656280
17. Bradley, A.P.: The use of the area under the roc curve in the evaluation of machine learning algorithms. Pattern Recogn. **30**, 1145–1159 (1997). https://doi.org/10.1016/S0031-3203(96)00142-2

SVM-RCE-R-OPT: Optimization of Scoring Function for SVM-RCE-R

Malik Yousef[1] [✉], Amhar Jabeer[2], and Burcu Bakir-Gungor[2]

[1] Department of Information Systems, Zefat Academic College, 13206 Zefat, Israel
[2] Department of Computer Engineering, Faculty of Engineering, Abdullah Gul University, Kayseri, Turkey
{amhar.jabeer,burcu.gungor}@agu.edu.tr

Abstract. Gene expression data classification provides a challenge in classification due to it having high dimensionality and a relatively small sample size. Different feature selection approaches have been used to overcome this issue and SVM-RCE being one of the more successful approach. This study is a continuation of two previous research studies SVM-RCE and SVM-RCE-R. SVM-RCE-R suggests a new approach in the scoring function for the clusters, showing that for some different combination of weights the performance was improved. The aim of this study is to find the optimal weights for the scoring function suggested in the study of SVM-RCE-R using optimization approaches. We have discovered that finding the optimal weights for the scoring function would improve the performance of the SVM-RCE- in most cases. We have shown that in some cases the performance is increased dramatically by 10% in terms of accuracy and AUC. By increasing the performance of the algorithm, it is more likely that we can extract subset genes relating to the class association of a microarray sample.

Keywords: Optimization · Gene expression classification · Machine learning

1 Introduction

Gene expression research is one of the major research areas in the field of bioinformatics. There is exponential growth in the biological data produced by DNA microarray technology [1–3]. This approach is high throughput, allowing scientists to measures multitudes of genes at the same time. Through this method, researchers can study and analyze numerous genes at the same time. DNA microarray technologies is providing great insight in genomic data and is changing the field of bioinformatics. Drug discovery, prevention of disease as well as cures, biological interactions, plant and animal metabolisms are underlying issues addressed by gene expression levels [4]. Additionally, there is widespread research in cancer studies to find potential biomarkers based on gene expression levels in order to find potential biomarkers [5–7]. The focus of research is on a small subset of genes that are relevant to the phenomenon under study among the different genes also known as the feature subset problem. DNA microarray technology are essentially the measurement of different genes at the stages of translation and transcription. There are two major methods of obtaining DNA microarray data: hybridization of

© Springer Nature Switzerland AG 2021
G. Kotsis et al. (Eds.): DEXA 2021 Workshops, CCIS 1479, pp. 215–224, 2021.
https://doi.org/10.1007/978-3-030-87101-7_21

sample to cDNA and high-density oligonucleotide chips [8]. Nevertheless, the data produced by these methods suffer from being highly redundant, large scale and the curse of dimensionality [9]. In order to solve the problems and dispel the curse, feature selection is the approach widely regarded by the bioinformatics community [10–12].

In general, feature selection can be categorized into three groups: filter approach, wrapper approach, embedded approach (combination of the previous methods) [13]. Filter methods focuses on the intrinsic characteristics of the genes in terms of their relevance or in their discriminative properties. The genes are ranked according to the filter method and the highest ranked genes are used are the remaining are eliminated. This methodology does not rely on any machine learning algorithm therefore the time complexity is quite low and can be used for large datasets. Moreover, the results are simplified and can be easily be verified in wet labs by biological domain experts. Thus, univariate filter approaches have widely leveraged to analyze and study gene expression levels [14]. Among the different filter approaches, Xing et al. [15] reports that IG (Information Gain) to be the best approach. However, this approach does not perform well for heterogeneous datasets whereas Bayesian Networks show their strength in this regard [16]. Therefore, different filter techniques outperform each other depending on the dataset. In wrapper approach, the genes are searched then judged based on the estimated accuracy of a classifier. The extracted genes are then used to train the classifier. Zhang et al. [17] asserted that wrapper methods outperform filter methods in terms of predictive accuracy of the classifier. Moreover, this approach also integrates the interaction of the gene selection with the classification that is independent in the filter approach. Nevertheless, this approach has cost of being computationally intensive and in some cases cause overfitting of the classifier [18]. Finally, we have embedded approaches wherein the search algorithm is rooted in the classification algorithm. Therefore, it has the advantage of the interaction of search algorithm with the classifier while being far less computationally intensive [19]. One of the more successful approaches is to use SVM (Support Vector Machines) with an embedded feature selection algorithm [20].

SVM-RFE (Recursive feature elimination) [21] was introduced where the authors achieved very high accuracy with their classifier in comparison to other discriminant methods using SVM. In this method, the genes are ranked as features and the lowest ranked features are removed. Yousef et al. [22] introduced SVM-RCE (Recursive cluster elimination); moreover, it was reported to outperform SVM-RFE. SVM-RCE uses KNN to cluster the genes and then uses SVM to rank the clusters with their respective scores while eliminating the lower ranked clusters. Based on its widespread interest, Luo et al. [23] recently improved the computation time by applying an infinite norm of weight coefficient vector to each cluster to score them. They removed the lowest performing genes instead clusters when the number of clusters are small. Additionally, we wanted to empower SVM-RCE and we introduced SVM-RCE-R (Rank) [24] that extended SVM-RCE with a user specific ranking function. Here the user can choose which clusters should be ranked higher based on different metrics (accuracy, sensitivity, f-measure, area under the curve and precision), thereby allowing scientists to explore the biological data in depth to their needs.

Based on improving this method on a greater scale, we are now introducing SVM-RCE-R-OPT which searches for the optimal set of weights resulting in an improvement in our classification results. We use Bayesian optimization to find the parameters for our six different weights. We compare SVM-RCE and SVM-RCE-OPT across 15 datasets to validate the findings that this approach does improve the classification results.

2 Methods and Implementation

We optimize SVM-RCE-R which is based on an early study SVM-RCE which lead us to the present approach of SVM-RCE-R-Opt. The methods and approaches used are described in the upcoming sections for SVM-RCE and SVM-RCE-R. We then describe in detail how we optimized SVM-RCE-R algorithm and the platform we used to implement SVM-RCE-R-Opt.

2.1 SVM-RCE

SVM-RCE is the first algorithm that suggests clustering genes using K-Means into clusters arranged according to correlation metric, in order to perform feature selection procedure by considering each cluster of genes as one unit. Then one needs to score each cluster of genes in terms of the classification of the training set that consist of two-classes. For that purpose, the training data was transformed to be represented based on the genes that belong to a specific cluster with the original class of the training set. Then an internal cross-validation is performed in order to compute the score. The score is the average of the accuracy performance of the cross-validation step. This step is applied for each cluster detected by k-mean. The next step is to rank all the clusters according to its score. The SVM-RCE removes the cluster with the lowest score or it can set to remove percentage of the lowest scored clusters. Thus, the results obtained is without the genes that are associated with the removed clusters as they do not contribute much to the prediction capabilities of the classifier.

2.2 SVM-RCE-R

Based on the interests of SVM-RCE in biological research, we decided to empower this algorithm with a user specific ranking function in SVM-RCE-R. In SVM-RCE, clusters were scored according to their accuracies. However, in data analysis of high dimensionality data with small sample size other metrics are preferred in the understanding of the features that contribute most to classification. This lead to the implementation of a user specific scoring function, in which researchers can choose the scoring function according to their needs. Therefore, we used the commonly used scoring metrics as described in Eq. 1 as our scoring function.

$$S(w1,w2,w3,w4,w5,w6) = w1 \times acc + w2 \times sen + w3 \times spe + w4 \times fm + w5 \times auc + w6 \times prec \tag{1}$$

where acc, sen, spe, fm, auc and prec refer to accuracy, sensitivity, specificity, f-mean, precision and area under curve respectively.

The ranking is then computed as a sorted list of clusters based on the score S(). We noted that we could achieve significant improvements in our results in comparison to

SVM-RCE. We also did notice that some combinations of clusters with different weights lead to better accuracy score even when the focus was solely on accuracy (Accuracy had the highest weight and the remaining metrics are zero). Therefore, the most important aspect is how one can compute the optimal weights w1,w2,w3,w4,w5,w6 such that it improves the overall performance of the algorithm. Therefore, we decided to focus on an optimization approach to find the best combination of weights for our next step in this approach.

2.3 SVM-RCE-R Optimal

Our new proposed approach SVM-RCE-R-OPT is implemented in KNIME [25] due to its user friendliness similarly to SVM-RCE-R. We split the gene expression dataset into train and test sets with a ratio of 30:70 respectively. Moreover, we used stratified sampling to make sure the training data and test data have the same ratio of negative to positive samples. The parameter optimization node in KNIME is used to find the optimal weights for our six different ranks which was used in SVM-RCE-R (acc, sen, spec, etc.). This node uses Bayesian optimization [26] as the search strategy to find the optimal weights for our six different ranks. The algorithm that is used for the maximization for the objective function is illustrated in Eq. 2 based on the original paper.

$$EI_{y*} = \int_{-\infty}^{\infty} \max(y * -y, 0) \, PM(y \mid x)dy \qquad (2)$$

The search strategy works in two phases: warm up phase and then the Tree-structured Parzen Estimation (TPE) phase. During the warm up phase, random combinations of the weights are used, and then based on the objective values found, the TPE phase starts. Moreover, users can specify the step size of each weight as well as the number of iterations for each phase. Meanwhile, the search algorithm draws weights with replacement from the search space.

Our objective function is based on our scoring function which was stated in Eq. 1. The means the scoring function across all the cluster levels (number of clusters) is used as our objective function, which was set to be maximized. We specified the step size to be 1000, since prior testing showed that there was an improvement by using heavier weights. After the optimal set of weights have been identified in the search space from the Bayesian optimization, they are then used in a separate node that runs SVM-RCE-R with those weights with the training split of the data. Similarly, we also ran SVM-RCE-R with only the weight of accuracy (acc) set to the maximum and the remaining weights set to zero on the same training set. This provides us a reference to validate whether the weights found are an improvement over the original SVM-RCE algorithm, since the algorithm uses accuracy as the ranking function.

2.4 KNIME Workflow

There the overview of the workflow that we programmed in KNIME [25] as reflected in Fig. 1. The user has to set the list file node to the folder that contains the datasets. The workflow then generates a folder with all the relevant output files.

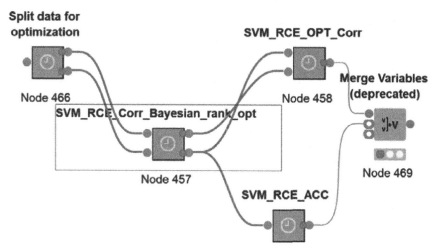

Fig. 1. KNIME workflow overview

The first step in the workflow is to split the data into two parts. One to calculate the optimal weights of the scoring function and the other for cross-validation of the standard approach (SVM_RCE_ACC meta node) and for the optimal approach (SVM_RCE_OPT_Corr meta node). The data that was used in computing the optimal weights is not used in the next steps to avoid overfitting.

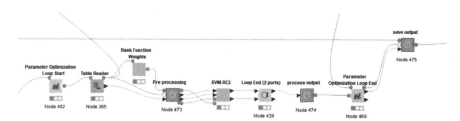

Fig. 2. Bayesian optimization of weights

The SVM-RCE-R is applied with different weights (Parameter Optimization Loop start node) on the training set (Fig. 2) where the results are collected at the loop end node. The maximum iterations used to find the optimum weights was limited to 15 iterations. The different weights are then computed according to the search algorithm mentioned in the previous section. When the optimal set of weights are discovered, then it is used for testing set of the data (Save output node).

3 Data

We have considered the same data used in the study of SVM-RCE-R and we have included two additional new datasets. The datasets represent a range of different diseases, cancers and studies. In terms of diseases: Early-stage Parkinson's disease (GDS2519), Ulcerative colitis (GDS3268), celiac disease (GDS3646), diabetes in children (GDS3875), effects of tobacco smoke in foetal cells (GDS3929), HIV (GDS4228), asthma (GDS5037), acute dengue (GDS5093), pulmonary hypertensions (GDS5499), multi-omic analysis of COVID-19 (GSE157103). In terms of different types of cancer: glioma (GDS1962), prostate cancer (GDS2547), colorectal cancer, (GDS4516_4718), fear conditioning studies in mice (GDS3900). All of the datasets have at least 100 samples except for GDS5093 that has 56 samples. These 14 gene expression datasets are downloaded from Gene Expression Omnibus at NCBI (GEO) [27]. The format of datasets contains sample IDs as the column names and the gene name (gene symbols), according to their respective platform, as the row names with their relevant gene expression values (Fig. 3). Since most of the datasets produced are based on different chips or platforms, the number of genes vary and the exact amount can be found by their GEO accession numbers.

Row ID	S class	S MIR4640	S RFC2	S HSPA6	S PAX8	S GUCA1A	S MIR5193	S THRA	S PTPN21	S CCL5	S CYP2E1	S EPHB3	S ESRRA	S CYP3A6	S SCARB1
GSM97800	neg	4701.5	282.7	769.6	1616.3	232.7	357.7	245.1	33.2	30.7	224.6	107.5	738.3	314.8	1074.7
GSM97803	neg	4735	347.9	287.9	1527.2	204.8	336.5	186.2	22.9	57.1	133.7	270.8	564.2	355.8	1114.3
GSM97804	neg	2863.9	355	199	1793.8	119.3	328.7	349.3	30	17.8	270.1	300.8	510.1	371.6	1191.8
GSM97805	neg	5350.2	319.9	182.8	1880	180.2	304.7	325.4	47.6	30.7	186.4	163.2	542	336.2	1019.8
GSM97807	neg	4789.4	294.2	204.3	1012	156.7	190.1	132	18.8	11.8	218.5	221.4	601.2	216.4	1342.5
GSM97809	neg	5837.8	257.5	184.9	1024.4	155.1	253.3	182.6	28.9	13.4	165.8	355.3	698.2	268.5	1196.6
GSM97811	neg	4446.7	321	107.5	1133.8	236.2	342.5	184.5	15.8	17.9	249.4	212.6	599.1	287.6	1356.5
GSM97812	neg	4264.1	317.9	196.9	1295	235.9	284.1	214.2	22.5	29.1	275.7	228.9	572.8	230	1442.5
GSM97816	neg	11011.5	283.2	225.8	1500.6	65.9	371.2	170.4	48.2	34.1	225.3	132.3	616.5	317.9	1737.6
GSM97817	neg	3832.6	330.9	274.1	1736.6	194.3	521.3	244.6	33.6	30.6	183.2	303.4	716.9	365.6	1085.8
GSM97820	neg	5227.2	340.8	253.6	1504.2	282.2	322.8	192.4	24	16.8	177.2	260.6	562	357.7	1247
GSM97825	neg	2935.6	327	157.9	1651.9	243.1	354	234.7	29.9	24.1	171.7	365	573	337	1370.9
GSM97827	neg	3561.5	363.4	94.3	1410.2	271.1	310.4	215.6	78.8	56.7	138.1	460.2	791.9	309.4	1322
GSM97828	neg	10728.8	268.4	245.4	1423.4	75	424.6	162.8	27.6	45.7	196.7	200.3	616.6	371.9	1834.8
GSM97833	neg	4156.6	266.5	232.8	1420.9	321.1	275	146.5	102.9	12.5	168.9	283.6	557.5	313.9	1456.4
GSM97834	neg	4278.4	224.7	245.2	1544.2	264.9	267.7	283.8	41.7	22.3	161.5	372.1	646.4	297.7	1283.3
GSM97840	neg	5916.2	303.7	217	1442	137.6	443.4	111.5	92.1	192.7	142.9	293.2	704.3	306.8	1518.8
GSM97846	neg	3136.6	353.9	247.2	1662.2	217.2	325.8	326.5	53.6	7.1	227.8	195.8	632	314.8	1095.9
GSM97848	neg	4415.7	303	180.9	1345.5	288.9	321.3	212.2	18.6	17.9	123.1	197.3	539.2	299.8	1128.7
GSM97849	neg	3313.4	331.7	174.6	1378.2	261.3	357.3	172.5	17.5	32.3	193.1	141	627.9	293.7	1397.5
GSM97850	neg	6011.4	258.6	188.8	1632.2	331.9	413	257.1	88.6	15.1	238.2	290.8	687.1	304.8	1191.7
GSM97853	neg	4107.2	248.6	32.2	1427.9	316.6	277.6	238.5	21.6	4.5	255.5	241.6	610.5	286.1	1043.4
GSM97855	neg	7053.4	330.5	182.4	1258.5	172.3	219.5	139.1	18.2	12.5	158.5	219.9	618	220	1260.3
GSM97878	pos	8196.2	288.5	453.9	1589.3	6.4	598.7	281.5	143.1	1519.7	61.2	191.8	599.8	373.3	1803
GSM97913	pos	6006.6	412.5	3748.5	1779.1	13.8	421.5	250.3	42.8	76.6	115.4	348.1	666.6	279.5	1723.7
GSM97932	pos	2619.5	330.2	850	1705.6	118.9	875.5	296	77.2	2111	120.8	136.6	784.5	321.5	969.9
GSM97939	pos	11699.2	349.9	138.8	1388.6	88	486.5	213.6	163.1	10.3	251.4	899	919.2	311.8	2359.5
GSM97951	pos	7718.5	394.9	267.3	1325.3	190.6	387.7	200.6	80.2	14.2	196.1	372.3	645	248.7	1833.5
GSM97957	pos	12700.4	440.8	201.2	1209.2	31.8	489.9	152.8	66.5	13.4	249.6	224.9	701.5	258	1558.6
GSM97793	pos	8816.4	286.9	167.8	1398.6	54.9	461.3	158	25.6	26	303	428.1	891.3	281.5	1131.6
GSM97793	pos	10178.1	388.2	227.3	1665.4	90.7	469.9	459.1	20.4	63.8	293.2	140.4	783.6	292.2	852.4
GSM97795	pos	7826.6	352.4	306	1967	106.4	203.8	266.3	24.3	38.4	396.9	282.2	705.2	315.5	1247.3
GSM97802	pos	6857.8	735.4	261.6	1740.9	316.7	282.6	265.3	25.8	14.4	44.9	575.8	678.4	317	1427.6
GSM97810	pos	8255	373.8	149.5	972.1	99	439.8	196	130.1	13.8	111.7	276.5	610	238	1092.7
GSM97815	pos	8016.8	383.8	250.3	1668.4	134.4	483.1	282.9	32	20.9	164.9	501.5	791.3	295	1234.8

Fig. 3. Input table (dataset) format in KNIME

4   Results

We have applied 100-fold Monte Carlo cross-validation [27] for the original approach and for the optimal approach. In each fold, we compute different performance metrics such as accuracy, specificity and area under curve (AUC). The average of all the 100 folds is computed for each metric. Accuracy and specificity is computed in Eq. 3 where TP is true positives, TN is true negatives, FP is false positives and FN is false negatives. Meanwhile AUC is calculated based on the probability that a classifier will rank a randomly positive instance higher that a negative one.

$$Specificity = TN \ / \ (TN + FP)$$

$$Accuracy = (TP + TN) \ / \ (TP + TN + FP + FN) \tag{3}$$

To validate the optimal weights found from the training, we compute the difference in accuracy between cluster level 90 of the optimal solution and the base accuracy used in the original study SVM-RCE [22]. Using the optimized weights from the training part of the algorithm, we observed that we have an improvement for seven of the datasets, while two of the datasets (GDS3900, GDS4516_4718) showed similar accuracy as shown in Fig. 4. The figure shows that in some cases the improvement over the standard approach might even reach to 10%; in most cases, the improvement is around 5%.

Since we are dealing with high dimensional data, we need to look at other metrics more specifically AUC and specificity. In terms of the specificity, Fig. 5 illustrates that ten out of twelve datasets outperformed or had similar performance as the original SVM-RCE algorithm. This could imply that we are not overfitting in this approach and the robustness of the classifier is still preserved. Additionally, when comparing the AUC in Fig. 6, we note that the optimal approach generally shows an even greater improvement. We can see that seven of the datasets shows either similar or better performance. We can see about a 10% increase in AUC performance for four of the datasets (GDS2519, GDS3646, GDS3875, GDS5093) which is quite a significant improvement. From these results, we can conclude that there is an overall increase in the performance of the datasets. We believe if the number of iterations to search for the optimal set of weights is increased, we may see improvements across all the datasets. However, this could have the drawback of being computational expensive as well as time consuming.

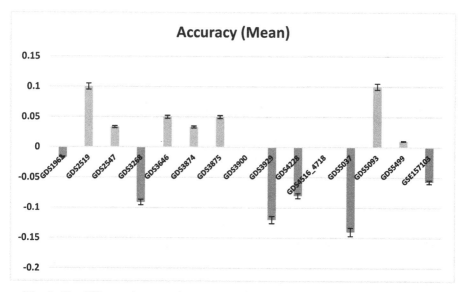

Fig. 4. The difference between the accuracy of the optimal weights to the base accuracy

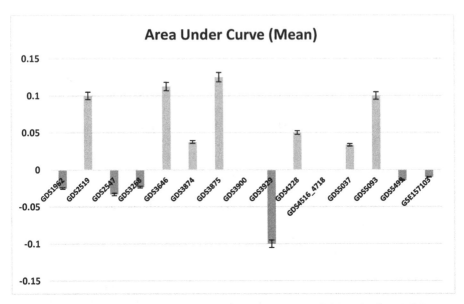

Fig. 5. The difference between the AUC of the optimal weights to the base AUC

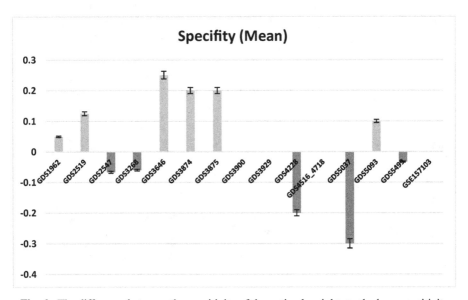

Fig. 6. The difference between the sensitivity of the optimal weights to the base sensitivity

5   Conclusions

In this study, we have proposed an optimization approach for computing the weights for the scoring function that would provide the optimal solution for ranking the clusters. We perform this by using Bayesian search optimization to find the optimal set of weights, then we compare the results with the SVM-RCE. Since SVM-RCE operated using a different ranking function, we wanted to validate whether this approach provides an improvement. When comparing the results across 12 datasets the overall performance is improved in most cases in terms of the accuracy, sensitivity and AUC. However, we would like to note that this algorithm is time consuming since the optimization procedure requires a long time in order to find the suitable weights in the search space. Moreover, approach also allows researchers to understand underlying genes related to biological research since it is based on the SVM-RCE. Therefore, we can find the genes that most contribute to the certain disease or specific research topic (e.g. fear factor). This would help us to find genes that help in identifying diseases in terms of expression levels, under expressed and overexpressed. This could potentially help in medical diagnosis of diseases and understanding of the role genes play in biological processes.

References

1. Chandra, B., Gupta, M.: An efficient statistical feature selection approach for classification of gene expression data. J. Biomed. Inf. **44**, 529–535 (2011)
2. McConnell, P., Johnson, K., Lockhart, D.J.: An introduction to DNA microarrays. In: Methods of Microarray Data Analysis II. Proceedings of the Second Conference on Critical Assessment of Microarray Data Analysis, CAMDA 2001, pp. 9–21. Kluwer Academic Publishers, Dordrecht (2002)
3. Dopazo, J.: Microarray data processing and analysis. In: Methods of Microarray Data Analysis II, Proceedings of the Second Conference on Critical Assessment of Microarray Data Analysis, CAMDA 2001, pp. 43–63. Kluwer Academic Publishers, Dordrecht (2002)
4. Riva, A., Carpentier, A.S., Torresani, B., Henaut, A.: Comments on selected fundamental aspects of microarray analysis. Comput Biol Chem **29**, 319–336 (2005)
5. Veer, L., Da, H., Bijver, M., et al.: Gene expression profiling predicts clinical outcome of breast cancer. Nature **415**, 530–536 (2002)
6. Zajchowski, D., et al.: Identification of gene expression profiles that predict the aggressive behavior of breast cancer cells. Cancer Res. **61**, 5168–5178 (2001)
7. Veer, L., Jone, D.: The microarray way to tailored cancer treatment. Nat. Med. **8**, 13–14 (2002)
8. Allison, D.B., Cui, X., Page, G.P., Sabripour, M.: Microarray data analysis: from disarray to consolidation and consensus. Nat. Rev. Genet. **7**, 55–65 (2006)
9. Ying, L., Han, J.: Cancer classification using gene expression data. Inf. Syst. **28**, 243–268 (2003)
10. Lazar, C., et al.: A survey on filter techniques for feature selection in gene expression microarray analysis. IEEE/ACM Trans. Comput. Biol. Bioinf. **9**, 1106–1119 (2012)
11. Li, T., Zhang, C., Ogihara, M.: A comparative study of feature selection and multiclass classification methods for tissue classification based on gene expression. Bioinformatics **20**, 2429–2437 (2004)
12. Ang, J.C., Mirzal, A., Haron, H., Hamed, H.N.A.: Supervised, unsupervised, and semi-supervised feature selection: a review on gene selection. IEEE/ACM Trans. Comput. Biol. Bioinf. **13**, 971–989 (2016)
13. Zhu, S., Wang, D., Yu, K., Li, T., Gong, Y.: Feature selection for gene expression using model-based entropy. IEEE/ACM Trans. Comput. Biol. Bioinf. **7**, 25–36 (2010)
14. Aris, V., Recce, M.A.: Method to improve detection of disease using selectively expressed genes in microarray data. In: Methods of Microarray Data Analysis, Proceedings of the First Conference on Critical Assessment of Microarray Data Analysis, CAMDA 2000, pp. 69–80. Kluwer Academic Publishers, Dordrecht (2002)

15. Xing, E.P., Jordan, M.I., Karp, R.M.: Feature selection for high-dimensional genomic microarray data. In: Proceeding of 18th International Conference on Machine Learning (2001)
16. Giallourakis, C., Henson, C., Reich, M., Xie, X., Mootha, V.K.: Disease gene discovery through integrative genomics. Annu. Rev. Genomics Hum. Genet. **6**, 381–406 (2005)
17. Zhang, H., Ho, T.B., Kawasaki, S.: Wrapper feature extraction for time series classification using singular value decomposition. Int. J. Knowl. Syst. Sci. **3**, 53–60 (2006)
18. Loughrey, J., Cunningham, P.: Overfitting in wrapper-based feature subset selection: the harder you try the worse it gets. In: Bramer, M., Coenen, F., Allen, T. (eds.) Research and Development in Intelligent Systems XXI, pp. 33–43. Springer London, London (2005). https://doi.org/10.1007/1-84628-102-4_3
19. George, V.S., Raj, C.: Review on feature selection techniques and the impact of svm for cancer classification using gene expression profile. Int. J. Comput. Sci. Eng. Surv. **2**, 16–27 (2011)
20. Li, F., Yang, Y.: Analysis of recursive gene selection approaches from microarray data. Bioinformatics **21**, 3741–3747 (2005)
21. Guyon, I., Weston, J., Barnhill, S., Vapnik, V.: Gene selection for cancer classification using support vector machines. Mach. Learn. **46**, 389–422 (2002)
22. Yousef, M., Jung, S., Showe, L.C., et al.: Recursive cluster elimination (RCE) for classification and feature selection from gene expression data. BMC Bioinformatics **8**, 144 (2007)
23. Luo, L., Huang, D., Ye, L., Zhou, Q., Shao, G., Peng, H.: Improving the computational efficiency of recursive cluster elimination for gene selection. IEEE/ACM Trans. Comput. Biol. Bioinf. **8**, 122–129 (2011)
24. Yousef, M., Bakir-Gungor, B., Jabeer, A., Goy, G., Qureshi, R., Showe, L.C.: Recursive cluster elimination based rank function (SVM-RCE-R) implemented in KNIME. F1000Research **9**, 1255 (2020). https://doi.org/10.12688/f1000research.26880.1
25. Berthold, M.R., et al.: KNIME - the Konstanz information miner. SIGKDD Explorations **11**, 26–31 (2009). https://doi.org/10.1145/1656274.1656280
26. Bergstra, J., Bardenet, R., Bengio, Y., Kégl, B.: Algorithms for hyper-parameter optimization. In: Proceedings of the 24th International Conference on Neural Information Processing Systems, pp. 2546–2554. Curran Associates Inc., Red Hook, NY (2011)
27. Barrett, T., et al.: NCBI GEO: archive for functional genomics data sets—update. Nucleic Acids Res. **41** (2013). https://doi.org/10.1093/nar/gks1193
28. Xu, Q.-S., Liang, Y.-Z.: Monte Carlo cross validation. Chemom. Intell. Lab. Syst. **56**, 1–11 (2001). https://doi.org/10.1016/S0169-7439(00)00122-2

Artificial Intelligence for Clean, Affordable and Reliable Energy Supply

Short-Term Renewable Energy Forecasting in Greece Using Prophet Decomposition and Tree-Based Ensembles

Argyrios Vartholomaios[1]($^{(\boxtimes)}$) (ID), Stamatis Karlos[1] (ID),
Eleftherios Kouloumpris[2] (ID), and Grigorios Tsoumakas[1,2] (ID)

[1] School of Informatics, Aristotle University, 54124 Thessaloniki, Greece
{asvartho,stkarlos,greg}@csd.auth.gr
[2] Medoid AI, 130 Egnatia Street, 54622 Thessaloniki, Greece
{lefteris.kouloubris,greg}@medoid.ai

Abstract. Energy production using renewable sources exhibits inherent uncertainties due to their intermittent nature. Nevertheless, the unified European energy market promotes the increasing penetration of renewable energy sources (RES) by the regional energy system operators. Consequently, RES forecasting can assist in the integration of these volatile energy sources, since it leads to higher reliability and reduced ancillary operational costs for power systems. This paper presents a new dataset for solar and wind energy generation forecast in Greece and introduces a feature engineering pipeline that enriches the dimensional space of the dataset. In addition, we propose a novel method that utilizes the innovative Prophet model, an end-to-end forecasting tool that considers several kinds of nonlinear trends in decomposing the energy time series before a tree-based ensemble provides short-term predictions. The performance of the system is measured through representative evaluation metrics, and by estimating the model's generalization under an industry-provided scheme of absolute error thresholds. The proposed hybrid model competes with baseline persistence models, tree-based regression ensembles, and the Prophet model, managing to outperform them, presenting both lower error rates and more favorable error distribution.

Keywords: Time series forecasting · Renewable energy sources ·
Signal decomposition · Prophet model · Tree-based ensembles

1 Introduction

Having achieved the liberalization of the energy market, Greece is working towards the development and operation of a competitive and economically viable energy model, through its admission into the unified European energy market. This transformation is guided by international directives that encourage the increased penetration of renewable energy sources (RES) into the local energy grid. Accurate RES forecasting is of utmost importance for transmission system

© Springer Nature Switzerland AG 2021
G. Kotsis et al. (Eds.): DEXA 2021 Workshops, CCIS 1479, pp. 227–238, 2021.
https://doi.org/10.1007/978-3-030-87101-7_22

operators (grid managers), in order to orchestrate the injection of RES into a robust energy grid.

In the energy generation domain, short-term forecasting ranges from one hour or one day to one week, and is used in regulating the energy market, determining energy imports and exports, and arbitrating energy prices. Whereas long-term forecasting ranges from one to multiple years, and it serves the grid manager in long-term planning in relation to maintenance and expansion of infrastructure, investments, security, economic issues, etc. Finally, medium-term forecasting stretches in a period from one week to one year and is usually applied for scheduling maintenance tasks.

Several scientific fields deal with signals that are governed by time-dependent relationships. In contrast to the typical machine learning (ML) task which is responsible for predicting continuous variables, namely regression, this kind of signals should be examined without violating their ordering. Time series forecasting is the most common term, under which such methods are categorized [1]. Classical ML regression has been extensively applied to the task in the last years aiming to provide better results for both short-term and long-term scenarios, offering also increased robustness compared to pure statistical approaches. Following this direction, several types of ensemble methods have been recently considered in the context of time series forecasting, as they are described in [2] and thoroughly investigated in [3].

An equally important procedure for capturing the underlying components of generic time series signals is decomposition. Although the classic additive and multiplicative methods are encountered in many applications, there is a need for integrating more sophisticated strategies either with or without the former ones, in order to capture the distinct and heterogeneous components of time series. Toward this direction, a recently developed approach by Facebook, namely Prophet [4], performs time series decomposition by employing generalized additive models (GAM) and Fourier series.

Despite the fact that Prophet has been used in several scientific papers as a competitor without actually managing to outperform various statistical and classical ML approaches (e.g., deaths caused by COVID-19 pandemic [5]), its striking success on more specific cases cannot be ignored (e.g., air pollution forecast [6]). This behavior is expected, if we consider that the original scope of the model was to forecast seasonal events that occur in the popular social media platform of Facebook. Hence, Prophet outperforms its competition when it comes to time-dependent signals that are governed by multiple seasonal effects. Such patterns are also encountered in RES, since their availability is affected by hourly, monthly, and seasonal variations.

To the best of our knowledge, this is the first work to exploit the decomposition properties of Prophet, combined with a regression tree ensemble for short-term forecasting of energy generation by RES. In our approach, after collecting historical energy generation and weather forecasts, we constructed artificial features for capturing the additional seasonalities as exogenous regressors. Code and link for our approach and the new Greek RES datasets that we compiled are available online[1].

The rest of this paper is structured as follows: Sect. 2 presents recently published work involving time series forecasting in similar domains or using ensemble methods. Next, we provide a brief description of our examined dataset and the proposed feature engineering process. A narrative of the proposed algorithm is posed in Sect. 4, while our produced results along with some meaningful comments on the corresponding experimental procedure follow in Sect. 5. Finally, we sum up with the most important points of our work and pose future directions.

2   Related Work

Regression ensembles for increasing the quality of time series forecasting have been explored in several approaches. Beyond the common methods of bagging and boosting, stacking was applied in [3], where two datasets from the field of agribusiness were examined over short-term price forecasting. Models based on Random Forest (RF), as well as extreme gradient boosting and a stacking variant achieved the best error reduction rates. Four different metrics were examined: Mean Absolute Percentage Error (MAPE), Root Mean Square Error (RMSE), Mean Square Error (MSE) and Mean Absolute Error (MAE). These findings support the powerful modeling capabilities of tree-based ensemble regression. Instead of searching exhaustively for fixed-size combinations, the concept of negative correlation was employed in [2] for selecting a subset of models among a predefined pool of candidates, without violating their bias-variance trade-off, but taking into consideration the covariance measure.

A work that combines the Prophet model with Gaussian Process regression (GPreg) [7], managed to outperform auto-regressive integrated moving average (ARIMA) and wavelet-ARIMA approaches for predicting traffic in wireless networks. This phenomenon presents great fluctuations and heavily depends on user profile. They assume that the first approach can model better the long-range trend of the underlying signal, in contrast with the second, which tries to model the short-range as a multivariate problem through a kernel choice. An inverse discrete wavelet transformation was used to produce the final array of predictions. The train-test split was defined as 7-1 days at a time scale of 1 h. Although the obtained results in terms of RMSE and MAPE were satisfactory, the main defect was the increased complexity of the GPreg model, a fact that may render this method infeasible when larger training datasets have to be tackled.

In the domain of RES forecasting, the decomposition of the energy time series using wavelet transformation techniques (WTT) is a popular method to model the intermittent nature of solar and wind phenomena. In [8] the authors

---

[1] https://github.com/intelligence-csd-auth-gr/greek-solar-wind-energy-forecasting.

experiment with several models in their attempt to forecast photovoltaic (PV) power generation during sunny and cloudy days. They propose a hybrid model based on a Random Vector Functional Link neural network and a seasonal ARIMA (SARIMA) model to manage PV generation forecasting during cloudy days. The hybrid model employs the maximum overlap discrete wavelet transformation for time series decomposition, which distinguishes the original signal in a set of 5 series: a low frequency *approximation* and four high frequency *details*. The predictions of both models are combined for the final forecast. Although SARIMA models are known to handle seasonal variations, they do not account for multiple seasonalities [9], which are inherent in solar energy. On the other hand, dealing with multiple seasonalities is an important property of the Prophet model.

In a similar fashion, in [10] the authors present a hybrid model applied to short-term wind forecasting by combining WTT, seasonal adjustment method (SAM), and a radial basis function neural network (RBFNN). The proposed WTT–SAM–RBFNN approach can be described in 4 steps: first the WTT is used to de-noise the original time series by identifying the high and low frequency components, secondly the SAM decomposes the low frequency component, then the trend component is modeled using the RBFNN model and finally the hybrid prediction is achieved by combining the modeled trend and the seasonal indices. The proposed model is trained and tested using mean hourly wind speed data for one month in Wuwei and Minqin in China. Although the proposed model demonstrates high accuracy, the evaluation is restricted by the small dataset, in contrast to our work, which is applied to a dataset that consists of 4 years of hourly energy generation and weather forecasts.

3   Dataset Description

The goal of this work is to establish a system that can consistently and accurately predict renewable energy generation in Greece, using historical solar and wind energy generation data along with weather forecasts. The modeling and performance of such a system, depends on the forecasting constrains set by the real life applications. The examined scenario assumes a forecast horizon of one hour and data availability up to 48 h. More specifically, previous information of wind and solar power generation is missing for the past 48 h prior to the target period, while weather forecasts are available up to 24 h after the target period. The historical RES generation data were collected by the European network of transmission system operators for electricity[2], an online platform that operates as energy data aggregator for the 42 countries that participate in the centralized European energy market. Weather data were retrieved by the Storm Glass weather API[3].

---

[2] https://transparency.entsoe.eu.
[3] https://stormglass.io/.

Subsequently, four years of hourly data (2017–2020) were collected and used to create two datasets for the 1-step-ahead solar and wind energy forecasting tasks using: a) temporal features, b) endogenous properties of the signal, and c) exogenous weather variables according to their correlation with each energy type. Specifically, time-related features such as the hour of the day, day of the week, day of the month, day of the year, and month are treated as cyclical features encoded as polar coordinates. On the other hand, previous (lagged) energy observations are employed from 96 to 48 steps prior to the target, along with weather forecasts for 24 steps after and prior to the target. In addition, the statistical properties of the time series are captured as features by applying a rolling window and calculating the minimum, maximum, average, skewness, variance, and standard deviation of each energy type. Finally, the energy values were scaled using min-max normalization.

Figure 1 illustrates the production for each hour and month, demonstrating the various seasonalities that are inherent to the energy data. Solar energy reveals consistent daily and yearly patterns, whereas a yearly pattern is present in the wind heat map.

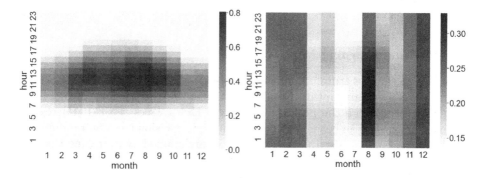

Fig. 1. Heat maps of scaled solar and wind energy generation for each hour of each month averaged over 4 years (2017–2020).

Each final dataset was formed after applying recursive feature elimination [11], using the feature importance as captured by ridge regression [12] and MSE as the evaluation metric. Finally, out of the total 176 engineered features, 150 and 160 features were selected for solar and wind energy forecasting, respectively, avoiding the noisy and/or redundant features of the original higher dimensional space. Lastly, the first 3 years of data (2017–2019) were used for training and the last year (2020) for testing.

4 Forecasting Models

This section presents the various forecasting approaches that are used to compare and evaluate the proposed model during our experiments. We start with baseline models, continue with a classic ML model based on tree ensembles, as well as the state-of-the-art Prophet model. Finally, we conclude with the introduction of the proposed hybrid model.

4.1 Baseline Models

The baseline approach for modeling renewable energy generation in Greece is a persistence model [13] based on the auto-correlation of the time series and the intuition that immediate past observations of a stochastic process will reflect the current observation better than older observations. This is formulated as:

$$\hat{y}_t = y_{t-n} \tag{1}$$

where n is the number of previous instances. Here, n indicates the number of days in the past. Different time lags were used to generate three models for $t - 2$, $t - 7$ and $t - 30$ days.

4.2 Machine Learning Models

According to the literature, nonlinear models can be very effective in RES forecasting since they can capture the intermittent nature of the resources [14]. In this paper, we explore the performance of the Extra Trees (ExTs) [15] regression model, which is an ensemble that fits multiple decision trees on randomized subsets of the training set. In regression, ExTs are applied by averaging the predictions of the decision trees. Its main difference with other popular ensemble models, such as RFs, lies in node splitting, where RFs depend on the calculation of a splitting criterion, whereas ExTs use a random splitting threshold. This random threshold decreases the computational burden, but usually makes the model depend on a greater number of estimators than RFs. In addition, ExTs use the whole feature space for training each estimator, while RFs use only a subset of features. The parameters for the ExTs model were selected using grid search parameter tuning, an exhaustive parameter optimization method that explores all possible configurations in a solution space.

Furthermore, we employed the model of Prophet, which promises to be an automated, user friendly, easily tuned tool for analysts that can handle multiple seasonalities (Fig. 1). This feature is important in energy generation, since seasonal patterns in energy data display multi-period seasonalities (e.g. daily, weekly and monthly). The Prophet is built as an additive regression model [4] in the form:

$$y(t) = g(t) + s(t) + h(t) + \epsilon_t \tag{2}$$

where $g(t)$ is the trend function, $s(t)$ the seasonal module that represents periodic changes, $h(t)$ the effect of holidays and ϵ_t is the error term. In addition, Prophet is customizable, allowing options such as the addition of custom seasonalities and the input of external regressors. By default, Prophet models seasonality using Fourier series which can be more efficient when it comes to periodic effects.

4.3   Proposed Hybrid Model

An additional property of the Prophet model is that it can act as a time series decomposition tool and offer insights into each examined problem. Here, we propose a hybrid model that exploits this property by removing the repeating temporal patterns from the energy time series, extrapolates the seasonality, and trains an ExTs regression model using the residual terms. The main intuition behind this modeling method is that the decomposable model can estimate the seasonal and trend components of the time series, while the ExTs model captures the non-linear patterns in the residual time series. Although a common method in time series decomposition literature is the employment of "approximations" and "details" extracted by wavelet transformation [8,10], Prophet uses a combination of GAM and Fourier series for the decomposition [4].

The implementation of the hybrid model for the Greek RES generation fore-casting system (see also Fig. 2), consists of four steps. First, we initialize Prophet by adding custom seasonalities and regressors, next the model is fitted to the training data and the seasonal component is calculated. Subsequently, the sea-sonal component is subtracted and the deseasoned time series is used as input to the ExTs model. The final forecast is produced by the residual forecasts plus the extrapolated seasonal patterns.

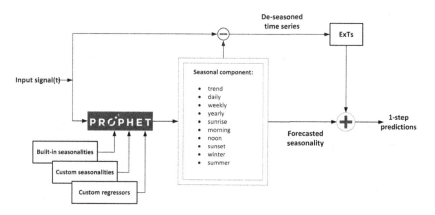

Fig. 2. Hybrid model using Prophet decomposition.

During the initialization of the Prophet model, apart from the default seasonalities, we introduced a biseasonal component to capture seasonal variations (winter, summer) and a time of day component (sunrise, morning, noon, sunset, night). Furthermore, the following features were added as external regressors:

- rolling statistics - mean, min, max, skewness, standard deviation, variance,
- previous energy values from 48 to 72 h in the past,
- previous weather values from 48 to 72 h in the past, and
- available forecasts for the next 24 h of temperature, humidity, visibility and wind speed (solar energy modeling) and gust, wind speed (wind energy).

5   Experimental Results

This section presents the results of the forecasting experiments for each energy type and each model along with a commentary of the findings. To be consistent with the literature, the metrics of RMSE and MAE were used to measure the performance of the models [3]. In addition, the models are compared in terms of error intervals. Specifically, the interest lies in the percent of the absolute error that remains under 10%, between 10% and 15%, and above 15%. These intervals are of great interest to energy producers, revealing a sense of the forecasting confidence.

Table 1 shows the MAE and RMSE for all models and energy types. We first notice that the volatile wind signal is more challenging to forecast than the solar one, where the baselines are competitive. In addition, we notice the positive effect of the proposed feature engineering (FE) process, which strongly boosts the accuracy of all models in both energy types. Prophet is slightly better than ExTs in terms of RMSE, while ExTs are better in MAE, especially in terms of solar energy. Notably, the proposed hybrid model achieves the best results in both measures and energy types.

Table 1. MAE and RMSE values for all models and both energy types.

Model	Solar		Wind	
	MAE	RMSE	MAE	RMSE
Hybrid Prophet+ExTs	**0.041**	**0.067**	**0.069**	**0.088**
Hybrid Prophet+ExTs w/o FE	0.077	0.117	0.106	0.136
1-step-ahead ExTs Regression	0.045	0.081	0.081	0.11
1-step-ahead ExTs Regression w/o FE	0.146	0.195	0.107	0.144
Prophet	0.055	0.08	0.083	0.104
Prophet w/o FE	0.091	0.138	0.182	0.225
Persistence t-2	0.049	0.107	0.226	0.287
Persistence t-7	0.052	0.114	0.25	0.317
Persistence t-30	0.062	0.125	0.243	0.307

Figure 3 shows the distribution of the absolute errors for each model in each of the two energy types. The proposed hybrid approach is the most robust, achieving the highest percentage of errors below 10% in both cases (85.3% for solar and 77.5% for wind energy) and the least amount of errors above the 15% threshold, again in both cases (5.3% for solar and 7.5% for wind energy), following a short-tailed distribution.

Lastly, Fig. 4 illustrates the actual and forecasted energy generation during a week in July and December. It becomes apparent that the consistent energy generation patterns are easily modeled by all models during summer, whereas during winter larger deviations can be observed.

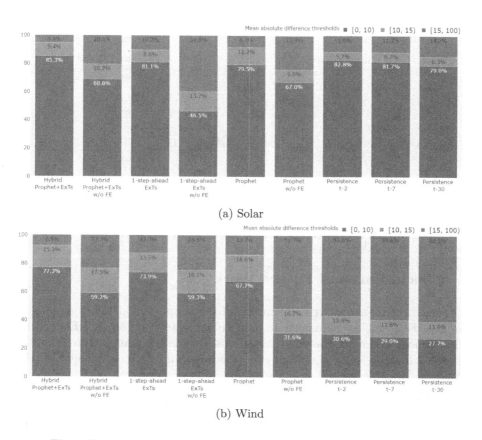

(a) Solar

(b) Wind

Fig. 3. Distribution of absolute errors for each model and energy type.

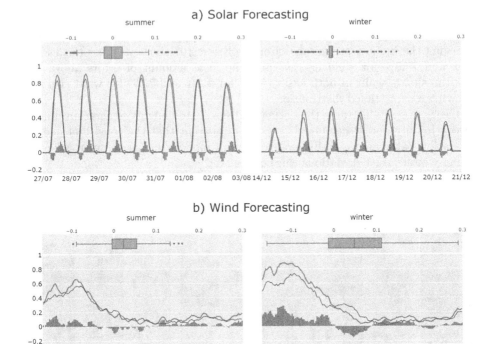

Fig. 4. RES forecasts during a week in July and December.

6   Conclusions and Future Work

We presented an innovative combination of the Prophet model with non-linear tree-based ensembles, managing to achieve accurate and robust RES predictions. Among the main contributions of this work is the manufactured dataset that describes the solar and wind energy generation in Greece along with the proposed feature engineering and selection strategy. Moreover, the focal point of this paper is the utilization of Prophet as a time series decomposition model and its combination with ExTs to predict RES signals.

Regarding future expansions of this work, one can experiment with the adoption of metrics that can select models with complementary predictive behavior and could operate as an asset for improving the performance of the proposed model [2]. In many cases, energy forecasting predictions are needed for multiple steps in the future. Adapting the proposed model to accommodate multi-step forecasts is a topic for future research. Furthermore, different non-linear models can be combined with Prophet decomposition, especially neural network architectures such as LSTM networks that are often employed in forecasting tasks, or exploit them under meta-learning schemes for creating robust ensemble models [16].

Finally, more innovative parameter optimization techniques could be explored, such as genetic algorithms, instead of the naive grid search used here, which is tedious and computationally intensive [17].

Acknowledgements. Part of this work is co-financed by the European Regional Development Fund of the European Union and Greek national funds through the Operational Program Competitiveness, Entrepreneurship and Innovation, under the call RESEARCH – CREATE - INNOVATE (project code: T2EDK-03048).

References

1. Hyndman, R.J., Athanasopoulos, G.: Forecasting: Principles and Practice (2018)
2. Allende, H., Valle, C.: Ensemble methods for time series forecasting. In: Seising, R., Allende-Cid, H. (eds.) Claudio Moraga: A Passion for Multi-Valued Logic and Soft Computing. SFSC, vol. 349, pp. 217–232. Springer, Cham (2017). https://doi. org/10.1007/978-3-319-48317-7_13
3. Ribeiro, M.H.D.M., dos Santos Coelho, L.: Ensemble approach based on bagging, boosting and stacking for short-term prediction in agribusiness time series. Appl. Soft Comput. **86**, 105837 (2020)
4. Taylor, S.J., Letham, B.: Forecasting at scale. Am. Stat. **72**(1), 37–45 (2018)
5. Kumar, N., Susan, S.: COVID-19 pandemic prediction using time series forecasting models. In: 11th International Conference on Computing, Communication and Networking Technologies, ICCCNT 2020, Kharagpur, India, 1–3 July 2020, pp. 1–7. IEEE (2020)
6. Samal, K.K.R., Babu, K.S., Das, S.K., Acharaya, A.: Time series based air pollution forecasting using sarima and prophet model. In: Proceedings of the 2019 International Conference on Information Technology and Computer Communications, ITCC 2019, pp. 80–85, New York, NY, USA. Association for Computing Machinery (2019)
7. Li, Y., Ma, Z., Pan, Z., Liu, N., You, X.: Prophet model and gaussian process regression based user traffic prediction in wireless networks. Sci. China Inf. Sci. **63**(4), 1–8 (2020)
8. Kushwaha, V., Pindoriya, N.M.: A SARIMA-RVFL hybrid model assisted by wavelet decomposition for very short-term solar PV power generation forecast. Renewable Energy **140**, 124–139 (2019)
9. Dokumentov, A., Hyndman, R.J.: STR: A seasonal-trend decomposition procedure based on regression (2020)
10. Zhang, W., Wang, J., Wang, J., Zhao, Z., Tian, M.: Short-term wind speed forecasting based on a hybrid model. Appl. Soft Comput. J. **13**(7), 3225–3233 (2013)
11. Guyon, I., Weston, J., Barnhill, S., Vapnik, V.: Gene selection for cancer classification using support vector machines. Mach. Learn. **46**(1–3), 389–422 (2002)
12. Cortes, C., Mohri, M.: On transductive regression. In: Schölkopf, B., Platt, J.C., Hofmann, T. (eds.) Advances in Neural Information Processing Systems 19, Proceedings of the Twentieth Annual Conference on Neural Information Processing Systems, Vancouver, British Columbia, Canada, 4–7 December 2006, pp. 305–312. MIT Press (2006)
13. Owens, M.J., Challen, R., Methven, J., Henley, E., Jackson, D.R.: A 27 day persistence model of near-earth solar wind conditions: a long lead-time forecast and a benchmark for dynamical models. Space Weather **11**(5), 225–236 (2013)

14. Voyant, C., et al.: Machine learning methods for solar radiation forecasting: a review. Renewable Energy **105**, 569–582 (2017)
15. Geurts, P., Ernst, D., Wehenkel, L.: Extremely randomized trees. Mach. Learn. **63**(1), 3–42 (2006)
16. Vaiciukynas, E., Danenas, P., Kontrimas, V., Butleris, R.: Two-step meta-learning for time-series forecasting ensemble. IEEE Access **9**, 62687–62696 (2021)
17. Romano, J.D., Le, T.T., Fu, W., Moore, J.H.: TPOT-NN: augmenting tree-based automated machine learning with neural network estimators. Genet. Program. Evolvable Mach. **22**(2), 207–227 (2021)

A Comparative Study of Deep Learning Approaches for Day-Ahead Load Forecasting of an Electric Car Fleet

ı

Ahmad Mohsenimanesh[1]($\boxtimes$), Evgueniy Entchev[1], Alexei Lapouchnian[2], and Hajo Ribberink[1]

[1] CanmetENERGY-Ottawa, Natural Resources Canada, Ottawa K1A 1M1, Canada
{Ahmad.Mohsenimanesh,Evgueniy.Entchev,Hajo.Ribberink}@canada.ca
[2] Digital Accelerator Group, Natural Resources Canada, Ottawa K1A 0Y7, Canada
Alexei.Lapouchnian@canada.ca

Abstract. The charging of electric cars affects the performance, efficiency, and required capacity of the electric grid especially where a large electric car fleet located close together simultaneously charges off the same local transformer. Therefore, an accurate load forecasting is required for the reliable and efficient operation of a power system. In this study, three deep learning algorithms, including long short term memory, bidirectional long short term memory, and gated recurrent units are employed and compared in forecasting the aggregate load for the charging of a fleet of electric cars. The developed models were trained and tested on a real-world data set that was collected from 1000 electric vehicles across Canada during 2017–2019. The bidirectional long short term memory algorithm possesses the lowest mean absolute error, mean absolute percentage error and root mean square error among the used methods and is best suited for forecasting the load of electric cars fleet.

Keywords: Electric cars · Charging load · LSTM · Bi-LSTM · GRU · Long range BEVs · Mid-range EVs · Short range EVs

1 Introduction

The global market for electric vehicles (EVs) is growing. A McKinsey report says worldwide sales of EVs reached 2.1 million in 2018, with a growth rate of about 65% from 2017 [1]. The International Energy Agency (IEA) predicted that the global EV fleet will reach about 130 million by 2030 [2]. Therefore, utilities and other power generators need to be prepared now for increased loads as the electrification of transportation grows. Since load forecasting is a pivotal part of the operation of power utility companies, decision-makers in the utility sector must forecast the future demand for electricity with a minimum error percentage. Accurate load prediction can save millions of dollars to the utility companies [3]. The forecast methods for EV charging loads broadly fall into three categories related to the time horizon: long-, mid- and short- term. Long-term load forecasting aims to assist in power system infrastructure planning, while mid-term and

---

The original version of this chapter was revised: The credit line has been corrected to "© Her Majesty the Queen in Right of Canada, as represented by the Minister of Natural Resources 2021". The correction to this chapter is available at https://doi.org/10.1007/978-3-030-87101-7_24

G. Kotsis et al. (Eds.): DEXA 2021 Workshops, CCIS 1479, pp. 239–249, 2021.
https://doi.org/10.1007/978-3-030-87101-7_23

short-term load forecasting can be essentially useful for system operations, dispatch of day-ahead energy market [4], regulation, scheduling and unit commitment of the power grid [5].

Over the past few decades, scholars have developed many modules to improve the accuracy of various short-term load forecasting methods, either based on a traditional approach or using Artificial Intelligence (AI). With the rapid development of AI technology and Machine Learning (ML), intelligent algorithms have contributed to the successful application of big data technologies in various applications. Although ML modeling techniques are widely used by many power and energy utility companies to predict the energy needed to balance generation and demand [3], it is still a difficult task. Firstly, because the load series is complex and exhibits several levels of seasonality; the load at a given hour is dependent not only on the load at the previous hour, but also on the load at the same hour on the previous day, and on the load at the same hour on the day with the same denomination in the previous week. Secondly, because there are many important exogenous variables that must be considered, especially weather-related variables [7].

With the diversification of modern power grid systems, an increasing number of factors, including weather, holidays, and electricity prices have various impacts on load demand [8]. Traditional load forecasting methods are unable to provide forecasting models with sufficient predictive accuracy [4]. These methods are based on mathematical models that often perform poorly when dealing with nonlinear problems. Deep learning methods successfully overcome this issue and are widely used in load forecasting. As opposed to shallow learning or traditional machine learning, deep learning refers to a large number of hidden layers, which endow stronger learning and self-adaptive ability [7, 8]. Recurrent neural networks (RNNs) are fundamentally different from traditional feed-forward neural networks. They are sequence-based models, which are able to establish the temporal correlations between previous information and the current circumstances [7, 9]. However, the conventional RNN would suffer from the gradient vanishing problem [10], non-stationary load data and long-term dependencies forecasting horizon [11]. Therefore, the long short term memory (LSTM) network which a variation of deep RNN, is an effective approach to address the issues and to meet the requirements of load forecasting accuracy [12].

The aggregated load forecasting of an electric car fleet is an important research topic within the energy sector that has not been fully explored from a deep learning perspective. Bouktif et al. [13] has recently used a LSTM-RNN-based model for aggregated demand side load forecast over short-and medium-term monthly horizons. Zheng et al. [11] applied a hybrid algorithm, including empirical mode decomposition (EMD) and the LSTM to accurately forecast the complex non-linear electric load time series over a long horizon. The bidirectional LSTM (Bi-LSTM) has been used in several areas of study to provide accurate aggregated power load forecasting results [7, 10, 14]. Du et al. [15] found that the Bi-LSTM has high robustness on time series use in short term load forecasting. They concluded that the two-way network has a positive effect on the accuracy of power load forecasting. Zhu et al. [16] used the gated recurrent units (GRU) model to predict the short-term charging load of EV charging stations. They recommended the GRU model as a useful tool of higher accuracy in terms of the hourly short-term EVs load forecasting. Huang et al. [17] used the GRU model to predict the state-of-charge of lithium-ion batteries under various ambient temperature conditions. They found that the convolutional GRU method outperformed popular deep-learning methods in terms of estimation errors.

In recent times, deep learning models namely, LSTM, Bi-LSTM, and GRU have undergone much development to forecast electrical loads. While most models concern the forecasting of residential and industrial loads [7, 11, 14, 15], some models were developed to forecast electric car loads [8, 16]. Clearly, the aggregate load of the charging of a fleet of electric cars with different battery capacities including long range (LR) Battery Electric Vehicles (BEVs), mid-range (MR) Electric Vehicle (EVs), and short range (SR) EVs is quite different from other loads. In addition, Canada is one the coldest countries on the planet. Its weather has a huge impact on car batteries, EV charging behavior and the resulting aggregated charging load during the winter period. Therefore, there is a need for high accuracy forecasting models for the load of a fleet of EVs in Canada. To address this need, three deep learning models were developed with the following objectives:

- To compare the models in forecasting the aggregate load of the charging of a fleet of electric cars in Canada,
- To verify the accuracy of the models with a real-world data set.

The remainder of this paper is organized as follows: Sect. 2 provides an overview of the three deep learning methods used in this study. Section 3 describes data pre-processing and feature analysis. Section 4 describes the experimental results and validation. Section 5 presents the conclusions.

2 Deep Learning Models

This section describes the three structures of recurrent neural networks investigated in this study.

LSTM is a kind of structure for sequential data developed by Hochreiter and Schmidhuber [18] as an improvement of RNN. It can learn to bridge minimal time lags in excess of 1000 discrete-time steps by enforcing constant error flow through constant error carousels within special units. Multiplicative gate units learn to open and close access to the constant error flow. LSTM has three gates: input, forget, and output. The forget gate is embedded to indicate how much the previous memory remembers and how much it has forgotten [9].

Gated recurrent unit (GRU) is a special type of a recurrent neural network based on optimized LSTM. Its internal unit is similar to the LSTM, except that the GRU combines the input gate and the forgetting gate of the LSTM into a single update gate [7, 11, 13].

Bidirectional LSTMs (Bi-LSTM) are an extension of traditional LSTMs that train two LSTMs on the input sequence – one on the original sequence and one on the reversed one. With this form of generative deep learning, the output layer can get information from past and future states simultaneously [7], which can improve model performance on sequence classification problems.

3 Data Pre-processing and Feature Analysis

For deep learning method applications, a large data set of charging loads was used that was collected by FleetCarma Inc. in cooperation with 10 utility companies and the University of Waterloo between 2017 and 2019, using FleetCarma C2 Datalogger through the OBD II port of 1,000 electric vehicles. The collected data include charging loads of thirty five vehicle models in nine provinces for three charging locations (home, public and other) and three charging levels (1, 2 & 3). The data captured the charging start and end time (hour, min, sec), energy consumption (kWh), energy loss (kWh), and the battery State of Charge at start time (%) and end time (%). Over 727000 charge events were collected, and Fig. 1(a and b) demonstrates the number of charge events

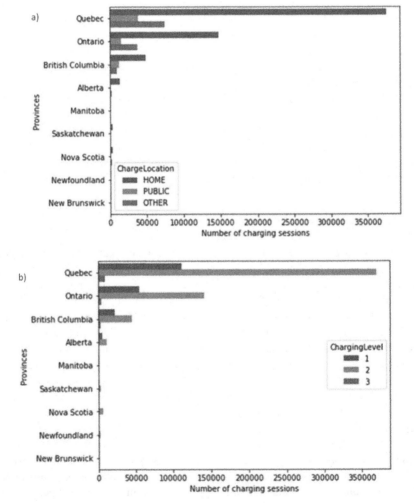

Fig. 1. Number of charging sessions a) per province and charging location, and b) per province and charging level

broken down by provinces, charging levels and charging locations. Provinces with the highest number of the charge events were Quebec, Ontario, and British Columbia. The majority of charging takes place at home (66%), and level 2 charging (82%) is more popular than level 1 and 3.

In this research, we have developed two individual models to process battery size and weather events into characteristic input parameters for the forecasting models (Tables 1 and 2). For the battery size, thirty-five electric vehicle makes and models used in this research work were categorized into three groups of EVs based on battery capacities. For the weather, thirty-three weather events were categorized in three groups, including rain, snow, and haze/fog/dust/smoke.

Several other influential factors were used as input for day-ahead load forecasting, including the charging load and time sequence of 24 time stamps per day from August 2017 to June 2019, charging level, charging location, electricity rates, seasonal category, temperature, and day type. When developing our machine learning models, we divided the dataset into training and testing subsets using the standard 80/20 ratio. For time interval processing, we used Python tools, including the pandas library to integrate all the charging events data based on the time stamps and split them into 24 time stamps every single day, thus producing a proper time series dataset.

Table 1. Electric Vehicles groups

LR BEVs (60–100 kWh)	Chevrolet Bolt (60 kWh), Kona EV(60 kWh), Tesla S60D (60 kWh), Tesla S70D (70 kWh), Tesla 3 (75 kWh), Tesla S75(75 kWh), Tesla X75D (75 kWh), Tesla S85 (85 kWh), Tesla S85D (85 kWh), Tesla SP85 (85 kWh), Tesla SP85D (85 kWh), Tesla S90 (90 kWh), Tesla SP90D (90 kWh), Tesla X90D (90 kWh), Tesla S100D (100 kWh), Tesla X100 (100 kWh), Tesla XP100D (100 kWh)
MR EVs (15–40 kWh)	X5 Hybrid (15.3 kWh), Pacifica hybrid minivan (16 kWh), Pacifica hybrid PHEV (16 kWh), iMiEV (16 kWh), EQ fortwo (16.5 kWh), ELR (17 kWh), Volt (18.4 kWh), Spark EV (18.4 kWh), Ioniq electric (28 kWh), Focus Electric (30 kWh), Leaf (30 kWh), i3 (33 kWh), e-Golf (35.8 kWh), Soul EV (39.2 kWh)
SR EVs (7–12 kWh)	Fusion Energi (7.6 kWh), C-Max Energi (8 kWh), A3 Sportback e-tron (8.8 kWh), Toyota Prius Prime (8.8 kWh), Ioniq electric hybrid (8.9 kWh), Sonata PHEV (10 kWh), BMW 330e & 530e (12 kWh), Outlander PHEV (12 kWh)

Table 2. Grouped weather events

Rain	Snow	Haze/Fog/Dust/smoke
Rain, Rain Showers, Freezing Rain, Freezing Drizzle, Drizzle, Moderate Drizzle, Heavy Rain, Thunderstorms, Moderate Rain, Moderate Rain Showers, Heavy Rain Showers, Moderate Hail	Snow, Snow Pellets, Blowing Snow, Snow Showers, Snow Grains, Ice Pellets, Moderate Snow, Moderate Snow Showers, Moderate Snow Pellets, Heavy Snow, Ice Crystals, Ice Pellet Showers	Fog, Freezing Fog, Haze, Blowing Dust, Smoke, Mainly Clear, Clear, Mostly Cloudy, Cloudy

4   Experimental Results and Discussion

In this section, we describe the model parameters of the three developed models, talk about model validation, and summarize the results. The GRU, LSTM and Bi-LSTM have two hidden layers, and all of the models' first hidden layers have 100 nodes. For the second layer, the GRU, LSTM and Bi-LSTM have 50, 50, 30 nodes, respectively. The epoch and batch size of the training process were achieved according to the data set size, and the network convergence. In this experiment, we set them as 100 and 30, respectively. To prevent over-fitting of the network, we added the dropout layer, which is usually set to a range of 0.3–0.8. Through experimentation, the dropout was set to 0.2 to achieve the lowest prediction error.

For performance evaluation and comparison, the preprocessed data was fed into three deep learning models. To access the effectiveness of the models, three metrics were employed including Root Mean Squared Error (RMSE), Mean Absolute Error (MAE), and Mean Absolute Percent Error (MAPE). The performance comparisons showed that MAE, MAPE and RMSE of the Bi-LSTM model were minimal, which were as small as 21.7, 5.4, 28.8 in training stage, and 22.5, 6.5, and 29.9 in testing stage, respectively (Table 3).

Table 3. Performance comparison of deep learning based methods. MAE: Mean Absolute Error, MAPE: Mean Absolute Percent Error, RMSE: Root Mean Squared Error, GRU, LSTM, Bi-LSTM

Model	Train (MAE)	Test (MAE)	Train (MAPE)	Test (MAPE)	Train (RMSE)	Test (RMSE)
GRU	26.0	26.7	7.7	8.6	31.5	33.3
LSTM	30.4	26.4	6.8	6.9	40.6	35.0
Bi-LSTM	21.7	22.5	5.4	6.5	28.8	29.9

Loss curves of the three models are presented (Fig. 2). The training set and the test set loss function of the three models converged very fast. All these methods achieved a very small loss value lower than 0.003 after 10 epochs, and this means that all the methods well learned the training set and achieved good performance at the test set. Such trends in loss curves have also been observed in reported experimental studies on the training data set of different deep learning models [8].

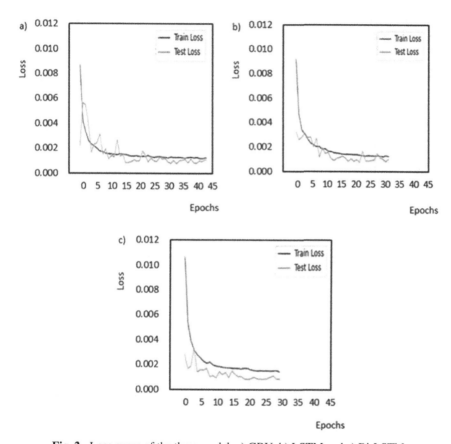

Fig. 2. Loss curve of the three model. a) GRU, b) LSTM and c) Bi-LSTM

Figure 3(a, b and c) illustrates the results of the aggregated charge power (kW) during the day. As can be seen from the Fig. 3, the peak load during the day reached around 7 p.m., and the real error which is the difference between actual and prediction is the largest at that point. Although all three models show good predictive results on peak loads, the Bi-LSTM model achieves a comparatively better performance. Such trends in load prediction curves have also been observed in reported experimental studies on the training and testing data set of different deep learning models [7, 8].

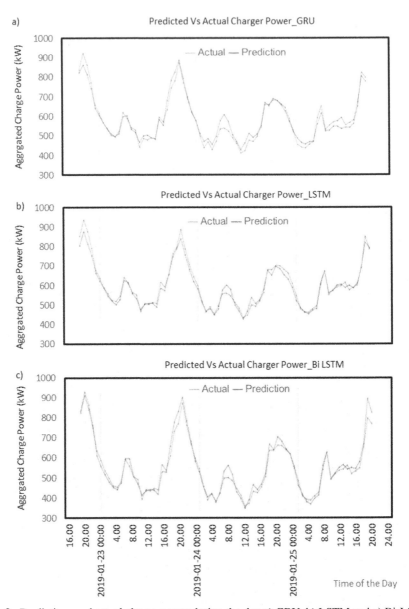

Fig. 3. Predictions and actual charge power during the day a) GRU, b) LSTM and c) Bi-LSTM

Figure 4(a, b and c) illustrate the results of aggregated charge power in spring and winter. It can be seen from the figures that the overall charge power in winter is higher than spring. This might be a result of higher load for cabin heating and more power per charging session in winter.

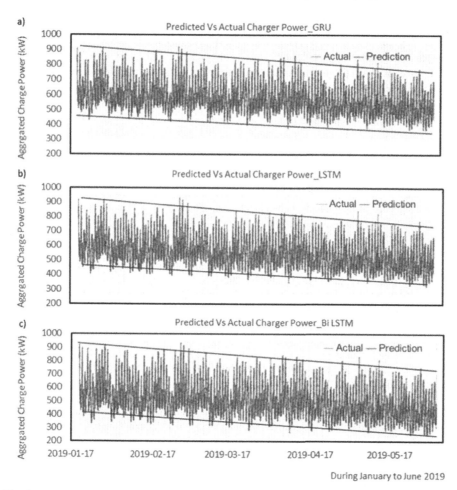

Fig. 4. Predictions and actual aggregated charge power during January to June 2019. a) GRU, b) LSTM and c) Bi-LSTM

5 Conclusions and Future Work

Accurate power load forecasting represents an essential part of energy management for sustainable electricity systems. Through analysis of the charging load characteristics obtained from vehicle side data of electric vehicles, several influential factors were selected as input for our forecasting models, including charging level, charging location, vehicles group based on battery size, electricity rates, seasonal category, temperature, weather condition, and day type.

In this study, we employed three deep learning algorithms including LSTM, Bi-LSTM, and GRU, and compared the forecasted EVs aggregated charging load to determine the effectiveness of the models. Three metrics were employed, including RMSE, MAE, and MAPE. The performance comparisons showed that MAE, MAPE and RMSE of the Bi-LSTM model were the lowest, which were as small as 21.7, 5.4, 28.8 in training stage, and 22.5, 6.5, and 28.8 in testing stage respectively. Although all three models show good predictive results on peak loads during the day, the Bi-LSTM model achieves a comparatively better performance.

We have modeled the power load forecasting as time series problem and thus the Bi-LSTM approach can be generalized to other time series data. Our future work will include applying Bi-LSTM modeling on the level of residential customers for the provinces with the highest number of charging events.

References

1. McKinsey   Homepage.   https://www.mckinsey.com/industries/automotive-and-assembly/our-insights/mckinsey-electric-vehicle-index-europe-cushions-a-global-plunge-in-ev-sales. Accessed 08 Apr 2021
2. IEA Homepage. https://www.iea.org/reports/global-ev-outlook-2019. Accessed 08 Apr 2021
3. Mamun, A.A., Sohel, M., Mohammad, N., Haque Sunny, M.S., Dipta, D.R. Hossain, E.: A Comprehensive review of the load forecasting techniques using single and hybrid predictive models. IEEE Access **8**, 134911–134939 (2020).
4. Haq, Md.R.: Machine learning for load profile data analytics and short-term load forecasting. Electronic theses and dissertations 3414 (2019)
5. Raza, M. Q., Khosravi, A.: A review on artificial intelligence based load demand forecasting techniques for smart grid and buildings. Renew. Sustain. Energy Rev. **50**(C), 1352–1372 (2015)
6. Mosavi, A., Salimi, M., Faizollahzadeh Ardabili, S., Rabczuk, T., Shamshirband, S., Varkonyi-Koczy, A.R.: State of the art of machine learning models in energy systems, a systematic review. Energies **12**(1301), 1–49 (2019)
7. Kong, W., Dong, Z.Y., Jia, Y., Hill, D.J., Xu, Y., Zhang, Y.: Short-term residential load forecasting based on LSTM recurrent neural network. IEEE Trans. Smart Grid **10**, 841–851 (2017)
8. Zhu, J., Yang, Z., Guo, Y., Zhang, J., Yang, H.: Short-term load forecasting for electric vehicle charging stations based on deep learning approaches. Appl. Sci. **9**, 1723 (2019)
9. Wikipedia   Homepage.   https://en.wikipedia.org/wiki/Bidirectional_recurrent_neural_net works. Accessed 08 Apr 2021
10. Bengio, Y., Simard, P., Frasconi, P.: Learning long-term dependencies with gradient descent is difficult. IEEE Trans. Neural Networks **5**(2), 157–166 (1994)
11. Zheng, H., Yuan, J., Chen, L.: Short-term load forecasting using emd-LSTM neural networks with a xgboost algorithm for feature importance evaluation. Energies **10**, 1168 (2017)
12. Apaydin, H., Feizi, H., Sattari, M.T., Colak, M.S., Shamshirband, S., Chau, K.-W.: Comparative analysis of recurrent neural network architectures for reservoir inflow forecasting. Water **12**(5) (2020)
13. Bouktif, S., Fiaz, A., Ouni, A., Serhani, M.: Optimal deep learning LSTM model for electric load forecasting using feature selection and genetic algorithm: comparison with machine learning approaches. Energies **11**(1636), 1–20 (2018)
14. Wu, L., Kong, C., Hao, X., Chen, W.: A short-term load forecasting method based on GRU-CNN hybrid neural network model. Math. Probl. Eng. **2020**, 1–10 (2020)
15. Du, J., Cheng, Y., Zhou, Q., Zhang, J., Zhang, X., Li, G.: Power load forecasting using BiLSTM-attention. IOP Conf. Series. Earth Environ. Sci. **440**, 1–11 (2020)
16. Zhu, J., et al.: Electric vehicle charging load forecasting: a comparative study of deep learning approaches. Energies **12**, 1–19 (2019)

17. Huang, Z.: Convolutional gated recurrent unit-recurrent neural network for state-of-charge estimation of lithium-ion batteries. IEEE **7**, 93139–93149 (2019)
18. Hochreiter, S., Schmidhuber, J.: Long short-term memory. Neural Comput. **9**, 1735–1780 (1997)

Correction to: A Comparative Study of Deep Learning Approaches for Day-Ahead Load Forecasting of an Electric Car Fleet

Ahmad Mohsenimanesh, Evgueniy Entchev, Alexei Lapouchnian, and Hajo Ribberink

Correction to:
Chapter "A Comparative Study of Deep Learning Approaches for Day-Ahead Load Forecasting of an Electric Car Fleet" in: G. Kotsis et al. (Eds.): *Database and Expert Systems Applications - DEXA 2021 Workshops*, **CCIS 1479, https://doi.org/10.1007/978-3-030-87101-7_23**

In the originally published version of chapter 23 the credit line was incorrect. The credit line has been corrected to "© Her Majesty the Queen in Right of Canada, as represented by the Minister of Natural Resources 2021".

The updated version of this chapter can be found at
https://doi.org/10.1007/978-3-030-87101-7_23

Author Index

Printed in the United States
by Baker & Taylor Publisher Services